The
Birth of Britain

A *History of Early Modern England*

General Editor: John Morrill

This new series provides a detailed and vivid account of the history of early modern England. One of its principle aims is to capture the spirit of the time from the point of view of the people living through it. Each volume will be broad in scope covering the political, religious, social and cultural dimensions of the period.

Published

The Birth of the Elizabethan Age
England in the 1560s
Norman Jones

The Birth of Britain
A New Nation 1700–1710
W. A. Speck

In preparation

England in the 1590s
David Dean

The Birth of the Jacobean Age
England 1601–1612
Pauline Croft

The Rule of Charles I
England in the 11630s
Kenneth Fincham

England in the 1650s
Ann Hughes

The Restoration
England in the 1660s
N. H. Keeble

England in the 1690s
Craig Rose

The
Birth of Britain

A New Nation 1700–1710

W. A. Speck

BLACKWELL
Oxford UK & Cambridge USA

First published 1994

Blackwell Publishers
108 Cowley Road
Oxford OX4 1JF
UK

238 Main Street
Cambridge, Massachusetts 02142
USA

British Library Cataloguing in Publication Data
A CIP catalogue record for this book is available from the British Library.

Library of Congress Cataloging-in-Publication Data
Speck, W. A. (William Arthur)
    The birth of Britain : a new nation 1700–1710 / W. A. Speck.
    p.   cm. — (A history of early modern England)
    Includes bibliographical references and index.
    ISBN 0 631 17544 X (alk. paper)
    1. Great Britain—History—Anne, 1702–1714. 2. Great Britain—
    History—William and Mary, 1689–1702. I. Title. II. Series.
DA495.S73   1994
941.06′9—dc20
                                                        93–45877
                                                           CIP

Copy-edited and typeset in 10 on 11½ Baskerville
by Grahame & Grahame Editorial, Brighton
Printed in Great Britain by Hartnolls Ltd., Bodmin, Cornwall
This book is printed on acid-free paper

To the Memory
of
Geoffrey Holmes

Contents

List of Illustrations

List of Maps

List of Abbreviations

Addison Corr	*The Letters of Joseph Addison*, ed. W. Graham (Oxford, 1941)
Add	Additional Manuscripts
ARA	Algemeen Rijksarchief, The Hague
BL	British Library
BIHR	*Bulletin of the Institute of Historical Research*
Boyer, *Annals*	Abel Boyer, *The History of the Reign of Queen Anne, digested into Annals* (11 vols, 1703–13)
Burnet	Gilbert Burnet, *History of my own time* (6 vols, Oxford, 1833)
CSPD	*Calendar of State Papers Domestic*
Churchill	W. S. Churchill, *Marlborough: his life and times* (4 vols, 1967)
Cobbett	W. Cobbett, *Parliamentary History of England* (36 vols, 1806–1820)
Cocks, Diary	Bodleian Library MSS Eng. hist. b. 210. The diary of Sir Richard Cocks
CJ	*Commons' Journals*
Cowper Diary	*The private diary of William Lord Cowper*, ed. E. C. Hawtrey (Edinburgh, 1895)
Coxe, *Marlborough*	W. Coxe, *Memoirs of the duke of Marlborough* (3 vols, 1905–8)
Divided Society	*The Divided Society: Party Conflict in England 1694–1716*, ed. G. S. Holmes and W. A. Speck (1967).
Hamilton, *Diary*	*The Diary of Sir David Hamilton* ed. P. Roberts (1975)
Heinsius Corr	*De Briefwisseling van Anthonie Heinsius*, ed. A. J. Veernendaal (11 vols, The Hague, 1976–1990)
HMC	Historical Manuscript Commission Reports
LJ	*Lords' Journals*

Luttrell	Narcissus Luttrell, *A Brief Historical Relation of State Affairs 1678–1714* (6 vols, Oxford, 1857)
NLW	National Library of Wales
Nicolson, *Diary*	*The London Diaries of William Nicolson, Bishop of Carlisle* ed. C. Jones and G. Holmes (Oxford, 1985)
POAS	*Poems on Affairs of State*, ed. George deForest Lord (7 vols, 1963–1975)
PRO	Public Record Office
RO	Record Office
Snyder	*The Marlborough–Godolphin Correspondence*, ed. H. L. Snyder (3 vols, Oxford, 1975)
Tory and Whig	W. A. Speck, *Tory and Whig: The struggle in the constituencies 1701–1715* (1970)
Trevelyan	G. M. Trevelyan, *England under Queen Anne* (3 vols, 1930–34)
TCD	Trinity College, Dublin
Vernon Corr	The Correspondence of James Vernon, Boughton Hall, Northamptonshire
Vernon Corr	*Letters illustrative of the reign of William III from 1696 to 1708 addressed to the duke of Shrewsbury by James Vernon*, ed. G. P. R. James (3 vols, 1841)
Wentworth Papers	*The Wentworth Papers 1705–1739*, ed. J. J. Cartwright (1883)

Note on Dates

The dating of events conforms to the Julian or Old Style Calendar, which during the decade was eleven days behind the Gregorian or New Style Calendar in use on the continent. New Style dates are also supplied for European events only where to employ Old Style dating alone might cause confusion. Where the Julian year officially began on 25 March, however, the year here is taken to have started on 1 January. As John Oldmixon observed in 1730, 'I begin the year always with the first of January, as it has always been in use among historians, a few instances of English writers excepted. The computation from the 25th of March is peculiar to law and commerce, and that too chiefly in England, tho' I know not for what reason, it having already occasion'd great confusion, especially in History' (*The History of England during the reigns of the Royal House of Stuart*, p. xvi).

Preface

The opening decade of the eighteenth century has been an obsession of mine for nearly 35 years. I first fell under its spell in the summer term of my second year at Queen's College, Oxford, when there was a relaxation of the previously remorseless essay-writing routine which allowed me the luxury of exploring a particular period in depth. During the long, hot summer of 1959, while other undergraduates were wisely punting on the Cherwell, I was in the Bodleian library pursuing the problem of the existence or otherwise of political parties in the reign of Queen Anne, which was the prevailing question of historical enquiry into the period. I still have the jejune essay which resulted, lovingly typed by my father, who perhaps vicariously experienced through it something of the student days he never enjoyed in reality. His support of my endeavours was essential in getting my foot on the ladder of scholarship.

The next step after graduating was to research a D.Phil thesis, inevitably on the House of Commons in the early eighteenth century, the bulk of it devoted to the years 1701 to 1710. The resulting thesis consisted largely of case studies of parliamentary politics between 1704 and 1708 and of general elections between 1701 and 1715. My first essays in professional writing were assisted by two major historians of the Augustan Age whose deaths I have sadly to record. The late Garry Bennett, whose contributions to Church history were seminal, supervised the thesis. And the late Geoffrey Holmes, whose works on so many aspects of the period were definitive, helped me, immeasurably, not only my his critical readings of the chapters of my doctoral dissertation but also of my first published article, as well as by collaborating with a much junior scholar in another article and in the edition of a collection of documents. I have sought to acknowledge a deeply valued friendship by dedicating this book to his memory. It was a matter of great regret to me that his illness made it impossible to share with him the writing of it as I would have liked to do. It would certainly have been much improved by his suggestions.

The electoral studies in the thesis formed the basis of a book, *Tory and Whig: The struggle in the constituencies*, published in 1970. Though some of the materials in the case studies was published in articles, the narrative that informed them never appeared in print. It has been used as the foundation of the present text, though fresh documentation has been added, particularly the splendid editions of the correspondence of the duke of Marlborough and Lord Godolphin by Henry Snyder, and of the London diaries of bishop Nicolson of Carlisle by Clyve Jones and Geoffrey Holmes. These are now the fundamental printed texts for the decade, indispensable to any scholar working in it.

I thank Leeds University for granting me study leave for the session 1992 to 1993, and the Netherlands Institute for Advanced Study in the Humanities and Social Sciences, which awarded me a Fellowship enabling me to complete the text in Wassenaar free from any distractions. I am also grateful to John Morrill for his enthusiastic response to the draft produced by the NIAS printer. Stephen Webb also gave the text a close reading and made many valuable suggestions, not least the suggestion that a basic theme in the text was the pursuit of 'moderation'. The final version owes much to Mary Geiter, who refreshed my views of a familiar decade. Any remaining errors are of course entirely my responsibility.

Williamsburg, Virginia
December 1993

Introduction: the 1700s

Decades do not acquire their distinctive characters from the fact that they begin and end at ten-year intervals. When we talk of the 1920s, the 1930s and the 1960s we do not refer to the exact years 1920 to 1929, 1930 to 1939 or 1960 to 1969. In England 'the twenties' really began with the armistice of 1918, while 'the thirties' started with the onset of the slump in 1929. As for 'the swinging sixties', the spirit which the expression conveys emerged, as Philip Larkin observed, in 1963, between the trial of *Lady Chatterley's Lover* and the Beatles' first LP.

Although the characterization of decades seems to have become fashionable in the nineteenth century, with the 'hungry Forties' perhaps being the first to be so treated, historians can retrospectively recognize distinctions before then. Thus the opening years of the eighteenth century have a coherence in English history which separates them from the closing years of the previous century and from the last four years of the reign of Queen Anne. But their coherence does not fit the precise span of 1700 to 1709. That would be a very artificial period to treat as an entity. Rather the distinctive era began in 1701 and ended with the ministerial revolution of the summer of 1710 and the subsequent general election in September.

General elections, indeed, give the decade 1701 to 1710 its distinctive character. For no other ten-year period in modern English history witnessed as many. Between January 1701 and September 1710 there were no fewer than six. Englishmen and even English women lived through an era of almost constant electioneering. For although only about a quarter of adult males had the right to vote in those days, contested elections frequently involved the unenfranchized in their turbulence and partisanship.[1]

This study therefore begins with the general election held in January 1701. A chapter is devoted to each year of the subsequent decade. But, just as it would be artificial to require decades to begin and end at exact intervals, so is it to conclude years on the 31st of December. Indeed in many respects the 'Old Style' of starting the year on the 25th of March, although it was obsolescent by the eighteenth century, was more in keeping with the rhythm of its opening decade. Certainly dating April the first month, as Quakers then did, fits more comfortably the political configurations of these years. For parliamentary sessions were generally held from the Autumn to the Spring, and these provided a more coherent shape to the political calendar than the chronological year.

By and large, then, the chapters extend from the weeks around the Spring equinox rather than the Winter solstice. Thus the first chapter ends with the death of William III on 8 March 1702, for though that might not have coincided with the last day of 1701 it completed an era. The second chapter also stops not on 31 December 1702 but in February 1703. On the second the earl of Rochester resigned from the Lord Lieutenancy of Ireland. On the third negotiations between English and Scottish commissioners for an Anglo-Scottish union were suspended. In the same month the first occasional conformity bill came to grief following disputes between the Lords and the Commons about its provisions. These three events made February 1703 a more natural transition in the political life of the nation than that from one year to another. The chapter on the year 1703 ends in April 1704, with the resignation of the earl of Nottingham from the Secretaryship of State and the simultaneous removal from the ministry of several high church tories, which contemporaries acknowledged was a major shift in political alignments. The chapter on the year 1704 ends the following April with the dissolution of Anne's first parliament. The general election of 1705 inaugurated another chapter in political history, which culminated with the appointment of English and Scottish commissioners in the Spring of 1706 to negotiate a union of their respective countries. The months from April 1706 to May 1707, which saw the Union of England and Scotland brought to a successful conclusion, the United Kingdom of Great Britain coming officially into existence on 1 May 1707, were far more significant in the life of the nation than the twelve from 1 January to 31 December 1706.

The next event to mark a significant turning point was the fall of Robert Harley in February 1708. The opening of the peace negotiations at The Hague in the Spring of 1709 also opened up a new chapter in the war which dominated the decade. Finally the trial of Dr Sacheverell a year later began a process which was to transform the political scene when it ended with the general election of 1710, with which this study also concludes.

Certain features of the political scene which are taken for granted might not be familiar to some readers and therefore require to be introduced here. In December 1700 the Prussian envoy wrote from London to Berlin:[2]

Though the English are nearly all divided into Whigs and Tories there
are many country members in Parliament who have never joined with
these parties to the extent of closely espousing either. These men speak
and vote in the House according to their lights, which rarely reach
beyond the shores of their own island. The principles which govern
their reasoning are their care for
1. the religion of this country
2. the liberty of the individual
3. the trade which enhances the value of their produce, and
4. the cultivation of their lands.
No matter which is the party in power, and no matter how eloquent
its appeal may be, it will never win over these members unless it can
convince them that one of these four points is under attack.

This letter neatly summarized the principal concerns not only of MPs
but also of their constituents on the eve of the first general election
to be held in the eighteenth century. They were not at that time
completely polarized into two parties. Although most could be identified either as tories or as whigs there were still significant numbers
who were not enlisted in their ranks. These independents could be
persuaded to join with either party if they could be convinced that a
vital interest was endangered.

Tories tried to convince them that the national religion was under
attack. The slogan 'the church in danger' was the rallying cry of the
tory or, as it was also significantly called, the church party. It had
been raised in *A Letter to a Convocation Man*, a tract published in
1697. This accused the largely whig government of presiding over
a virulent attack on the established Church of England and on its
clergymen from dissenters, deists and even atheists. The remedy for
this, a meeting of the Church's representative body Convocation, had
been deliberately denied to its members. Such a denial, it alleged, was
illegal, since Convocations should have been convened along with
parliaments. This was constitutional nonsense but political dynamite.
For it was true that Convocation had not met since 1689, when it
had demonstrated a degree of rancour towards Protestant dissenters.
Thus an attempt to open the Church's ranks by relaxing the Anglican
liturgy so as to accommodate moderate Presbyterians, at least, had
been thwarted by the intransigence of high churchmen. Since then
Protestant nonconformity, legally allowed under the Toleration Act of
1689, had seemed to flourish, while the numbers communicating with
the established church had declined alarmingly. Even more alarming,
perhaps, were the onslaughts upon Anglican orthodoxy from the press
after 1695. Until then publication was subject to state censorship given
statutory authority by the Licensing Act. The failure to renew the Act
in that year had led to the press being unmuzzled. There had ensued

a spate of pamphlets challenging the basis of the church's authority and even the role of its clergy. Those who felt threatened by these developments sought in the machinery of Convocation to reverse these trends. Thus when the tory earl of Rochester took office as Lord Lieutenant of Ireland in December 1700 he did so on condition that elections for Convocation should be held simultaneously with those for parliament in the new year.

When Convocation at last met in 1701, however, it turned not against free-thinkers so much as against whig bishops. Burnet of Salisbury was singled out for attack for having published an analysis of the Thirty-nine Articles which his enemies claimed was heretical. When they proceeded to censor it in the Lower House the archbishop of Canterbury, Thomas Tenison, prorogued their sittings. The dispute showed that the clergy were divided into two parties, the so-called 'high church' party, which was dominant among the elected representatives of the clergy in the Lower House, and the 'low church' party which had a majority of the bishops who formed the upper. These were the equivalent of the tory and whig parties in the state. Indeed tories in the House of Commons identified the bishops bench in the Lords as a bloc vote for the whigs. Led by Sir John Pakington they tried to prevent careerist low church clergy from toeing the whig line to obtain preferment to it by introducing a bill in 1701 to prohibit bishops being translated from one see to another.

Another religious trend which alarmed the tories was the resort to the practice of occasional conformity by dissenters in order to hold office. Strictly speaking the Church of England had a statutory monopoly of offices under the Crown or in municipal corporations guaranteed by the Test Act of 1673 and the Corporation Act of 1661. Both made communion according to Anglican rites a qualification for office-holding in national and local government. Protestants, however, unlike Catholics, could take communion in the established church, and many Presbyterians did so in order to qualify themselves for office. Apart from presenting themselves at a communion service in order to receive a certificate to satisfy the legal requirements, however, they generally attended their own services. A particularly flagrant example of this practice occurred in 1697 when the Lord Mayor of London, Sir Humphrey Edwin, went to a conventicle 'attended by the sword-bearer with the city sword and the other officers'.

Such affronts swelled the cries that the church was in danger. Where the remedy for other challenges was seen to lie in Convocation the threat from occasional conformists was to be dealt with in parliament. John Howe, a recent convert from the whig to the tory ranks, first moved for legislation to outlaw the practice in March 1701 'to ingratiate himself with his new friends the Church or to be revenged upon his old friends the Dissenters'.[3]

If tories maintained that the Church was endangered from dissent, whigs asserted that it was threatened more by Catholicism. The Revolution of 1688 indeed had in their eyes only narrowly averted the threat posed by the arbitrary acts of the Catholic James II. He had fled into exile in December and his rule set aside by the Convention parliament which met in January 1689. In the Bill of Rights provision had been made for a Protestant succession to the crown. First children of William and Mary were to succeed, then children of Mary's sister Anne, and failing them heirs William might have by another wife should Mary die childless. At the time it seemed as though every eventuality had been covered. But in fact Mary died in 1694 leaving no children, William clearly would never marry again, and in July 1700 the duke of Gloucester, the only one of Anne's many children to survive babyhood, died. Once again the succession was open, and if the claims of the exiled James and his son James Francis Edward were to be thwarted further statutory provision would have to be made to maintain the Protestant line in the house of Hanover. Whigs were to champion the cause of the Protestant succession more wholeheartedly than tories, some of whom still maintained allegiance to James, while many were suspected of doing so and were therefore dubbed Jacobites.

Whigs were also more likely to claim that individual liberty was threatened. During the debates on the Bill of Rights they had been keener than the tories on curbing the royal prerogative. Thus tory members of the Convention wished only to include in the Bill abuses of the prerogative which could be attributed to James II, while whig members had wanted to add other restrictions on the power of the Crown. In the event it had been agreed to proscribe the alleged illegal actions of James and to leave out reforms which required new laws. Thus Macaulay could claim that in the Revolution settlement 'not a single flower of the Crown was lost; not a single new right was given to the people'.[4]

That stretched a point a little, for the clause in the Bill which made it illegal to maintain a peace-time standing army without consent of parliament did indeed make new law and clipped a major bloom. Nevertheless William's reliance on parliament, and particularly on the whigs in the Commons, to sustain his war effort led to further pruning of the prerogative. Thus the price he paid for such vital sinews of war as the Bank of England was the Triennial Act of 1694, which limited his prerogative of summoning and dissolving parliament at pleasure since it necessitated a general election to be held every three years. William was determined to retain as many prerogatives as possible, and he used the royal veto in 1693 to reject a triennial bill which had passed both Houses of parliament. The following year, however, he accepted that his consent was necessary as a condition of appointing whigs as ministers.

There was one aspect of the tension between the prerogative of the Crown and the liberty of the subject which cut across the party lines. As we have noted, both tories and whigs maintained that a standing army was illegal in time of peace without consent of parliament. Since war was declared with France in 1689 this did not become an issue until after the treaty of Rijswijk in 1697. Then, however, it emerged with a vengeance. Most tories came out openly in opposition to a request by the king to maintain at least 30,000 men in the armed forces. By then his ministers were mainly whigs, and they tried to fulfil his wishes. But a significant minority of back-bench whigs, led by Robert Harley and Paul Foley, joined with tory opponents of the standing army. These Country whigs were most vociferous in the ensuing pamphlet war, which took the form of an argument between Country writers such as John Trenchard and Court apologists like Lord Somers. Trenchard argued that standing armies were inconsistent with English liberties, and drew on historical and contemporary examples to demonstrate that they had been used by tyrants to suppress their subjects. Somers, the Lord Chancellor, denied that the government planned to use the army except to defend English liberties against tyrants like Louis XIV. But he argued in vain. The new Country party, as the alliance of tories and opposition whigs was called, cut the army to 10,000 in the session 1697 to 1698, and, after a general election fought mainly on this issue, cut it further in the following session to a mere 7,000.

Trade had also created tensions between Court and Country during the 1690s. Concern was expressed in the Commons about the disruption of commerce brought about by the war and the government's apparent failure to protect it. This came to a head in the session 1695–6 when some Edinburgh merchants launched the Scottish East India Company which seemed to threaten English trading interests. To protect English commerce against these threats the Country party urged the setting up of a Council of Trade responsible to parliament. To counter this move the Court proposed the establishment of a Board of Trade answerable to the Crown. In the event the Court prevailed and the Board of Trade and Plantations was set up in 1696.

Trade to the Far East had also caused friction between tories and whigs in the years after the Revolution. The monopoly of the East India Company incorporated by James I had often been challenged by merchants wishing to breach it. Charles II and James II, however, had resisted these challenges and confirmed the privileges of the Company. Its close identification with those monarchs caused it to be under a cloud after 1689, and William III granted a charter to its rivals who formed the New East India company in 1698. Thereafter there were two companies engaged in trade with the Far East. Their interests were espoused by members of parliament, quite a few of whom were also members of one or other of the companies. On the whole the old company was championed by the tories and the new by the whigs. In 1700 their disputes came to a head when the old company proposed to outbid the new in a loan to the government of £2,000,000. Since the Commons had to approve one or other of the bids the two companies were to make every effort to secure representation in parliament.

The rivalry between the two companies was to inform some of the proceedings in the new parliament when it met in 1701. But this was a storm in a teacup in comparison with the row which exploded over foreign policy as war with France again became imminent. Tory politicians came out in opposition to renewed hostilities while whigs clamoured for war.

It was clear that something would have to be done to avert a major conflict when the long anticipated death of Carlos II of Spain finally occurred. For he ruled over a vast empire, which included in Europe the southern Netherlands (modern Belgium), much of Italy as well as all of the Iberian peninsula except Portugal, while across the Atlantic, Spanish sway was upheld in Mexico and Peru. Carlos had no direct heir, so these possessions were claimed by his Habsburg cousins in the Holy Roman Empire and by the Bourbons headed by Louis XIV of France. If either claimant obtained the whole it would produce a European hegemony unacceptable to England and the Dutch Republic. William III, the stadhouder-king, had tried to prevent the Spanish inheritance being gained by either, and had negotiated two partition treaties in 1698 and 1700 aimed at dividing it between rival claimants. In October 1700, however, as his final act Carlos published a will which left his empire intact to the principal Bourbon claimant, Louis XIV's grandson, Philip, duke of Anjou. In November news reached England that Louis XIV had accepted the will and that thereby the attempts by William III and his allies to partition the Spanish king's empire to avoid the whole going either to the Habsburg or the Bourbon claimant were rendered void. Tories professed indifference to this development. As one put it:[5]

> I am commenced so violent a sportsman that my satisfaction to continue in the country two months longer than usual has not been interrupted by the death of his Catholic Majesty (Carlos) nor am I a jot concerned whether the widow accepts the hancher of Monsieur le Dauphin to dry up those tears or whether the original papers for partition of the Spanish monarchy be allotted to the politicians or to the tobacconists for the use of their best Virginia does not trouble my head.

William's tory ministers, Lord Treasurer Godolphin and Rochester, the Lord Lieutenant of Ireland, were prepared to accept Louis' decision. They urged William to recognize Philip as king of Spain. Leading whigs, then in opposition to the largely tory ministry, advocated resistance to French expansion.

To the whigs Louis XIV represented a threat to the balance of power, the Protestant interest and to what they called the liberties of Europe. They saw the fate of the country as being intricately involved in these ideological concepts. The more insular tories were much less enthusiastic for the involvement in European politics that such notions implied.

The reluctance of tories to renew hostilities was partly provoked by their allegations that they bore the brunt of war taxation. Tory propagandists asserted that the fiscal measures brought about to finance the war effort were detrimental to the landed interest, while whigs defended the Bank and the new system of public credit. This was one of several trends which converged in the opening years of the eighteenth century to end the confusion of William's reign, when Court and Country frequently cut across tory and whig, and polarized parliament and society into tories and whigs under Anne.

The year 1701 was indeed to become a watershed in this transition. The issues of religion, the succession and above all of peace or war were to realign politicians into two parties, the tories and the whigs, whose rivalry was to provide the main dynamic of politics not only at Westminster but also throughout the country.

What polarized the parties above all was the attempt by the tories to impeach the whig leaders for their role in the partition treaties of 1698 and 1700 whereby William III had tried to avert war over the Spanish succession. Whig ranks closed against this onslaught. The impeachments were long remembered as the issue which set the two parties in the mould they were to occupy for the rest of the decade and beyond. When the whigs were coming into power during Anne's reign James Brydges, Paymaster of the forces abroad and a Court tory, felt threatened. As he explained to Godolphin:[6]

> It was my misfortune to come very young into Parl[iament] during our heats and divisions in the late reign; and my natural temper carrying me to pursue with warmth their measures and interest with whom I am engaged, I made some steps which may be remembered hereafter to my disadvantage . . . I was pitch't upon by the House of Commons to carry up their impeachment against my L[or]d Halifax . . .

Brydges was the more concerned when he learned that 'not contented with the distinction of tacker or no tacker they [the whigs] had brought it in their discourse everywhere to that of impeachment or no impeachment, and that whoever were for the first were not fit to be employed, in their opinion, in the Queen's service'.

Something like a two-party system appears to have operated in this decade. Indeed it seems as though the politics of the period between 1701 and 1710 can be explained exclusively in terms of the rivalry between the tories and the whigs, and how the latter gradually overcame the former to gain power by 1708 only to have it snatched from them in 1710.

This view, however, is to some extent illusory. The Crown possessed great resources which could be used effectively to offset the tendency towards a two-party system. Before investigating their use in these years it is important to establish precisely what is meant by such a system. The concept is meaningful only in the sense of an alternation in power by two parties. Thus since 1945 Britain has seen the effectual operation of a two-party system, even despite the existence and rise of minor parties, with the monopolization of power by successive Labour and Conservative governments. At any given time the Cabinet is composed either of Labour or Conservative politicians, while their rivals are in opposition.

By contrast in the reigns of William III and Queen Anne the Cabinet can only be described as having been composed exclusively of members of one party for very brief periods. William preferred coalition ministries of both parties. It is true that he was persuaded that the whigs were more inclined to back his war effort, and gave key Cabinet posts to the Junto after 1693.[7] As a result by the mid-1690s the ministry became predominantly whig. However, after the peace of Rijswijk the Junto failed to retain control of parliament, and William reverted to his former policy of appointing mixed ministries by 1700. During 1701, as war clouds gathered and the tories seemed more inclined to pursue vendettas against the whigs than to prepare England for a renewal of hostilities against Louis XIV, he showed signs of turning again to the Junto.

This process was far from complete, however, when the king died in 1702. Queen Anne, though she was inclined towards the tories, was no less anxious to avoid complete dependence on one party than her predecessor. Consequently, while appointing tory leaders to the more influential posts, she included whigs in the Cabinet in 1702. As the high church tories began to demand their removal, she instead removed them. From 1704 to 1708 her ministry was able to retain the confidence of parliament on most occasions without conceding more than a minimum of Cabinet posts to the Junto and their adherents. In 1708 she was obliged to make major concessions to them. Between 1708 and 1710 it could be said that there was an all-whig Cabinet, provided we are prepared to ascribe the duke of Marlborough and lord Godolphin to that party by then – though earlier they had passed for tories. Thus for only two years, a fifth of the decade, can the Cabinet ministers be allocated exclusively to one party or another. When one descends to junior ministerial posts the situation even between 1708 and 1710 is not clear-cut, for there were tory ministers despite Junto ascendancy, like James Brydges the Paymaster of the forces. In the choice of Cabinet ministers, therefore, William and Anne got their way for most of their reigns, choosing to retain the services of politicians despite the rage of party in parliament.

The fact that most Cabinet ministers were peers is a clue to the importance of the House of Lords in this decade. When dealing with how the monarchs employed the resources of the Crown to influence the proceedings in parliament it is right to start with the upper chamber.

The presence of twenty-six bishops there gave the Crown over the years the opportunity to create a bloc of Court supporters. William III had used the unique opportunities which the Revolution had given him to remodel the episcopal bench. Several bishops had refused to recognize the validity of his right to the throne, for which they had been deprived of their sees and replaced, for the most part by low church men whose votes could be relied on by the whigs. Anne tried with archbishop Sharp of York to promote high churchmen to bishoprics who would, as she put it, 'vote right'.

Where voting right in William's reign had usually meant supporting Court whig measures, as far as Anne was concerned it involved supporting Court tory policies. Here she was handicapped by the fact that a slight majority of lay peers were whiggishly inclined. Her most drastic solution to this problem, the creation of a dozen tory lords, was in what might be anachronistically called the New Year's Honours list of 1712, after the decade ended. But before that she had ennobled four tories in 1703 in an attempt to redress the balance in the Upper House. This balance was disturbed again after 1707 by the arrival at Westminster of sixteen Scottish lords elected by their peers under the terms of the Act of Union. The Court, however, could exert considerable influence on the outcome of these elections, so that the Scottish contingent swelled the prevailing majority. In 1708 it strengthened the Junto's hand in its dealings with the ministers.

Promoting men to bishoprics or peerages involved the Crown directly in the business of managing the House of Lords. Other methods of influencing proceedings in parliament were, by and large, left to political managers. Thus William III relied heavily upon Robert Spencer, earl of Sunderland, while Anne employed such politicians as Lord Godolphin and Robert Harley to get her business through both Houses. And although he was abroad too often to get involved in the day-to-day management of parliament the duke of Marlborough exercized enormous influence on its proceedings.

The tremendously powerful political position held by the duke in the middle years of Anne's reign has never received the attention it deserves. It was entirely owing to the war. As long as the queen was committed to the war of the Spanish succession Marlborough was indispensable at the head of the armies of the Grand Alliance. By threatening to resign, his ultimate weapon in any showdown with the queen, Marlborough could virtually blackmail Anne into taking in ministers she did not like and even into parting with ministers she did. As we shall see he 'persuaded' her to appoint his son-in-law the earl of Sunderland as Secretary of state in 1706 and, after a tremendous struggle, to dismiss Robert Harley from the other secretaryship in 1708.

In this respect the decade was dominated by the 'duumvirs', as Marlborough and Godolphin were known. They survived several changes of ministry, which transformed the Cabinet from a predominantly tory body in 1702 to a largely whig one by 1710. Their control of the political machine is a key to the political changes of the 1700s.

One way in which managers like Godolphin and Marlborough used the Crown's influence was by patronage. The Treasurer had at his disposal resources which could be employed to build up a nucleus of support in parliament. The Captain General also had a handful of followers in both Houses. Army officers like William Cadogan, lieutenant of the Tower and Member for Woodstock on the duke's interest, Adam de Cardonnel his Secretary, James Craggs of the ordnance office and General Thomas Erle were loyal lieutenants in the Commons. Marlborough even had a few dependents among Admiralty officers and naval officers, including his brother George, and Henry Killigrew, both of whom owed their seats at St Alban's to the Churchill interest in the borough.

But the chief patron in the Admiralty was Anne's husband, Prince George of Denmark. George played a much more prominent part in the politics of her reign than has been acknowledged. Indeed Anne's devotion to her husband has been underestimated. Thus some historians speak of her being left alone to fight her political battles once she had parted company with her former friend, the formidable duchess of Marlborough. Yet she had 'the Prince, her turtle mate' as a contemporary poem put it, to lean on until his death in 1708.[8]

The involvement of George in politics has largely gone unnoticed because he was a shadowy figure. He is mostly dismissed in a few well-known anecdotes. Thus Charles II is alleged to have said of him that he had tried him drunk and had tried him sober and drunk or sober there was nothing in him. James II, on hearing that his son-in-law had gone over to William of Orange in 1688 repeated what George had said when learning of other desertions, 'est-il possible?' Lord Godolphin once complained that an audience with Anne would have lasted forever 'if after the clock had struck 3, Prince George had not thought fit to come in and look as though it were dinner time'.[9]

Yet George had more political clout than these anecdotes suggest. Thus he had significant patronage at his disposal not only having his own household but also the posts of Lord Admiral and Warden of the Cinque ports. This was used to build up a nucleus of support in parliament. For instance, the earl of Westmorland, who was gentleman of the Prince's bedchamber and deputy warden of the Cinque ports, was 'an obedient follower of the Prince' until George's death in 1708.[10] On one occasion Westmorland was summoned by the Prince to Kensington Palace at eight o'clock in the morning to be instructed how to vote in the Lords. Lord Stawell, lord of the Prince's bedchamber, was less loyal than Westmorland, for though Lord Godolphin boasted that he could 'govern him in every vote' he was dismissed for opposing the Court in parliament.[11]

Prince George's patronage was not confined to the Upper House. As Lord Admiral he presided over a unique Council of Admiralty which was intended to cover up but rather compounded his administrative incompetence. Members of this Council were also members of the House of Commons, and were expected to toe the line in debates. When one of them, George Clarke, the Council's Secretary, flagrantly voted the wrong way in 1705 he was actually dismissed from the Prince's service in the very division lobby. Another member of the Council, Sir George Rooke, was sacked shortly afterwards. Two other dependants of the Prince's who defied his wishes in the same division were also dismissed: Thomas Conyers, his equerry and Henry Grahme, a gentleman of his bedchamber.[12]

Prince George even enjoyed some electoral interest, since the Cinque Ports, which were all parliamentary boroughs returning two members each, were in the words of a contemporary 'much guided by the Lord Warden'. In 1705 he gave his interest to his deputy, Lord Westmorland, who boasted 'such success that the members were almost all changed to the principles I was of'.[13]

George thus had a small but not inconsiderable connexion of peers and MPs whose parliamentary behaviour he could influence. Indeed so influential was he held to be that when financial provision was being made for him by parliament in 1703 a motion was proposed to add a clause disqualifying his dependants from sitting in the Commons. Anne, ever protective of her close friends and family, resented opposition to this bill, 'saying that she had rather an affront were given to her self than to the Prince'. This motion was easily defeated in the Lower

House by 209 votes to 37. But it demonstrated some concern that the Prince's patronage was influencing proceedings in parliament.[14]

George seems to have had even more influence than his patronage provided. This can only be deduced, for the documentary evidence is scanty to say the least. Consequently his role remains obscure. Even his obituarists were hard put to it to find much to say about him. Thus his chaplain admitted in his funeral sermon that 'as to his behaviour in public affairs, which were very difficult and intricate, the many years which he was engaged in them, he always steered his course with such wisdom and judgement that no one with any justice can discover a real fault or blemish in his management'. Nevertheless he provided clues to George's priorities. Thus he stressed the Prince's belief in Providence, which was expressed 'in moving discourses on the glorious battle of Blenheim, the marvellous relief of Barcelona and the last delivery from the intended invasion' – the last a reference to the Jacobite attempt at a landing in Scotland. George is thus revealed firmly committed to the allied cause in the war of the Spanish succession and to the Protestant succession in the house of Hanover. As a former military man who was related to the elector of Hanover and whose very position depended on the Revolution settlement of 1689 this is scarcely surprising. But it does suggest that he reinforced Anne's commitment to both as well. Again his chaplain emphasized these aspects of Prince George's contribution to public life when he observed: 'let Germany lament for the high alliance and near relation to this Crown.' 'Europe hath reason to bemoan this loss', he concluded, 'for Her Majesty's sake.'[15]

Prince George's death devastated Anne, who, incapacitated with grief kept the Court in mourning until December 1710, the maximum time prescribed by custom. It was as much a turning point in her reign as the death of Albert was in Victoria's. Previously she had been redoubtable in having a stomach for the political fight. For many months she had held out against giving office to leaders of the whig Junto. Now suddenly all the fight was taken out of her. Immediately after George died Somers and Wharton were given Cabinet office. She had as little as possible to do with parliament, her speeches at the opening of the session in November 1708 and at its close in April 1709 being delivered by commissioners. When she again addressed the Houses at the opening of parliament in November 1709 'it was observed that she spoke in a much fainter voice than she used to have, and her manner was more careless and less moving than it has been on other occasions.'[16]

The trauma of her husband's death led to the whigs storming the closet. Had he not died she might well have stood out against them longer. While it is always dangerous to use a counter-factual argument it is not altogether clear that she would have been obliged to capitulate her prerogative of ministerial appointments to them.

Certainly there were reserves of parliamentary strength to draw upon. In addition to the placemen, who made up half the House of Lords and about a quarter of the Commons, there were peers and MPs whose loyalty to the Crown could still offset the pull of party. In the Upper House there were lords like the earl of Cholmondeley, a moderate whig who claimed in 1712 that 'he was an impartial man, and in pure respect for her majesty should be for complying with her majesty's desire.' In the Commons too there were moderates whom the Court employed in an effort to offset the Junto. These were called 'lord treasurer's whigs' since they were managed by Godolphin. Among them was Robert Monckton, who was so inclined to support the Court that in 1710 he told his fellow whigs that 'he wou'd not fly in the Queen's face for them'.[17] Another was Robert Walpole, who served his political apprenticeship participating in these efforts to build up a Court party in parliament. He was to apply the lessons he learned far more effectively than lord treasurer Godolphin. As prime minister Walpole employed patronage to build up a Court party in parliament far more dependable than were the placemen of Anne's day. The 'Old Corps' whigs whom he directed were a disciplined army in comparison with the dependants of the Court under the queen. As we have seen in the case of Prince George's servants many felt their first loyalty was to a party rather than to the Crown. The whigs especially stayed loyal to the Junto, keeping up the pressure on the Queen in 1708 until she collapsed when her husband died.

Anne's bereavement paralyzed the Court and led to the triumph of the Junto. But when she recovered her fighting spirit she showed that Robert Harley was right to claim that 'there is not one party, nay not both of them, can stand against the Queen's frowns'.[18] Early in 1710 some whigs planned to move a resolution in parliament requesting that she dismiss Abigail Hill, the lady of the bedchamber whom they suspected of intriguing against them. Anne was livid. She closetted peers and MPs telling them plainly that they would incur her wrath if they supported the resolution. The tactic worked, and the motion was dropped. Even though the whigs boasted a majority in both Houses they flinched from using it to try to force the queen to remove what one called 'such a slut' as Abigail.[19]

As long as she was committed to the war, however, Anne was obliged to work with the whigs. Until Prince George's death she fully upheld her commitment to the Grand Alliance. Thereafter she began to waver. In 1709 Robert Harley noted the effects of what was termed 'the butcher's bill' on 'her sex and Christian horror of bloodshed'.[20] The following year he was able to persuade her that an honourable peace could be negotiated and that she could dispense with the services of the whigs. Over the summer he engineered the ministerial revolution which replaced an entirely whig Cabinet with one predominantly tory under his own leadership. In September the Queen dissolved parliament and in the ensuing general election a tory majority was returned to the Commons.

A dissolution was the ultimate weapon which the queen could use to free herself from dependence upon a particular set of politicians. For the Crown had considerable influence over the outcome of elections, so much so that the party which it backed usually triumphed at the polls. As Lord Cowper advised George I in 1715, with the experience of Anne's reign still very fresh, "tis wholly in your Majesty's power by showing your favour in due time (before the elections) to one or other of them to give which of them you please a clear majority in all succeeding parliaments'.[21]

Such had not been the case in William's reign. As we shall see he tried to get a different result from that which came about when he decided on the 'snap' dissolution of parliament in 1701. And in 1710 public opinion was swinging against the whigs and in favour of the tories, so that Court influence simply helped the process whereby a House of Commons with a whig majority was replaced by one with a tory majority. And even then it could not control the size of that majority, so that the tories came back to Westminster in greater numbers than Harley had anticipated or desired. 'Those who got the last parliament dissolved,' gloated a whig, 'are as much astonished and they say troubled for the glut of tories that will be in the next as the whigs themselves.'[22] It meant that Harley's ministry would be more dependent upon them than he wished, and possibly even the Queen herself.

For the Queen had definite ideas about the constitutional and political roles of the Crown and parliament. She resented the 'merciless men of both parties' who insisted on office as a reward for their support. Early in her reign she told the House of Lords firmly 'that it was her own undoubted prerogative to retain or displace those that attended her'.[23] Yet she had to yield that prerogative in order to get her way with her parliaments.

Nevertheless in the end she did get her own way. Such achievements of her reign as the Union with Scotland and the preservation of the Protestant succession in the House of Hanover owed not a little to her dogged determination to secure them. A less determined monarch might have given in to the rage of party. Anne set up the Crown as a third force against the parties. By doing so she offset the tendency towards a two-party system. She did what she could to make sure that the parliaments of her reign were loyal to her rather than to the party leaders.

To describe politics in this decade as a two-party *system* is therefore misleading. Any model of the political structure of the years 1701 to 1710 must take the Crown's influence into account. A triangle would best serve the purpose, with one side for the tories, another for the whigs, and a third for the Court.

The influence of the Court was perhaps most forcibly felt in the greatest single achievement of the decade, the Union of England and Scotland in 1707. Both William III and Anne were devoted to its accomplishment, and the Queen counted it a greater blessing of her reign than the victories in the war with France.

Traditionally the Court had had more influence over the Scottish parliament than it had over the English. This was due to many considerations. For one thing the northern body was much smaller, perhaps half the size of the English. It also met in one House, where the three estates of nobles, barons from the counties and burghers from the towns assembled together. Since many of the Scottish nobility were impoverished, while the electorates even for the shires were small and therefore more amenable to electoral interest than most English constituencies, the Court could exploit its patronage to build up a considerable connection in the Estates. The Court party thus generated had taken its lead from the Lords of the Articles, a committee of the Scottish Privy Council which controlled the proceedings of the Edinburgh parliament.

But the traditional means of influencing the outcome of debates in Edinburgh had been seriously weakened by the Revolution. The settlement of 1689 had been much more radical in Scotland than in England. Thus the Lords of the Articles had been abolished and with them a steering device for procedure which had served the Court well under the Stuarts. The Presbyterian church had been established and episcopacy abolished which was a further blow to the Court, especially under Anne who sympathized with the episcopalians. Country ideology, even Republicanism, had been ascendant in the Revolution, the Scottish Convention making no bones about the notion that James VII had forfeited his Crown by breaking the original contract. At the same time support for the deposed monarch in the form of Jacobitism was much stronger in the northern than in the southern kingdom.

All these considerations made the situation very different from that which faced the Court in England. There was a resurgence of Scottish independence from the Crown, which was increasingly identified with the power structure in England. Where James VII had spent some time in Scotland as duke of York, building up a clientele there, neither William nor Anne ever visited the country. They were held to be remote from the concerns of their northern subjects, a feeling intensified by William's attitude towards the Scottish Company for trading with Africa and the Indies. The launching of the company had been seen as a direct threat to its interests by the English East India company, which had sought help from parliament. Their political supporters managed to prevent English investors buying stock in the new company. William had taken the side of the English merchants, even intervening personally to stop the Scottish company raising capital in Europe. It had nevertheless aroused the enthusiasm of Scottish investors, especially for its scheme to plant a colony at Darien on the isthmus of Panama. But New Caledonia had been a disaster, and had to be abandoned. Its failure was partly due to the fact that William had listened to Spanish objections to the scheme.

All these developments made it difficult to create a Court party in the Scottish parliament. The political groupings in the Estates which developed when the Court's influence declined were very different from those in the English parliament. While the terms tory and whig were used to define them they did not mean the same thing in Edinburgh as they did at Westminster. Although whigs were those who stood 'on the Revolution foot' this could apply to a wide gamut of politicians from staunch Presbyterians and even Republicans to careerists. And even a Scottish nobleman could admit that 'the greatest difficulty is how to describe a Scots Tory'.[24] Again it spanned a spectrum from episcopalians to out and out Jacobites, who were far more numerous in Scotland than in England. Most contemporary commentators seem to have preferred a different vocabulary. George Lockhart, for instance, saw a turning point in 1698 with the debates in the Scottish parliament on the Darien disaster. This 'raised a hot debate in the House, the Courtiers defending the King; but the Country party, which then began to get that title . . . at last prevailed'. When a new parliament met after the elections in 1703[25]

> there were different parties or Clubs; first the Court party; and those were subdivided into such as were Revolutioners, and of anti-monarchical principles, and such as were any thing that would procure or secure them in their employments and pensions; and these were directed by the Court in all their measures. Secondly the Country party, which consisted of some (tho but few) Cavaliers, and of Presbyterians, of which the Duke of Hamilton and the Marquis of Tweeddale were leaders. Thirdly the Cavaliers . . . of whom the Earl of Home was the chief man. All these had their several distinct meetings and projects . . .

This was the parliament which was eventually to ratify the Union. There are many problems associated with the final form which the Union took which are dealt with in the appropriate passages in the narrative. One aspect, however, needs to be spelled out here to put the transaction in context. That is the relative resources of the two countries. For at the time these were extremely disproportionate, with England being among the wealthiest nations in Europe while Scotland was one of the poorest. Lord Belhaven stressed the superiority of the English in a celebrated speech attacking the Union:[26]

> Their circumstances are great and glorious, their treaties are prudently managed both at home and abroad, their generals brave and valorous, their armies successful and victorious, their trophies and laurels memorable and surprising, their enemies subdued and routed, their strongholds besieged and taken, sieges relieved, marshals killed and taken prisoners, provinces and kingdoms are the results of their victories; the royal navy is the terror of Europe, their trade and commerce extended throughout the universe, encircling the whole habitable world, and rendering their own capital city the Emporium for the whole inhabitants of the earth; and which is yet more than all these things, the subjects freely bestowing their treasure upon their sovereign; and above all, these vast riches, the sinews of war, and without which all the glorious success had proved abortive, the treasures are managed with such faithfulness and nicety, that they answer seasonably all their demands, though at never so great a distance.

By contrast Scots were 'an obscure, poor people ... removed to a remote corner of the world, without name and without alliances'.

Belhaven was paying tribute to the great power status which England had acquired since the Revolution of 1688. Before then she had appeared to be a mere satellite of France. Afterwards she emerged as the linchpin of alliances formed to defeat alleged French threats to the balance of power and 'the liberties of Europe'. During the 1690s the allies had not distinguished themselves under William III, the nine years' war being a hard slog of sieges. In the 1700s, however, under the leadership of Marlborough, the Grand Alliance achieved a series of notable victories against the Bourbon powers. The autumn of 1706, when the Edinburgh parliament was debating the terms of union, saw England's reputation at its zenith after Marlborough's victory at Ramillies had led to the expulsion of French forces from most of the Spanish Netherlands.

England had had the potential for great power status before, as Cromwell had shown with his intervention in the last stages of the struggle between France and Spain which had started during the Thirty Years War. By throwing English resources behind the French he had assisted in the process whereby Habsburg hegemony was replaced by Bourbon ascendancy during the reign of Louis XIV. Since then, however, those resources had not been geared to military intervention in Europe. After 1689 they were, and revealed how formidable they could be. They can be summed up as the results of three Revolutions: Agricultural, Commercial and Financial.

The basis of England's wealth was still mainly agricultural. Of her five million or so inhabitants at least a quarter were directly or indirectly involved in agriculture. During the seventeenth century an Agricultural Revolution had occurred which had transformed the productivity of English farms. Whether it was the adoption of alternate husbandry in the Midlands or of crop rotation in East Anglia, the result had been a massive increase in output which had made England not only self sufficient in foodstuffs but able to export a surplus.

Since the population had remained relatively stable after the middle of the century, ending a period of growth, the increased output had led to a fall in food prices which gave most people more money in their pockets to spend on items which had previously been considered luxuries. Some of these were imported from across the oceans, such as tea and coffee from the east and sugar and tobacco from America. Others were manufactured at home, improving the quantity and quality of domestic possession from clothes and bed linen to kitchen utensils and even reading matter. The resulting stimulus to trade and industry had created wealth in other sectors of the economy than the agricultural.

Government had sought increasingly to tap this wealth in the form of customs and excise. These formed the main taxes under Charles and James, who had stimulated commerce and manufacturing deliberately to increase the yield from these sources. They were helped by a boom in the 1680s which has been seen as a Commercial Revolution. It particularly affected trans-Atlantic trade, leading to the remarkable growth of the English colonies on the eastern seaboard of North America and in the West Indies.

After the Glorious Revolution the government was even keener to maximize its revenues in order to sustain the war effort. In addition to the customs and excise the land tax was introduced at the war-time rate of four shillings in the pound, which in theory at least was a twenty per cent tax on rents. This alone yielded £2,000,000 a year, while the other taxes brought in on average £1,640,000. But since the war budgets soared to £5,454,555 there was a shortfall between revenue and expenditure, exacerbated by the slowness with which revenues were collected. By 1697 the gap reached £16,700,000. This huge sum was raised in anticipation of future taxes in the form of loans. A system of public credit was created which has been dubbed the Financial Revolution. At its heart was the Bank of England, founded in 1694. The Financial Revolution provided England with the sinews of power which were to transform its role in Europe. During the War of the Spanish Succession they were able to sustain a navy of nearly 43,000 men, an army of nearly 93,000, and massive subsidies to foreign states.[27]

They were also to make Scotland seem puny in comparison. Since the Revolution of 1688 the Scottish economy had taken a downturn.

Harvest failures in the 1690s seriously disrupted her agriculture. Some of the country's million or so inhabitants had actually starved, in sharp contrast to her English neighbours. Scotland's traditional trading links were seriously weakened by the war with France. Above all the Company of Africa and the Indies incurred the disaster of Darien, with an estimated loss to Scottish investors of £153, 631, which was perhaps a quarter of the liquid capital assets of the kingdom.

The basic problem at the time of the Union was what form of association could there be between an emergent great power, which had just won the shattering victory of Ramillies over one of the finest armies Louis XIV ever put into the field, and a country with an army of only 3000 men and a navy of two frigates? Few in either country wished to continue as they were, with a Union of Crowns only in a composite monarchy. Even those Scots who were prepared to consider the succession of the same person to the two thrones after Anne's death included many who wished to limit the prerogatives of the Crown in that event, for instance by making declarations of war by the king of Scotland dependent upon the approval of the Scottish parliament. Others advocated a federal union, but support for this seems to have been rather nebulous. No blueprint of how the kingdoms were to be federated seems to have survived. It is not known whether there was to be a federal parliament with powers superior to those of the parliaments in Edinburgh and London, let alone what those relative powers were to be. There are only vague references to such federal polities as the Dutch Republic, which would scarcely recommend itself as a model of effective government to members of the English ministry such as the duke of Marlborough, who had to endure the inertia produced by the slow workings of the constitution of the United Provinces.

The alternative to the Union of the Crowns or an incorporating Union of the parliaments was that Scotland would somehow go her own way upon the death of Queen Anne, as a sovereign state with a separate monarch. But this was surely unrealistic? If the Union had been rejected by the Edinburgh parliament there could be little question but that confusion would have ensued, possibly civil war, certainly a breakdown of the Queen's government. And that would have provided the occasion for the restoration of order by the troops which the English ministers had stationed on the borders and in northern Ireland for just such a contingency. In the last analysis it was not a choice between Union and independence for Scotland, but between the treaty and an English conquest. As Lord Chancellor Cowper observed on the occasion of the treaty being presented to the Queen, the 'great and main consequence' of the Union was 'the continuation of peace and tranquility instead of bloodshed and distraction.'[28] These were the realities of the relative status of the two nations in international power politics.

Their uniting into the Kingdom of Great Britain was the most significant feature of the decade. Not only did the Union create a new nation; it brought into being a Great Power. The birth of Britain forged a state which more than any other forced the superpower of the Age, Louis XIV's France, to recognize a fresh and formidable challenger to its hegemony.

Although the making of the treaty of Union forms a centrepiece to this study it is set in a discussion of political developments throughout the decade. While the principal actors are the monarchs and their Cabinets, they are placed in a wider context of parliamentary debates and election campaigns. Thus the emergence of the new nation is examined against the background of the interaction of the state and society.

1

1701

Just before Christmas 1700 parliament was dissolved and a general election took place early in the new year. There were then 269 English and Welsh constituencies which, since most of those in England returned two members, accounted for 513 seats in the House of Commons. Today, when political parties maintain rival electoral organizations in every constituency, almost all seats are contested in general elections, even if they are considered 'safe'.

In the early eighteenth century there were no official party machines, and electoral campaigns were organized by local activists who did not incur the trouble and expense of a contest if their prospects of success were hopeless. Consequently in any general election only a minority of constituencies went to the polls. Thus in January 1701, though there were rumours of 3,000 candidates standing, only 86 contests are known to have been fought to a poll. Their distribution geographically produced an unusual pattern. At most general elections held during the decade the South East witnessed the highest proportion of contests and the South West the lowest. On this occasion, the first of six contests to take place between 1701 and 1710, the South West had a slight edge on the South East.[1] This was due to a drop in the number of polls held in the south-eastern counties to the lowest number in these years. It is hard to account for this anomaly, especially in view of contemporary perceptions of a hard-fought election.

The Court did its best to whip up interest in the outcome of the election, distributing electoral literature to animate the voters. Such attempts appear to have met with mixed success. In Worcestershire national issues were raised in the contest for knights of the shire, with the tories objecting to bishops and placemen.[2] In the neighbouring county of Herefordshire local concerns seem to have predominated. 'As to whig or Church' observed Robert Price 'that is not the question. I believe all parties serve an interest'.[3] Such cynicism was probably provoked by the efforts of the two East India companies to get representation in the Commons.

Some elections in the south-west were hard fought as rival candidates from the two strove to get into parliament.[4] Wiltshire boroughs provided one of the main battlefields as Lords Halifax and Wharton of the whig Junto used their extensive interests in the county to help new Company candidates led by Samuel Shepheard junior. Thus Chippenham went to the polls for the only time in William's reign, due to Edward Montague's unsuccessful bid to wrest a seat from one of the sitting members there. Others were more fortunate. 'Certainly the new Company men did quite well; 67 have been identified in the list of returns, including a core of 28 active supporters, as compared to 17 old Company sympathizers, six of them active supporters.'[5]

The overall result of the general election, however, was not auspicious for the new Company. Although contemporary analyses differed from seeing it as a whig victory to claiming tory gains, when the Commons met on 10 February to elect a Speaker the tories and placemen carried it for Robert Harley against Sir Richard Onslow, the Country whig candidate, by 249 votes to 125. One of Onslow's supporters objected to Harley's nomination being arranged with the king by 'the Lord Rochester, now prime minister of state'.[6] The alliance of Courtiers and tories augured ill for whig members whose returns had been controverted by rival candidates. It was particularly ominous for new East India Company men since the Commons resolved on 12 February 'that where it shall appear any member has got himself elected by bribery or corruption the House will punish them.' That this was aimed primarily at the new Company was driven home when Samuel Shepheard senior, the director of its electoral strategy, was accused of bribery and ordered to appear at the bar. He was subsequently found guilty of bribery in several elections and sent to the Tower, along with two of his sons. In total, ten members sponsored by the new East India Company lost their seats on petition.[7]

However, the alliance which backed Harley's candidacy for the Speakership, and apparently controlled the committee of elections under the chairmanship of the Court whig Sir Rowland Gwynne, was not firmly cemented. There were issues which drove a wedge between the tories and the placemen, causing some at least of the latter to vote with the Country whigs. One such issue surfaced in the first division to take place after the choice of a Speaker. This was on the reply to the king's speech. William had asked parliament 'maturely to consider the present state (of affairs abroad) and make no doubt but your resolutions thereupon may be such as will be most conducing to the interest and safety of England, preservation of the protestant religion in general, and peace of all Europe'. When they came to consider their reply on 14 February the Commons echoed William's words, resolving to 'take such effectual measures as may best conduce to the interest and safety of England the preservation of the protestant religion and peace of Europe'. Some tories moved to leave out the words 'peace of Europe' but were outvoted 181 to 163.[8]

William's speech had also drawn attention to the vexed question of the succession. 'Our great misfortune in the losse of the duke of Gloucester', he observed referring to the death the previous July of princess Anne's only surviving child, 'hath made it absolutely necessary that there should be further provision for the succession to the crown in the protestant line after me and the princess. The happiness of the nation and security of our religion seems so much to depend upon this that I cannot doubt but that 'twill meet with a general concurrence.' And by and large it did.

Contemporaries commented on the consensus which arose over providing for the succession. 'I was apprehensive that the business of this day would have broke the unanimity of the House', John Verney admitted on 1 March. 'But it has happened quite contrary and produced two votes in the fullest committee I ever saw and passed in the most solemn manner and without any dispute (viz) that the crown should be settled . . . upon the next protestant line; and that a farther declaration should be made of the rights of the people in the same bill.'[9]

The clauses declaring the rights of the people were debated before the successor was named. These were a 'farther declaration' since they picked up where the Bill of Rights had left off in 1689. Thus on 5 March three clauses were agreed. The first required all matters concerning the government of the realm to be transacted in the Privy Council and resolutions taken there to be signed by counsellors. The second disqualified foreigners from being Privy counsellors, members of parliament or civil and military office-holders. The third debarred foreigners from receiving property from the Crown. It was surprising that few objected to these proposals since all three could be construed as a criticism of William III's practices. The first was aimed at his use of a cabinet of ministers, and the others at the influence of his Dutch favourites. Some Courtiers did raise objections, for instance pointing out that no man with any sense would accept membership of the Privy Council on the terms prescribed. Yet the great majority insisted on the clauses being incorporated in the bill of settlement.

On 10 March four more restrictive clauses were added to the bill. One restricted the royal prerogative of declaring war by insisting that it could not be used to commit England to the defence of foreign possessions of the Crown. The second required the successor to be a member of the Church of England. The third made parliamentary approval necessary for the monarch to leave the realm. The fourth disallowed royal pardons as pleas in cases of impeachment. A fifth would have confined confiscation of goods from traitors to those who committed treason, exempting their descendants, but this was rejected.

On 11 March two final restrictions on the prerogative were resolved. One incapacitated any placeman or pensioner from sitting in the House of Commons. The other removed the right of the Crown to appoint judges at pleasure and required them to be appointed on good behaviour. And then the successor was named as the dowager electress Sophia of Hanover. 'The question passed unanimously and without a debate.'[10] It was, however, a fragile consensus. Whigs genuinely regarded the restrictions of the royal prerogative as safeguards of English liberties. Some Jacobite tories hoped so to restrict the prerogative that the Crown would become unattractive to the prospective successor and thereby keep the door open for the Pretender.[11] Tory sincerity during the passage of the bill of settlement was queried by several contemporary commentators on these proceedings. Gilbert Burnet objected that the chair of the committee was given to Sir John Bolles, who was already displaying the symptoms of madness for which he was later confined, and that attendance at debates on its measures was desultory.[12] Roger Coke noted that though it was mentioned in the king's speech on 10 February, no notice was taken of it until 3 March 'tho of the last importance'. He claimed that Somers related how the tories hoped the Lords would amend the restrictive clauses and that when the bill went back to the Commons unamended some tory members 'said aloud, the Devil take you and your bill'.[13]

Shortly after the passage of the bill of settlement the consensus disintegrated. 'All our fair ideas that arose from the unanimity of the House,' lamented John Verney in mid-April, 'are now changed into a melancholy prospect of the ill consequences of division and parties as near equal in number as they are in rage one against another.'[14] One of the first signs of this breakdown occurred on 21 March. Three days earlier the king had laid before both Houses copies of papers presented to the French demanding securities in case war broke out. The Commons agreed to draw up an address of thanks for this information, but the Court pushed its luck by moving for a clause to be inserted in it thanking William 'for his care of these nations and peace in Europe'. This wording was opposed by the tories, and on a division it was rejected by 193 votes to 187. It was claimed that the Court lost so narrowly because some of its supporters were attending a music concert.[15]

The tories followed up their triumph by condemning the partition treaty of 1700 for its alleged role in precipitating the European crisis. This allegation had first been raised in the Lords, though tory attempts there to accuse former whig ministers of negligence in allowing William to negotiate it without their advice backfired. It was proved that not only had Lord Somers been consulted about it but so had other ministers, including the tory Lord Jersey. While this stopped the investigation in the Upper House in its tracks, it did not prevent the tories in the Commons from pursuing a vendetta against the late ministry in general, and Somers in particular, whom they accused of putting the great seal to the treaty while it still contained blank spaces for the king to fill when negotiations were completed. Some used language so strong that the Prussian envoy excused himself for not repeating it in his despatch.[16]

On 24 March the tories drew up an address attributing the 'dangers which now threaten both this kingdom and the peace of Europe' to the treaty, which one tory compared to 'a combination of three robbers to rob the fourth'. On 29 March they moved a resolution in a committee on the state of the nation that Somers had been guilty of high crimes and misdemeanours for his part in the partition treaty of 1700. The Speaker, Robert Harley, being free to express his views in committee, revealed a strong animus against Somers, saying that 'if the question should be carried in the negative farewell England farewell Constitution . . . our posterity will curse us and our children here after blame us'.[17] Notwithstanding this impassioned plea the motion was lost by 189 votes to 182. Despite this set-back the tories proceeded on 14 April to move the impeachment of the former Lord Chancellor for his role in the first treaty of 1698. When the resolution was passed by 198 votes to 188 they followed it with impeachments of the earl of Orford and Lord Halifax. Next day they agreed by 162 votes to 107 to address the king to remove the three lords and the duke of Portland from his presence and councils for ever.

The impeachments not only polarized the Commons into two very even sides but also drove a wedge between the two Houses. For in the Lords the impeached ministers could rely on a majority to protect them. Their friends in the upper chamber moved a contrary address to the king, asking him not to remove them from his councils unless and until the Commons proved the charges against them. William tried to remain non-committal. He ignored the Lords' address but replied ambiguously to that from the Commons 'that I will employ none in my service but such as shall be thought most likely to improve that mutual trust and confidence between us, which is so necessary in this conjuncture both for our security and the defence and preservation of our allies'. Deadlock ensued between the two Houses as the Lords challenged the Commons to make good their charges against the impeached ministers. When the Lower House failed to present its case the Lords heard the accused peers and acquitted them.

The clash between the two Houses provoked a paper war outside. Daniel Defoe and Jonathan Swift joined the fray on the side of the Lords, the first with a *Memorial* and the second in his *Discourse of the Contests and Dissensions between the Nobles and the Commons in Athens and Rome.* Below these luminaries lesser fry entered the lists. On 29 April five lines of verse were 'found in the lobby of the House of Commons':[18]

> Ye True-Born *Englishmen* proceed,
>   Our trifling Crimes detect.
> Let the Poor starve, Religion bleed,
> The *Dutch* be damn'd, the *French* succeed,
>   And all by your Neglect.

The alleged neglect of foreign affairs was taken up in a petition to parliament from the grand jury of Kent which urged the Commons to vote supplies so 'that his Majesty may be enabled powerfully to assist his allies before it is too late'. On 8 May the petition was presented to the House, which voted it 'scandalous insolent and seditious' and ordered the five men who presented it into the custody of the sergeant at arms.[19] Nevertheless despite their treatment of the Kentish petitioners, who became celebrated figures, the very next day the Commons resolved to support the king's allies 'in maintaining the liberties of Europe'. A tory member noted that the resolution was passed 'with more spirit and unanimity than has appeared on any one subject these many years'.[20] The tories were clearly rattled by the furore which the petition had aroused. Many members were pressurized to take action to resist French aggression.[21] On 12 June, when the king visited parliament to give the royal assent to the bill of settlement and asked the Houses to finish their business quickly as he was urgently needed abroad, the Commons agreed to 'unanimously assure' him that they would welcome alliances with the Dutch and the Emperor 'for the preservation of the liberties of Europe, the prosperity and peace of England and for reducing the exorbitant power of France'. When they presented their address to the king at Kensington on 14 June, William 'heartily thankt them for the same, saying it would be a great encouragement to the emperor and states'.[22] Although the dispute between the Houses threatened to hold up supply, by 24 June, the bills to raise it were ready for the royal assent. In presenting them to the king, Speaker Harley pointed out 'that they had granted more money this sessions than ever was given in one year to any of his majesty's predecessors in time of peace'. William then passed them and prorogued the parliament.

Over the summer the whigs waged a two-pronged campaign to persuade William to make ministerial changes in their favour and to dissolve parliament. The earl of Sunderland, who had acted as a broker between them and the king earlier in the reign, came out of retirement to press upon him again the treachery of the tories and the worthiness of whigs like Somers, 'the life the soul and the spirit of his party'. Meanwhile the whigs orchestrated addresses from several constituencies urging a dissolution. William, abroad in the Netherlands, took little notice of their efforts initially. Indeed the few alterations he did make were rather in favour of the tories. Thus Edward Northey became attorney general while the duke of Somerset was added to the Lords Justices appointed to administer the realm in the king's absence. As one rank tory put it 'this present alteration in the ministry will prove so advantageous to the nation . . . that all mankind that are for the monarchy and the Church of England . . . are resolved to exert their utmost interest to support it and to prevent those Presbiterian ratts from infesting the government and plundering it any more.'[23]

The death of James II at St Germains in September transformed the situation. Louis XIV played into whig hands by recognizing his son as James III. The common council of London drew up an address to the king pledging that, since Louis' recognition of the pretender had 'affronted his majesty and his government this city declares they will stand by, assist, and support his majesty and government vigorously against the power of France'. When William received this in Holland he ordered it 'to be translated into all languages, to be sent to the several courts of Europe'.[24] On his return to England early in November William was presented by Somers with arguments for dissolving parliament. These persuaded the king to inform the cabinet on the 9th that he had resolved on a dissolution. Godolphin resigned as Treasurer on hearing the news, while other tory ministers registered their disapproval of the decision in the Privy Council on 11 November when those present only approved of it by three votes.[25]

William's decision to dissolve a parliament which had only been elected the previous January was therefore taken very quickly after his return from the continent. Indeed, just the day before he told the cabinet of it, he had led Godolphin to assume that the old parliament would be reconvened. The snap dissolution consequently took many people by surprise.

This possibly accounts for the fact that there were relatively few contests. Only 91 are known to have occurred, five more than at the previous election. Their geographical distribution, however, was rather different. Proportionally fewer took place in the south-west while more occurred in the south-east. In Wiltshire the number was halved, from eight to four. This was almost certainly due to the fact that the second election of 1701 did not witness a contest between rival East India Companies, which had been fiercely fought in that county. On the contrary, on the eve of the polls the old and new Companies were engaged in negotiations for a merger. The increase in the south-east from 26 in January to 33 in December particularly affected Kent. No polls had occurred in the county and only one in its boroughs at the first election, whereas six took place at the second.[26] Presumably the furore aroused by the Kentish petition accounted for the upsurge in electoral activity between the two elections.

The issues raised by the petition indeed played a major role in the election campaign. William himself set the tone in his proclamation dissolving parliament, which urged the electorate to return 'good Englishmen and Protestants'. According to one disgruntled tory the result was to send them 'into the country with libels affixed to our backs'.[27] Among the libels was a black list of tory MPs who were alleged to have met at the Vine Tavern in Long Acre. These were nicknamed 'Poussineers' in a guilt-by-association technique which linked them with three tories who had been seen in the company of Monsieur Poussin, a French agent, at the Blue Posts tavern. Two of these, Charles Davenant and Anthony Hammond, failed to secure election because, according to a newsletter, of 'the story of Mons Poussin'.[28] Whig propaganda swayed the voters in the metropolitan district. 'I wish the people all over England would choose with the same spirit they have done in Westminster, London and Southwark,' James Vernon wrote to the duke of Shrewsbury, 'where they have shewn great aversion to Jacobitism and a French faction, notwithstanding the powerful endeavours to support it.'[29] These three boroughs expressed whiggish sentiments in 'advices' which they gave to their new representatives. At least nineteen constituencies issued instructions to their members after their elections.[30] Not all the advice was along whig lines. Thus Cornish voters, 'being of opinion that the late parliament was entirely in the king and kingdoms interest', desired their knights of the shire 'to enquire who advised the dissolution in so critical a juncture'.[31] Most of the instructions, however, clearly came from whig voters. The freeholders of Buckinghamshire, for instance, gave very different advice to their members from that given by those in Cornwall. They were 'exhorted charged and required' to 'heartily concur in such alliances as the King has or shall make for pulling down the exorbitant power of France'[32]

The outcome of the general election was very close. While the whigs made gains in the south-east the tories held their own elsewhere, especially in the west country, which made it difficult for contemporaries to gauge which party had won. The whigs calculated that they had gained overall about thirty seats more than they had held in the previous parliament.[33] Given the narrow tory majorities in the Commons in 1701, such a gain should have ensured whig control in the new House. But others felt that the tories had more than held their own. 'Notwithstanding the innumerable lies which they [the whigs] have endeavoured to serve themselves in the late elections,' claimed Richard Goulston, 'the majority runs against them.'[34] All in all the best verdict was that of John Ellis, who thought the elections 'seem pretty equal on both sides.'[35]

Both sides therefore made every effort to get their supporters to London for the choice of a Speaker. 'The parties are preparing to give one another battle the first day of the parliament,' John Ellis observed, 'one side to make Sir Thom[as] Littleton speaker the other to have Mr Harley again.' Pressure was brought to bear on individuals to get up to town in time for the vote, even though it was to take place on 30 December, in the midst of the Christmas season.[36] In the event 'after a great struggle for a speaker Mr Harley . . . carried it, he had 216 to Sir Thom Littleton 212, which was one of the fullest Houses the first day that ever was known.'[37]

The vote dumbfounded the whigs for they had been confident that with the backing of the Court they could carry it for Littleton. Yet though the king clearly indicated his support for Littleton, the tories managed to seat Harley in the chair.[38]

Had William shown more favour to the whigs before the election, they might have fared better at the polls. As it was he had awaited the outcome of the contest before committing himself to them. Thus the approval of Littleton was one of the first overt signs that he designed a whig scheme. He now made further moves in that direction. When the tory Secretary of State Sir Charles Hedges resigned rather than vote against Harley he was replaced by the whig earl of Manchester. The duke of Somerset, who had ostentatiously transferred his allegiance from tory to whig during the election campaign, became Lord President of the Council. Above all on 25 January William dismissed Rochester from the Lord Lieutenancy of Ireland.

The whigs hoped that these moves would improve their parliamentary situation. In the Commons they set some store on the committee of privileges and elections to retrieve it. Thus the duke of Newcastle wrote to whig members to make sure that Sir Rowland Gwynne was again elected as chairman.[39] They feared that a tory would chair it instead, and use his influence to reject petitions from whigs against sitting members and carry those from tories against whig MPs. In the event Gwynne was chosen unanimously.[40] But this did not mend the fortunes of the whigs. For the committee showed partiality to tories anyway, and when its resolutions were conveyed to the Commons the House upheld them. As one tory put it after the hearing of the first

Verbeelding
der Stervende Koning van Engeland,
Schotland, Vrankryk en Yrland, etc. etc. etc.

WILHELM DE III.

den 10. Maart 1702.

Hier Daald d'Oranje Zon, 't ontzachlykst Weirelds Wonder,
Beschermer van 't Geloof, de Regterhand van Staat,
Te vroeg voor Albion en Nagebuuren, Onder,
Waar door gantsch Nederland en 't Ryk aan 't kwynen staat,
En 's Konings Dood Betreurd, terwyl elk Smelt in Traanen,
Zo wel de Bondgenoot als Britsche Onderdaanen.

Figure 1 Death of William III, 1702.

two petitions 'it seems by the two elections one for Malden the other for Hertford that the Court party are the weaker side.'[41] The crucial vote on the Malden election was carried by 226 to 208, a remarkably high number of members which a disgruntled whig put down to the tories' carrying men into the House to vote, claiming that 'there was not one man that could get out of bed absent on the other side'.[42] Another straw in the tory wind was the choice of the high church preacher George Smalridge to deliver the sermon on 30 January, the anniversary of the execution of Charles I, 'king and martyr'.

Even when the whigs found an issue they thought would confound the tories the latter were able, albeit by the smallest possible majority, to hold their own. This was a move to get people to abjure allegiance to the son of James II. The House accepted the notion of an abjuration oath, but on the question of whether it should be compulsory or voluntary it divided along party lines. The whigs wanted it to be voluntary so that crypto-Jacobites would be revealed when they refused to take it. The tories, aware of the tender consciences in their ranks, wished it to be made compulsory. On 20 January a committee vote was taken on this issue and a compulsory oath was resolved by 188 votes to 187.

After that narrowest of victories the tories seemed to carry all before them. On 22 January the committee of privileges and elections heard a petition from Thomas Bliss against Thomas Colepepper, one of the Kentish petitioners who had been returned for Maidstone. The tories got their revenge – a big majority finding for Bliss. When their resolutions that Bliss was duly elected, and that Colepepper was guilty of corruption, were reported to the House they had a field day. The Commons 'resolved that the aspersing of the last House of commons or any member thereof with receiving French money, or being in the interest of France, was a scandalous, villainous and groundless reflection, tending to sedition, and to create a misunderstanding between the king and his people; that Mr Colepepper is guilty thereof, and to be committed to Newgate and prosecuted by the attorney general'. Having started a retrospective vindication of their proceedings in the previous parliament, the tories followed it up on 17 February by passing three resolutions upholding their rejection of the Kentish petition and the Legion Memorial. Such triumphs led one observer to claim that 'in 3 years we have had 3 parliaments, great struggling in point of party, and notwithstanding all the management of the Court, which leans entirely to the interest of the Whiggs, yet the Church (or Country) party have at this time an actual majority in the House of Commons'.[43]

Then on 26 February the whigs were able to seize the advantage in a debate before a packed House which went on unusually late into the evening. By 235 votes to 221 they got the Commons to agree that the Lords had done justice to them in the impeachments, that anybody impeached should be brought to a speedy trial, and that subjects could petition the king to dissolve parliament. Quite how the whigs achieved this reversal is not easy to explain. As one whig put it 'it was the first day that party had been victorious'.[44] Clearly they pulled out all the stops, in the biggest division of the reign. But another possibility is that some tories, who had gone along with the defence of the previous parliament, and denunciation of attempts to influence its proceedings from outside, got cold feet and changed their votes at the prospect of fresh elections.

Between the votes of 17 and 26 February William suffered a fall from his horse and fractured a collar bone. This occurrence concentrated minds on the succession. Two days after, on 23 February, the Lords added an amendment to the abjuration bill making it treason to try to exclude Anne from it. Although William recovered sufficiently to propose to parliament consideration of a legislative union with Scotland, his condition gave grounds for anxiety. He could not appear in person to give his assent to the abjuration bill but had to appoint commissioners to do so. Some tories objected to this procedure. 'The abjuration was past on Saterday night in such a manner as never was done in any reign in the world' a witness complained to the earl of Nottingham. 'For the k[ing] was in so ill a condition that he could not write his name. Therefore a stamp was put into his hand and that by help of others lifted upon the paper.'[45] This was his last public act. On 8 March he died.

William's death marked the end of an era. The stadhouder-king was the architect of the Glorious Revolution and of England's emergence as a Great Power. At first he had been welcomed as the saviour of English liberties. But his commitment to the containment of French aggression had placed a heavy burden on his new domain. While his wife Mary lived his unpopularity had been overshadowed by the favourable image which she projected. Her death in 1694, however, was a major blow and he had not endeared himself to his subjects by his coldness, arrogance and obvious preference for the Dutch. His favouritism to his fellow countrymen became a political issue in the late 1690s when his grants to them in Ireland were resumed by parliament. Such considerations lay behind many of the implied criticisms of foreign connections in the Act of Settlement. However, Louis XIV's recognition of the Stuart claimant aroused more favourable sentiments towards William in the last year of his reign. While he never inspired warmth and affection he nevertheless was lamented by all but the most hardened Jacobites. They rejoiced at his demise, devizing a drink made from champagne and stout to toast 'the little gentleman in black velvet', the mole which made the molehill over which the king's horse Sorrel stumbled.

2

1702

On 11 March 1702, three days after the death of William III, Queen Anne appeared before parliament. She made the most of the occasion, the first time a monarch had addressed the Houses which were sitting when the previous king died. Before the Revolution they had been dissolved by the ruler's death; but by an Act of 1696 provision had been made for parliament to survive William for six months. Anne wore the crown, the ribbon of the Garter and the badge of St George. Her robe, red velvet lined with ermine and edged in gold, was modelled on a portrait of Queen Elizabeth I. Queen Anne deliberately cultivated an Elizabethan image in other ways, for instance by adopting the motto *Semper Eadem*.

Unlike Elizabeth, however, she was nervous about addressing the peers and MPs, and blushed when she made her speech, so that some hostile observers likened her to the sign of the Rose and Crown. Nevertheless, speaking in the clear voice which became her hallmark, she 'charmed both Houses ... for never any woman spoke more audibly or with better grace ... and raised a hum from all that heard her'.[1] 'My Lords and Gentlemen,' she began, 'I cannot too much lament my own unhappiness in succeeding to the crown so immediately after the loss of a king who was the great support, not only of these kingdoms but of all Europe.' 'It shall be my constant endeavour,' she concluded, 'to make you the best return for that duty and affection you have expressed to me, by a careful and diligent administration for the good of all my subjects: and as I know my own heart to be entirely English I can very sincerely assure you there is not anything you can expect or desire from me, which I shall not be ready to do for the happiness and prosperity of England; and you shall always find me a strict and religious observer of my word.'[2] The projection of an Elizabethan image was not lost on observers. Anne announced that she was giving £100,000 of her own money for public purposes, which was held to be 'a true imitation of Q. Elizabeth's maxims'.[3]

Some historians have detected in the words 'I know my heart to be entirely English' another Elizabethan motif, an echo of Elizabeth's speech at Tilbury claiming that she had 'the heart and stomach of a king, and of a king of England too'. They also observe that Anne was the first monarch since Elizabeth to have both parents born in England. Contemporaries, however, were more struck by the way it echoed a speech of her father, James II. They also regarded the expression as a reflection on Dutch William, the 'Mr Caliban' whom Anne detested. His admirers resented this insult, Lord Spencer exclaimed in a debate a few days later that 'those that reflected upon that king for not being English had French hearts'.[4] This was not taken to be a reflection upon the Queen. As John Oldmixon observed, 'every one knew that her majesty's speeches were drawn up by those counsellors in whom she most confided; and it was matter of concern that any of them should presume so much on the influence they had over her as to put words in her royal mouth so unworthy of king William's glorious memory'. The controversial expression was in fact inserted in the speech by her uncle, the earl of Rochester, one of the ministers who helped draft it.

Rochester kept his post as Lord Lieutenant of Ireland since 'his commission . . . was never superseded'.[5] His virtual reinstatement was a sign that the Queen intended to promote tories to her first ministry. As she informed parliament on 26 May 1702, she would countenance those who had the truest zeal to support the Church of England. So in the opening days of her reign she appointed the earl of Nottingham to the post of secretary of state for the south. The secretariat dealt with France and southern Europe, and was held to be the senior of the two secretaryships at a time of friction and conflict with the French. The other, which dealt with northern Europe, went to Sir Charles Hedges. Other tories were brought into the ministry. Thus the earl of Jersey became Lord Chamberlain and Sir Edward Seymour became comptroller of the household. The latter replaced the Junto whig Lord Wharton whom the queen cordially detested. So great was her aversion to him held to be that she reputedly struck him off the privy council at the same time, a particularly vengeful act since it was customary to retain privy counsellors whatever their politics. However, it appears that Anne did not take her dislike of him to the extreme, for his name occurs on the lists of those attending her privy council throughout the decade.[6]

Indeed the extent to which Anne made a clean sweep in favour of the tories can be exaggerated. In the sensitive areas of the admiralty and the army her crucial appointments did not benefit that party. She wished to put her husband Prince George at the head of naval and military affairs, but his incompetence made this an embarrassing decision, and diplomatic ways had to be found round it. So George was given the grandiloquent but empty title of generalissimo. While he was indeed made Lord High Admiral the executive business of the admiralty was placed in a commission known as the Prince's Council. This was a most anomalous situation, since normally there was either a Lord Admiral or a commission of the admiralty. The validity of having both at the same time was to raise questions when the admiralty came under attack later in the reign.

It is true that one of the admiralty commissioners who emerged as the most influential was a tory, George Churchill. But he owed his position to his brother, John Churchill, earl of Marlborough, the Captain General of the armed forces. For Marlborough was virtually prime minister. 'We look upon it,' the bishop of Clogher observed to William King, the bishop of Derry, 'that Lord Marlborough has the greatest share of affairs.'[7]

While Marlborough was still a tory of sorts, his toryism differed markedly from the high church variety. Although in the early 1690s he had been stripped of his commission and placed under arrest for alleged complicity in Jacobite schemes, he had come back into favour towards the end of William's reign, and in 1701 the king had given him the posts of commander in chief of the English forces in Holland and ambassador extraordinary to the Dutch Republic. To some extent this was part of a belated reconciliation between William and Anne, for Marlborough and his wife Sarah were intimates of the princess. The 'Cockpit group', as historians have labelled Anne and her husband George, the Marlboroughs and Lord Godolphin, had formed a nucleus of opposition to William for most of his reign. Their private nicknames for each other – Mr and Mrs Morley, Mr and Mrs Freeman, Mr Montgomery – confirmed their intimacy, while their sobriquet for the king, Mr Caliban, indicated their intense dislike of him. The appointment of Marlborough was therefore a very significant sign of improving relations.

But it was also William's tribute to Marlborough's military skill and commitment to the aims of the Grand Alliance. This inevitably drove a wedge between him and the high church tories, who still suspected massive military commitments on the continent and hankered after a sea war in which England would play the role of an auxiliary rather than of a major power. Thus in December 1701 he wrote to the Pensionary of Holland, 'wee have here noe talk but of elections; I hope in God thay will be such as will doe their utmost power against France'.[8] These differences surfaced early in the new reign at a meeting of the privy council to debate the declaration of war. Rochester endeavoured to confine the English contribution to that of an auxiliary, but was outvoted by Marlborough supported by the earl of Pembroke, a moderate tory, the duke of Somerset, a recent convert from the tories to the whigs, and the whig duke of Devonshire.

The retention of Devonshire and Somerset in the ministry revealed that a complete purge of the whig ministers was not undertaken at the outset of the reign. Anne was persuaded not to confine appointments entirely to tories by such confidantes as the Marlboroughs.[9] Sarah was herself a rabid whig, and urged the merits of that party on every occasion, until her pleas and blatant partisanship became counter productive. Marlborough's advocacy of the case for retaining some of them was more subtle. He maintained that from a managerial point of view it would be an error to commit the crown to the services of one party, which might use its monopoly to reduce the royal prerogative. In this policy he was abetted by Lord Godolphin, whom Anne put in the key position of Lord Treasurer. Again Godolphin had been a zealous tory earlier, but like Marlborough he emerged more as a manager in the reign of Anne, who saw that to retain control of the war effort it was vital not to give power to a party which lacked enthusiasm for it. Godolphin and Marlborough thus acted more as managers than as partisans. They played the role of brokers between the Crown and the parties. So closely were they united in this managerial policy that for the rest of the decade they were known as the duumvirs.

For a time they were joined by a third, Robert Harley forming with them a triumvirate for the first years of the reign. At this time Harley was still only Speaker of the House of Commons, a position he had acquired despite the efforts of the Court on behalf of a rival. Now he was in favour at Court. The accession of Anne had completed his transformation from a Country to a Court politician. Previously he had been a leader of those MPs who were thorns in the flesh of ministers, always ready to detect corruption and executive tyranny in their actions and policies. Now Harley used his influence to the Queen's advantage. Thus the Commons voted her a civil list of £600,000 a year for life, even though the whigs wanted it to be granted on a yearly basis.[10] Members were anxious to create a favourable impression to the country, conscious that another general election was imminent. Thus they began making interest in the constituencies early in the spring.[11] It was clear that public opinion was enthusiastic about the change from William to Anne. Although some members of parliament could not refrain from tears on the king's death, outdoors it was noted that 'among the mob where one is concerned there are forty rejoicing'.[12] Among the downcast on 8 March had been those with stock in the Bank, the value of which plummeted on news of William's death. However, the stock market soon rallied when Anne succeeded without incident.[13] Investors were probably reassured by the determination expressed by the House of Commons in its address of condolence to Anne on William's death 'to maintain her alliances for preserving the liberties of Europe, and reducing the exorbitant power of France'.[14]

Another sign of continuity with the previous regime which might also have boosted confidence was the express determination to seek an Anglo-Scottish union. One of the last communications King William had made with parliament was a message 'that there was nothing that [he] desired more than an union with Scotland'. He was particularly anxious to avoid the succession to the thrones of the two kingdoms going to different monarchs on the death of his successor. Yet this contingency seemed highly likely given that the Scots had not offered their Crown to the house of Hanover, and were moreover incensed because the English parliament had settled the Hanoverian succession without consulting them. They were also aggrieved in the closing years of William's reign with his preference for English over Scottish commercial concerns as displayed in his overt interference in the affairs of the Edinburgh-based company trading with Africa and the Indies. These developments seemed to typify the subordinate status to which England had arrogantly reduced Scotland ever since the union of the Crowns in 1603. It appeared as though the two kingdoms were heading for a rupture, a prospect which gravely concerned William even on his deathbed. Anne announced her support of his proposed remedy of union in her first speech to parliament. Members of both Houses responded by approving the appointment of commissioners to negotiate the terms of a union. It was noted, however, that whigs were enthusiastic for it while tories were at best lukewarm.[15] Nevertheless there was enough parliamentary support for it for an act to be passed naming English commissioners to treat for a union.

The attitude of the Edinburgh parliament was similar, with whigs led by the duke of Queensberry wholeheartedly in favour of negotiations, while the Cavaliers or Jacobites led by the duke of Hamilton were opposed to them. Hamilton and 74 other members took their opposition as far as denying that the assembly of the Scottish parliament was legal, and seceded from it. They had a point, for a statute of 1696 required parliament to meet within twenty days of William's death, a requirement not met in practice. Nevertheless the remaining whigs proceeded to act as though they were a legal body and also passed an act appointing Scottish commissioners for a union.

While Anne flinched from a dissolution of the Scottish parliament, she had no qualms about dissolving the English parliament, issuing writs for a new one on 2 July 1702. Her known preference for tories, rejoicing at the death of William, and the reconciliation of former non-jurors, many of whom were prepared to take the oaths to the queen who had refused them to her predecessor, augured well for the tory party and ill for the whigs when elections were held.

High summer found the candidates on the hustings in a general election campaign. There were, however, fewer contests than there had been the previous December, resulting in as many polls as there had been at the first election of 1701. It seems that the almost constant spate of electioneering over a period of eighteen months had established the state of parties in all but a few constituencies, where either the influence of the Court or public opinion could sway the result.

The third earl of Shaftesbury was convinced that Court influence was the deciding factor in bringing about a tory victory. 'That party whom the Court has favoured have obtained their victory in almost all parts,' he informed a friend in Holland, 'the justices of the peace, the sheriffs, the officers of all the militia of cities and counties, with all the rest of the civil and military offices, were in the hands of the high church party, and the changes reserved to the very instant of the elections.'[16] Although he was a disgruntled whig, tories were inclined to agree with him. 'We could not wish better elections than those in the North,' Lord Weymouth exulted to Nottingham, 'which shows that the power of some great men sprang from the influence of the Government.'[17] Other evidence, however, points to less blatant use of Court patronage.[18] One of the northern elections which Weymouth must have had in mind was that for Westmorland. There the whig earl of Carlisle remained as Lord Lieutenant. Nevertheless, there was a major change. In 1701 the Junto supporter Sir Richard Sandford had topped the poll with 652 votes, while Sir Christopher Musgrave came bottom with 525. In 1702 Musgrave polled 712 against Sandford's 299. Here the tide of public opinion was at least as strong as the pull of the Court in ousting a whig and installing a tory.[19] According to Burnet, 'the conceit which had been infused and propagated with much industry, that the whigs had charged the nation with great taxes, of which a large share had been devoured by themselves, had so far turned the tide, that the tories in the House of commons were at least double the number of the whigs'.[20] In fact the overall effect of the changes was to produce a majority for the tory party of about 133 before the petitions on controverted elections were decided. These were to boost the tory majority quite substantially.

Parliament had been summoned for 8 October but on 8 September a proclamation was issued proroguing the meeting until 20 October. The reason for the further delay was spelled out in a letter from Sir Charles Hedges at Bath to the earl of Marlborough, who was then in the duchy of Limburg.[21]

Today the gentlemen of the counties of Dorset and Somerset came to pay their duty to her Majesty. Those that are members of parliament took occasion to speak of the inconvenience it would be to them that the parliament should meet on the 8th of October in regard that it was the time of their quarter sessions and that being in the commission of the peace they were obliged to attend there to take their oaths and could not therefore be at the meeting of the parliament . . . I am told the Quarter sessions of almost all the counties of England happen to be about the same time and the generality of the members are uneasy at it especially in the North and West.

The Queen was at Bath along with her husband, who suffered badly that summer from asthma, for the good of their healths. She was accompanied not only by Lord Treasurer Godolphin and Secretary of State Hedges but also by Marlborough's wife Sarah. They seem to have taken advantage of the opportunity of six weeks' access without a high church tory presence to impress upon Anne the necessity of relying upon moderate tories and even whigs to pursue the war effort. Britain, the United Provinces and the Holy Roman Empire declared war on France simultaneously on 4 May. As we have seen, the tories in the cabinet were not enthusiastic about a land war, and wished to make the main British contribution at sea.

Marlborough, who was fully committed to a continental campaign, was on the continent commanding the opening campaign of the war of the Spanish Succession. He was not only Captain General of the English forces but since 1 July had become Deputy Captain General of the Dutch Republic too.

The United Provinces were threatened by a French army under Boufflers, who advanced between the rivers Maas and Rhine to put pressure on the Dutch. Marlborough sought to relieve it by attacking the French. His Dutch employers, however, were anxious that he avoid pitched battles and concentrate instead on siege warfare. So Marlborough, frustrated at lost opportunities to engage the French in the field, spent the summer taking the fortresses of Venlo, Stevensweert, Roermond and Liege, which gave the allies control of the rivers Maas and Rhine where they flowed through the Low Countries.

Meanwhile a naval descent on Spain commanded by the duke of Ormonde and Admiral Sir George Rooke had been far less productive but much more spectacular. They set out to capture Cadiz as a base for the British fleet and as a foothold for the Habsburg claimant to the Spanish throne, the so-called Charles III. But forces loyal to the Bourbon king Philip successfully defended the port, and the allied forces attacked nearby St Mary's instead, where they distinguished themselves by their pillaging and rape. An officer in attendance admitted that 'the soldiers were civil the first night, but finding the town wholly abandoned and the houses richly furnished they began their plunder the next day and that for a week following there was nothing but drunkenness and confusion amongst them'.[22] So far from doing Charles a service their depredations left a lasting detestation of his cause in Spain. When they abandoned the siege on 16 September after a month in order to return home, however, they were lucky enough to encounter the silver fleet in Vigo bay. Although the Spaniards managed to get most of the silver off the ships before the allies captured the fleet, the booty was still considerable enough to offset the loss of prestige, if not of honour, at Cadiz. At least it captured the imagination of the general public in England more than the slow-moving continental campaign. As Defoe put it:[23]

> The Learned *Mob* bought Compasses and Scales
> And every Barber knew the Bay of *Cales*,
> Show'd us the Army here, and there the Fleet,
> Here the Troops land, and there the Foes Retreat,
> There at St *Maries* how the *Spaniard* runs,
> And listen close as if they heard the Guns,
> And some pretend they see them Swive the Nuns.

The fiasco at Cadiz and the triumph at Vigo even featured on playing cards sold at the time.[24]

These events also had an important impact on politics. 'I believe 'tis an uncertainty in the Court itself how the Parliament will open and which way they will steer', Edmund Gibson wrote to the bishop of Carlisle in October. 'The business of Cadiz (no doubt) will be one of their first subjects, and in all probability will form the parties of the House some weeks before the usual time; no opposition being made . . . by Sir Tho Littleton's party in the choice of a speaker.'[25] And so it proved. Harley was elected Speaker again unopposed. The tories were unanimously behind his choice. He was proposed by Edward Finch, Nottingham's brother, and seconded by Lord Cheyne, a prominent Buckinghamshire tory. The whigs prudently decided that it would be futile to oppose him.

Reflections on the summer's campaigns, however, led to partisan sniping. There was a Court view, held by Marlborough and Godolphin, and supported by moderate tories, that the continental campaign was paramount, though the expedition to Cadiz was also strategically important. It had been proposed and planned under William III. To Marlborough it was a complement to, rather than a diversion from, the continental campaign. Nottingham was a consistent enthusiast for the Iberian theatre. A naval descent suited Rochester's 'blue water' strategy, especially since it was commanded by two of his associates, Ormonde and Rooke. Because it was botched, with the fiasco at St Mary's, this could be used against him. The whigs certainly planned to do so, holding tactical meetings at the home of Charles Spencer, who had just succeeded his father as earl of Sunderland, to concert their attack. In the opening days of the parliament this put Rochester and the high church tories on the defensive. When news of Vigo reached London, however, they could claim the credit.

News of the success did not reach London before the Houses assembled on 20 October. The Queen in her speech at the opening of parliament, which had been vetted by Godolphin, Harley, Nottingham and Rochester, informed the Houses that 'she could not without much trouble take notice of the disappointment we have had at Cadiz: I have not yet had a particular account of that enterprise, nor of all the difficulties our forces may have met with there; but I have such a representation of disorders and abuses committed at Port St Maries as hath obliged me to give directions for the strictest examination of that matter'. Her speech reflected the Court view. The Houses then made their separate replies. The Lords in theirs made no mention of Cadiz but congratulated the success of the British army and of the allies, which was very much the whig line. The Commons downplayed the Spanish descent and complimented 'the wonderful progress of your Majesty's arms under the conduct of the earl of Marlborough', claiming they had 'signally retrieved the ancient honour and glory of the English nation'. The whigs objected to the word 'retrieved' as a slight on the late king, and moved instead for the word 'maintained'. A debate on this motion lasted three hours, during which heated speeches were made on both sides. The young Henry St John distinguished himself by asserting that the country's honour had been lost not by William but by his whig advisers. He was challenged to a duel by Colonel Godfrey for insulting the memory of the dead monarch. Other whigs retaliated by asking whether English honour had been retrieved before Cadiz.[26] In the event the motion was defeated by 100 votes.

The tories tried to pass off the Cadiz expedition as a legacy of the previous reign, during which it had been planned. The whigs, on the other hand, kept up the pressure on the commanders responsible for the disgrace, Wharton in particular pursuing the matter in the Lords to the point where the tories in the Commons threatened to revive the impeachments against the Junto if they did not back off. The 'victory' at Vigo was a great relief to those tories who supported the duke of Ormonde and Admiral Rooke against the whig accusations. News of Vigo reached London on 31 October and was immediately greeted by their high church members as the greatest triumph of the campaign. They congratulated Ormonde and Rooke as well as the Captain General in a Commons address on 10 November and included Vigo among the victories which the state celebrated in St

Paul's on the 12th – a magnificent state occasion when the members of parliament, the judges, the lords spiritual and temporal accompanied the queen in a procession across Westminster which met the mayor and aldermen of London at Temple Bar to proceed to the cathedral. The Dutch envoy l'Hermitage noted that the whole cavalcade took several hours to pass and that the crowds were enormous, there not having been a similar ceremony since the reign of Elizabeth – another Elizabethan echo in the new reign. The duke of Ormonde's coach was followed by a throng of people who greeted it with loud cries of joy and acclamation.[27] The Marlboroughs were livid at this public rejoicing for Vigo since it detracted from the continental campaign. Queen Anne tried to reassure Sarah that it did not really matter, writing to inform her that 'you know I never looked upon the sea fight as a victory, & I think what has bin said upon it as rediculous as any body can do'.[28]

Anne also indicated publicly her greater regard for Marlborough than for the 'heroes' of Vigo by elevating him to a dukedom, granting him an annual pension of £5000 from the post office, and by attempting to persuade parliament to make it perpetual to his heir. Unfortunately the latter proposal backfired, since grants to favourites had formed a major plank of the tories' platform against the king in the previous reign, and they could hardly support a similar move by the queen. The attempt to introduce a bill to realize the Queen's intentions was thwarted by Sir Christopher Musgrave and other tories.[29] The resulting embarrassment was defused by Marlborough agreeing to waive Anne's recommendation. He himself blamed Rochester for his humiliation and pledged himself to the earl's destruction. Here he found a powerful ally in the queen, who was alienated from her uncle by 'what has been so maliciously hindered in parliament'.[30]

Anne was also irritated with Rochester for his opposition to an increase in the numbers of troops and for his lax attendance of Cabinet meetings. When Marlborough returned from the continental campaign in December he was anxious to obtain an augmentation in the number of troops for that theatre for the following year. He was thwarted by Rochester, who argued that the supplies had all been agreed and voted before the duke made his request. Marlborough put pressure on the Queen, and got the allies to back up his insistence that the increase was necessary. He encountered difficulties in getting parliamentary backing for the proposed increase until Rochester left office.[31] Rochester's irregular attendance of the Cabinet, and preference for caballing with high church tory ministers, which occasioned gossip in the last weeks of 1702, played into Marlborough's hands in his campaign to get rid of the troublesome Lord Lieutenant of Ireland.[32] Anne's patience with her uncle finally wore out in February 1703, when she ordered him to go to his post in Dublin. He preferred to resign rather than comply.

Rochester's resignation coincided with the collapse of the negotiations for an Anglo-Scottish union. The commissioners appointed by the Acts of parliament in both kingdoms held meetings from 27 October 1702 to 3 February 1703. At their first quorate meeting on 10 November Lord Keeper Nathan Wright expressed the hope 'that by this congress the great business for which her majesty has been pleased to grant these commissions may be happily effected that England and Scotland, already united in allegiance unto one head the Queen, may forever hereafter become one people, one in heart and mutual affection, one in interest and one in name, or in deed, a work which if it can be brought to pass promises a lasting happiness to us all'.[33] The duke of Queensberry, head of the Scottish commission, replied that he considered a union 'to be highly advantageous for the peace and wealth of both kingdoms and a great security for the Protestant religion everywhere'. Negotiations proceeded on the basis of extending the English Act of Settlement to Scotland to ensure the same successor to Anne in both kingdoms, and the union of the two parliaments into one. These were acceptable to the Scottish commissioners provided agreement could be reached on giving Scotland free access to English commerce. The English commissioners at first held off admitting Scots into the colonial trade, arguing that 'the plantations are the property of English men; and that this trade is of so great a consequence and so beneficial as not to be communicated as is proposed, till all other particulars which shall be thought necessary to this Union be adjusted'. However such access was so fundamental to the Scots that the principle was conceded on 2 January 1703. After that decision the negotiations ran into difficulties on the question of compensation for Scottish losses in the Darien venture. Virtual deadlock had been reached on this point when Anne sent them a letter on 3 February adjourning their sitting to 4 October. They were then to consider such important points as 'the constitution of the parliament, the affairs of the church, and the municipal laws and judicatories of Scotland, for security of the properties of the subjects of that kingdom'. The announcement of that formidable agenda indicates that the adjournment was not intended to wreck the proceedings but that a breathing space was thought to be needed before they were resumed.

Anne's reasons for postponing the deliberations of the commission are not easy to ascertain, especially since she was sincerely committed to the Union. She was about to change her Scottish ministry; the very next day sweeping removals and replacements were made, many commissioners being dismissed in the process. It could be that these changes weighed heavily, since her new Scottish advisers recommended that she dissolve the controversial Edinburgh parliament and hold fresh elections in Scotland. The seceders of the previous summer had continued to protest against the legality of the proceedings from which they had withdrawn by witholding taxes voted afterwards. How to cope with this tax strike was a thorny legal problem. The Cabinet discussed the possibility of forcing compliance by making some examples of prominent evaders, but shrank from this course.[34] Only a new Scottish parliament could clear the legal issues involved. At the same time the religious implications of a union with a predominantly Presbyterian country were increasingly unacceptable to the majority of tories. Some tory ministers among the English commissioners had demonstrated their hostile attitude to the negotiations by absenting themselves from meetings, which were often not quorate. And in the Commons tories were on the warpath against Presbyterians in England who practised occasional conformity with the Church of England.

The practice had been condemned the previous May in a characteristically intemperate sermon preached by the high church firebrand Dr Henry Sacheverell at Oxford University. In it he had upheld the mutual interdependence of church and state and held out 'the bloody flag and banner of defiance' against those 'crafty faithless and insidious persons', occasional conformists.[35] Hearings of petitions upon controverted elections had also inflamed high church wrath against them. One in particular had confirmed their worst suspicions. Twenty-one voters in Wilton had allegedly not qualified themselves by taking communion in the Anglican church in accordance with the Corporation Act. One witness testified to the committee of privileges and elections that 'he had heard the mayor say that he would make none burgesses that were not dissenters from the dam's teat'.[36] It was the opportunity which occasional conformity gave dissenters to vote in borough elections that perturbed tories most, since they invariably voted whig. Thus though William Bromley condemned the practice as 'abominable hypocrisy' and 'inexcusable immorality' he was prepared to consider the disfranchizing of dissenters as an alternative to the penalizing of occasional conformists. Failing such a measure, however, an occasional conformity bill was introduced into the Commons on 4 November. Burnet claimed that 'all believed that the chief design of this bill, was to model corporations, and to cast out of them all those who would not vote in elections for tories'.[37] Officials in borough corporations who qualified for their offices by receiving communion in the Church of England, and thereafter frequented a dissenting conventicle, were to be fined £100 and £5 for every day they continued in their employments from the time they attended a nonconformist service. Prosecutions could be initiated by common informers and no time limit was placed on their informations. The bill passed the Commons with huge majorities and was carried up to the Lords on 2 December by William Bromley, accompanied by forty or fifty members.

On its arrival in the Upper House Wharton immediately opposed it, 'as *haveing nothing good in it but its preface*'.[38] When it was given a second reading Somers moved that its provisions should be confined to the Test Act of 1673, which related to office holders under the Crown. Since this would have omitted reference to the Corporation Act the motion wrecked the real aim of the bill. It nevertheless passed the Lords, albeit very narrowly. Among the minority was Anne's husband Prince George, who as a Lutheran and Lord Admiral was of necessity an occasional conformist himself. This fact caused some embarrassment to the earl of Nottingham when it was pointed out to him in the Lords by Lord Halifax, just after the earl had supported the bill on the grounds that it was against hypocrisy. It added to Nottingham's discomfiture that the Prince was present in the House at the time. The queen apparently pressed her husband to vote even though he was suffering from asthma quite badly. An apocryphal story claimed that he remarked to Wharton 'my heart is vid you', though how sincerely he was sympathetic to the whigs at this time can be questioned. The tories were in the process of voting him the swingeing pension of £100,000 a year should he outlive his wife, a proposal which some whigs, including the earl of Sunderland, opposed.[39] Moreoever when the tories offered to put a clause in the bill exempting him from its provisions he declined it, saying that if his conscience did not permit him to communicate with the Anglican church he would renounce all offices, a reply which was much approved. He even undertook to have the liturgy translated into Danish for use in the royal chapel. Possibly he felt obligated to vote with the tories on the bill, though he also voted with them against a motion that 'every one bearing office might receive the sacrament four times a year, and come to church at least once a month'. Since this amendment to the bill was defeated by only one vote his contribution, which merited a rebuke from the whig Lord Halifax, was crucial.[40]

Other amendments required two witnesses to testify against those accused of occasional conformity and that time limits should be imposed on their testimony. A more substantial amendment made in the Lords was the rejection of the huge fines levied by the bill against occasional conformists. Thus they reduced the initial levy from £100 to £20. The reduction was held to be essentially a rejection of the measure since, although the Lords searched the records of parliament for over two centuries to establish that the Upper House had altered fines, financial clauses constituted revenue which the Commons claimed could only be voted by them. Thus substantially amended the bill was read a third time on 9 December and returned to the Lower House. Suspecting that the Commons might try to force it through the Lords by 'tacking' the bill to a supply bill the whigs got the peers to resolve that tacking was

Figure 2 Defoe in the pillory, 1703.

'unparliamentary and tends to the destruction of the constitution of this government'.

The Lords' amendments exacerbated the friction between the two Houses which had marked the session. As the Dutch envoy noted, 'the tory party was so superior in the House of Commons that the whigs counted for nothing there, whereas in the Lords they were the stronger'.[41] One of the many sources of conflict between them was Sir John Pakington's attack on the bishop of Worcester for interfering in the county election against him. The Commons had resolved that the interference of peers in the choice of members of parliament was a breach of the privileges of the House of Commons. The octogenarian bishop's meddling in Worcesteshire on behalf of whig candidates and against the high church tory Pakington was severely censured by the tories, who addressed the queen to remove him from his post of almoner. Their treatment of an episcopal colleague so incensed the bishop of Carlisle that, though he was still regarded as a tory, he went down to the door of the House of Commons and got the sergeant at arms to call out Sir Christopher Musgrave, whose son's election the bishop had assisted. He upbraided Musgrave for hypocrisy in supporting Pakington against the bishop of Worcester.[42] Though the Lords tried to persuade Anne not to yield to the Commons she did oblige the tories by removing the bishop of Worcester from his post, a move which was a hostage to fortune as it seemed to demonstrate her willingness to trade the Crown's patronage to political influence.

The row over the bishop of Worcester was a trifle compared with the clash over the occasional conformity bill. Each House nominated managers for a conference to discuss their differences. Though the MPs were prepared to accept many of the peers' amendments they objected to the changes made to the level of fines. Deadlock ensued over the Christmas season, and more conferences were held in January, including a free conference on the 16th which according to Burnet 'was the most crowded upon that occasion that had ever been known; so much weight was laid on this matter on both sides'.[43] After the exchange of views the Lords adjourned to their own House where they agreed to adhere to their amendment of the fine by 65 votes to 63, which 'being the cardinal question which determined the fate of the whole bill, the rest of the points were given up without coming to any division'.[44] The only amendment which the Lords were prepared to rescind was that which confined the bill to the Test Act. When the Commons insisted on it, including the Corporation Act too, their lordships conceded on 29 January, in a very thin House, by 34 votes to 20. At a conference held by the two Houses on 1 February they insisted on all their other amendments. On 5 February the Commons similarly stood by theirs, and so the bill was aborted.

While the bill was provoking heated exchanges in parliament it also precipitated a pamphlet war. Among the many tracts to take sides on the issue of occasional conformity one attracted more notice than the rest both from contemporaries and from posterity. Just after Christmas an anonymous pamphlet was published with the provocative title *The Shortest Way with the Dissenters*. It recommended that nonconformists should be exterminated, like toads or snakes whose venom only harmed the body while they poisoned the soul. Such outrageous views led to speculation about the author. Some thought it must be a Jesuit in disguise. Others surmised that it was a high church tory who had the courage to state in public what many thought privately but few dared to express. Among the few was Henry Sacheverell, whose violent language against dissent Daniel Defoe used as a model for his own satirical attack. The earl of Nottingham took it seriously enough to put a notice in the *Gazette* offering a reward of £50 for the arrest of those responsible. Defoe's hoax backfired, for he was apprehended, tried and imprisoned for his authorship of the piece.

The passions released by the dispute could only be cooled with the prorogation of parliament. Queen Anne closed the session on 27 February. Among the bills which received the royal assent on that day was an Act for enlarging the time for taking the abjuration oath. The last bill to receive William III's assent had been one to enjoin office holders to swear that they repudiated any allegiance to James Edward Stuart, the son of James II, and since his father's death self-styled James III. They had been given a year to take an oath abjuring him. With the time expiring, and many tories not yet having sworn in accordance with the Act, their friends sought to give them another year by this bill. When this bill reached the House of Lords in November 1702 the whigs, suspecting that its sponsors were sympathetic to Jacobites in the tory ranks, moved three amendments. The first stipulated that anybody who had lost office for refusal to take the oath should not be restored even if they took it in the extended time. The second made it treason to try to thwart the Protestant succession to the throne. The third extended the scope of the measure to Ireland. When these were debated in the Commons on 13 February some tories divided the House on the first amendment, but it was carried by 118 votes to 117. This was regarded as a significant split in the tory ranks. It was noted that the greatest strength the whigs could muster in this session was 85 votes. Consequently some 33 tories had voted against their colleagues. Having failed by one vote to defeat it the latter, led by Sir Christopher Musgrave, tried to persuade the House that the second amendment should be a separate bill rather than a clause in the current one. This too failed, for as its opponents pointed out it was an obvious gambit to defeat the proposal since there was not sufficient time left that session to carry a whole new bill. And Musgrave was reminded that the extension of the crime of high treason to cover attempts to prevent Anne's accession had been effected by adding a clause to the abjuration bill which William III had passed.[45] Consequently the amendments were all carried in the Commons and passed into law. As Burnet observed: 'all people were surprised to see a bill that was begun in favour of the Jacobites turned so terribly upon them; since by it we had a new security given, both in England and Ireland, for a protestant successor.'[46]

3

1703

The resignation of the earl of Rochester symbolized the strength of the ties between the queen and the duke and duchess of Marlborough. For Anne had parted with the services of her uncle in order to gratify the Churchills. It was Marlborough who first suggested that the way to get rid of Rochester was to order him to go to Ireland.[1] Now he had got his way. Yet just at this moment an event happened which, though it ought to have cemented the bond between 'Mrs Morley' and 'Mr and Mrs Freeman', drove the first fateful wedge between Anne and Sarah. This was the death on 20 February of the Marlboroughs' only son, John, Lord Blandford, at the age of sixteen.

Both parents were distraught, but the mother seems to have been more so than the father. She rushed to her son's bedside in King's College, Cambridge the minute she heard he was ill, with the smallpox. John stayed away until all hopes of a recovery were lost, and then joined his wife at the last moment. Blandford's death mocked his ambition to perpetuate his family. However, though this left him feeling there was nothing more to live for, he found solace in activity, going abroad as soon as he could after the funeral to throw himself into the campaign. Sarah, deprived of his presence, retreated into herself. It was rumoured that her son's death 'hath near touched her head'.[2] She spurned the queen's offer of condolence. 'It would have been a great satisfaction to your poor unfortunate faithful Morley, if you would have give me leave to come to St Albans,' Anne wrote, 'for the unfortunate ought to come to the unfortunate.'[3]

Anne knew all too well the afflictions of losing an only son. The death of the duke of Gloucester had blighted her world too. Almost two years after it a Dutch envoy observed that she had ever since been under a very great affliction. Where before she had enjoyed music and always dined accompanied by a recital of oboes and violins, she never employed musicians at her table thereafter. Indeed he thought that the event had so affected her that her reign would not be long.[4] In fact Anne contrived to overcome her grief, partly by devoting herself to her duties as Queen. It was observed at Court that 'the Duchess of Marlborough bears not her affliction like her mistress'.[5] Instead Sarah isolated herself, rarely attending Anne even during the sickness of Prince George the following November. This isolation, broken by letters lambasting the tories as Jacobites and extolling the whigs more stridently than ever, led gradually but perceptibly to a psychological estrangement.[6] Thus although Anne promoted the whig John Hervey to the peerage in March as a favour to Sarah, at the same time she also ennobled four tories.

The promotion of the marquis of Normanby to the dukedom of Buckingham, and the elevation of Nottingham's brother to the earldom of Guernsey, and a relative of Sir Edward Seymour's to the barony of Conway, together with the ennoblement of two more moderate tories to the upper House, struck contemporaries as a signal that the Queen intended to redress the balance of forces in the Lords in favour of the tory party. It was clearly a sign that, although she had parted with the services of Rochester, she was not turning her back on the high church men. On the contrary, it appeared that she was aiming to get the occasional conformity bill through both Houses in the next session.[7] The ennoblement of Hervey might have been a sop to Sarah, but the other creations were anthema to her. Even her husband must have found the favour shown to Buckingham and Seymour disagreeable. Shortly after the announcement of the new peerages Marlborough wrote to Godolphin 'if Buckingham continues being so impertinent to joyn with Seymour and others to obstruct business, I should think it were much better to be plain with him, than to suffer him to goe on in that way.' 'Wee are bound not to wish for anybody's death,' he acknowledged in a letter to his duchess a few weeks later, 'but if Sir Edward Seymour should dye, I am convinced it would be no great lose to the Queen.'[8] Whatever else the peerages signified, they did not indicate Anne's complete reliance on the Churchills at this juncture.

While the growing rift between the Queen and the duchess of Marlborough was as yet a secret hidden from all hearts except those of Anne and Sarah, and perhaps the duke's, his deeds were the talk of Europe. What was being talked about in the spring of 1703 was the siege of Bonn, which the duke undertook at Dutch insistence. He would rather have besieged Ostend and Antwerp, but the allies had prepared to take the Rhine citadel, so as he opined to Godolphin 'you know in my opinion I was never fond of this siege, but itt has now made soe much noyse that I think itt would be scandolous to avoyde the making itt now, soe that I have given the orders for the investing it'.[9] He went on to express gloom about the news from Germany, where the elector of Bavaria had thrown in his lot with the French and taken Regensburg.

During the course of the campaign the Bavarians advanced deep into Austrian territory, taking Innsbruck in the Tyrol without resistance from the Emperor's forces. Their advance was only repulsed by local levies. While this gave some comfort to the allies the successful siege of Augsburg by the Bavarians plunged them into further gloom. Marlborough was meanwhile concerned about French advances up the Maas which threatened Maastricht, though they retreated from it just before he himself took possession of Bonn.

After taking Bonn he renewed his 'great design' to take Ostend and Antwerp. Unfortunately it depended on Dutch willingness to give priority to the siege of Ostend, which they failed to do, preferring to pillage the country between the two towns instead. They were suspicious of Marlborough's aims in taking the port anyway, regarding it as a bid to give the British influence in the Low Countries to offset their own. The duke wished also to engage the French in battle but the Dutch again preferred a different strategy, especially after a surprise French attack on their own forces came close to inflicting a complete defeat on them. They therefore supported instead the sieges of Huy and Limburg, which Marlborough took in August and September. Their capture ended what was for him a very frustrating campaign.

This frustration has been seen as the motive for Marlborough's contemplating laying down his command in September 1703. The Captain general periodically considered resignation, especially in the year following his son's death. Historians tend to treat these as passing moods, but a man of Marlborough's unbridled ambition was not the type to throw it all away on impulse. However in this depressing year he seems to have come nearer to it than at any other time. In May the Queen took the prospect that both the duke and duchess would resign sufficiently seriously to send Sarah a desperate appeal to them to reconsider the matter.[10]

> The thoughts that both my dear Mrs Freeman & Mr Freeman seems to have of retyering gives me no small uneasyness & therfore I must say something on that Subject, it is no wonder at all people in your posts should be weary of ye world who are soe continually troubld with all ye hurry & impertinencys of it, but give me leave to say, you should a litle consider your faithfull freinds & poor Country, which must be ruined if ever you should putt your melencoly thoughts in execution, as for your poor unfortunat faithfull Morly she could not beare it, for if ever you should forsake me, I would have nothing more to do with the world but make another abdycation, for what is a Crown, when ye support of it is gon, I never will forsake your dear self, Mr Freeman nor Mr Montgomery, but allways be your constant faithfull servant, & we four must never part, till death mows us down with his impartiall hand.

This could be attributed to Sarah's despair at the death of Blandford leading her to take her husband's expressing a desire to resign more seriously than it deserved. But in the autumn the duke mentioned to Godolphin the strong possibility that he would not serve in the ensuing campaign.

Insofar as his feelings have been taken seriously by historians they have been attributed to his dealings with the Dutch. Certainly they were tense at this time. Not only did he feel that they had thwarted his desire for a battle, but one of their commanders who had been hard pressed by the French openly blamed the duke for not coming to his assistance. The authority given by the States General to their field deputies was a source of great annoyance to the duke in this year. 'If I might have millions given mee to serve another yeare,' he wrote to the Grand Pensionary Heinsius, 'and be obliged to doe nothing but by the unanimous consent of the Generals, I would much sooner dye.' English historians tend to take such expressions at their face value, however, and to see Marlborough as a Gulliver hampered by the Lilliputian Dutch. In fact he had an excellent relationship with Heinsius, and knew that his friend would exploit his complaints to get the States General to make concessions for the next campaign. What Marlborough wanted he spelled out later in the same letter. 'If the States can think my being here can be of any use, I hope they will approve of the onely expedient I can think of, which is my being att the head of the troupes payde by England, and thay joyning such of theirs to mee as they shall judge for the good of their service. Att the same time I shall be very desirous to have as many Deputys in the army with mee as thay please. for I shall never have a thought but what I should be glad theay should be judge off.'[11] This was more or less what he got for the ensuing campaign.

It was not what happened in the United Provinces that unsettled him so much as developments elsewhere. In particular he was stung by a letter from the Speaker, Robert Harley, to Lord Godolphin, which the Treasurer sent to him. In it Harley summed up conversations he had recently had 'with the hot people of both sides'. Among their complaints was 'the uselessness of an offensive war in Flanders'. It was galling to Marlborough that his efforts were discounted by both tories and whigs. In his view the Low Countries were vital to England's security. As he put it to Heinsius: 'if I had been born att Amsterdam, I could not be more desirous for the prosperity of Holland then I am, being truly convinced that when you are unfortunate, England must be undone.'[12]

Many tories shared the earl of Rochester's view that England's main effort should not be on land at all, but by sea. To them the disappointing continental campaign of 1703 was further proof of this proposition. Unfortunately for them the major naval expedition of the year had been a disaster rather than just a disappointment. Admiral John Graydon had been despatched with a squadron of five ships to the West Indies to equip an expedition from the colonies for an attack on the French in Newfoundland. Even on the way out he incurred criticism for failing to engage four French ships, arguing that his orders forbade him to delay. On arrival in Barbadoes and Jamaica, however, he delayed his departure to Newfoundland several months, not arriving there until August. By then the state of the ships and the men, in the opinion of the admiral, was inferior to the enemy, and he abandoned the expedition to return to England. The voyage across the Atlantic encountered severe weather, and the ships limped into English ports during October. Graydon's conduct was investigated by the House of Lords, and censured as 'a prejudice to the queen's service and a great dishonour to the nation'. They recommended that he be cashiered and never employed by the Queen again, which she agreed to, even stopping Graydon's pension. The 'blue water' theorists did therefore not offer much of a challenge to Marlborough's strategy in the Low countries.

Among the tories who thought the campaign there was 'useless', however, was the Secretary of State, Lord Nottingham.[13] He had advocated from the outset of hostilities opening up the Mediterranean and the Iberian peninsula to combined naval and military operations.

In 1703 he planned a joint Anglo-Dutch expedition for the Mediter-ranean, which would help the Protestants who had risen up against the French government in the Cevennes, and confirm the duke of Savoy when he calculated the pros and cons of deserting Louis XIV for the allied cause. As he wrote to the Pensionary of Holland, 'I have long bin of opinion that no war can be of great dammage to France but that which is prosecuted in the way I have proposed, that is, by a fleet and an army accompanying it.'[14] Unfortunately the ships from the United Provinces took until June to arrive, much to Nottingham's annoyance. By that time it was too late to do any-thing to help the Cevennois rebels. Instead the expedition protected a convoy of merchant ships to the Mediterranean. It stayed a few days in Livorno in September and then sailed back again, having accomplished very little, though it might have helped to confirm the duke of Savoy's decision to break his alliance with France and join the allies instead.

Nottingham's involvement in the Iberian theatre was much more successful. The abortive expedition to Cadiz had rather tarnished England's reputation in the Iberian theatre the previous year. But in 1703 a new opportunity to retrieve that fiasco was presented by the entry of Portugal into the war on the side of the Grand Alliance. Although the treaty with the Portuguese has ever since been associated with John Methuen, the diplomat who negotiated it, as Charles Davenant remarked at the time 'no minister can take a thing more to heart and labour it more industriously than my Lord Nottingham has done the Treaty with Portugal'.[15] To persuade the Portuguese to declare war on Bourbon Spain the treaty committed the allies to supplying them with 12,000 troops. The Dutch and English contribution to this force could only be obtained by reducing their armies in the Low Countries, and Nottingham put pressure on Marlborough to release men from his army for this service. The Captain General shared the Dutch view that men could hardly be spared from the Flanders theatre to go to the Iberian. He therefore sent as few men as he thought he could get away with to make up the English quota.

A further implication of involving the Portuguese in warfare against the Bourbons was a qualification of allied war aims. Initially the signatories of the Grand Alliance had merely committed themselves to getting a reasonable share of the Spanish inheritance for the Habsburg claimant, without specifying Iberian territories. But as a result of the treaty with Portugal they pledged themselves to obtaining the throne of Spain itself for the archduke Charles. This was immeasurably to complicate the character of hostilities and even more so the conduct of negotiations for their conclusion. The slogan 'no peace without Spain' encapsulated the policy which the allies undertook as the price of getting the Portuguese to join them.

For England, however, economically the Methuen treaty seemed to be pure gain. The commercial agreement which Methuen hammered out arranged for the exportation to Portugal of English manufactures, especially woollen cloth, in exchange for Portuguese products such as port wine. Since this resulted in an unfavourable balance of payments for Portugal she made up the difference with bullion, particularly with gold discovered in Brazil during the 1690s. This influx of precious metals was a godsend at a time when English trade with other parts of Europe produced a deficit because of the war effort, and the need to provide for an army based on the continent. It was partly because the Low Countries theatre drained money from England that Nottingham considered the continental campaign to be useless, much to Marlborough's chagrin.

What probably annoyed the duke even more, however, was to learn that some of the 'hot people' on the whig side shared Nottingham's views. Marlborough seems to have been especially sensitive to whig criticisms at this time. In July he complained about a whiggish libel, *A Prophecy*, which contained the lines:

> When *Marlborough, Godolphin, Lory,*
> Have acted over the old Story,
>
> . . .
>
> *England* will be, or I'm an Ass,
> The strangest Queendom ever was.

The poem allied the Captain General and the Lord Treasurer with Rochester, whom they had recently ousted from the ministry. As Marlborough observed those who wrote the libel 'are not very well acquainted with the notions I have of government'.[16] Nevertheless it revealed that he was still regarded in whig circles as a tory, a characterization which his support for the occasional conformity bill seemed to reinforce.

The fact that the tories were committed to bringing in a second bill when parliament met in November presented the 'duumvirs' with a dilemma. The duke had never liked the bill, and had even tried to prevent its introduction the previous session. But his attitude was that, once introduced, he was bound to vote for it, though 'he was afraid it would break us'.[17] As he put it to Sarah when anticipating the arrival of the second bill in the Lords, 'I must be careful not to doe the thing in the world which my Lord Rochister would most desire to have mee doe, which is to give my vote against this bill; but I doe promiss sollemly that I will speak to nobody living to be for itt.'[18] Previously, moreover, Godolphin had tried to do all he could to stifle it in the Commons before it reached the upper House. Prior to the session great efforts were made to get a maximum attendance of whigs and placemen with a view to defeating the bill when it was first introduced. News of these efforts reached the high church tories who put pressure on their own supporters to thwart the attempt to quash the measure. Thus Lord Weymouth wrote to Colonel James Grahme to muster up all his parliamentary colleagues, informing him that 'Sir Chuffer [Edward Seymour] will be in town . . . and our West Saxons will come up early'. In order to drive home the importance of attending he stressed, 'you never yet knew the whigs throw up the game'.[19] On the day the session opened Godolphin informed Harley 'I have sent about severall of those you call orderly men. I have spoken to Mr Lowndes [the Secretary to the Treasury] to ply his coffee house and to diffuse . . . All appear to be very well convinced of the unseasonableness of this bill; but all seem to bee apprehensive the matter is to[o] far engaged.'[20]

The second bill was less draconian than the first. Thus the fines were reduced from £100 to £50. If this was done to stave off criticisms the tactic did not succeed for it was noted that the bill provoked more opposition than the first had done. Nevertheless it passed the Lower House by 223 votes to 140. Marlborough was told that the bill would be thrown out of the Lords, unless he and Godolphin made efforts to get it passed, which they did not do. 'More importantly,' as Anne's biographer notes, 'the queen's attitude towards the bill had changed during the summer. She now believed that its reintroduction was a "pretence . . . for quarelling".'[21] Sir John Pakington, in a speech in favour of the bill which was for the most part a ranting denunciation of dissenters, pointed out that 'her desire to see this bill succeed the last sessions of parliament was sufficiently shewn by the prince of Denmark's constant attendance upon it'.[22] Instead of sending her husband to vote for it a second time, however, she took him off to Windsor the day before the bill was debated in the Lords.[23] Such moves led the whigs to muster all their strength to defeat the bill not by clogging it with amendments as in the previous session, but on a straight vote. The earl of Sunderland drew up lists calculating the probable outcome. The calculations led Wharton to boast that 'by proxies his party was now able to fling out the bill against occasional conformity'.[24] And so it proved. On 14 December it was agreed by a majority of twelve votes not to give it a second reading. 'Everybody sees too late', Godolphin had observed after the bill passed the Commons; 'wee were in the right that would have kept the bill at a distance. Like an unruly muskett it might serve to frighten those against whom it was presented, but not hurt any but those who give fire to it.'[25]

Queen Anne tried to remove some of the ammunition from the high church tory blunderbuss by relieving the plight of poor clergymen. For the inadequate stipends of many Anglican ministers fuelled the paranoia expressed in their slogan 'the Church in danger'. The discrepancies in clerical incomes from the richest to the poorest livings had been notorious at least since the Reformation. A few below the bishops lived comfortably on incomes of several hundreds of pounds. But most had to survive on considerably less than this, many receiving under £50 a year and some no more than £20. Moreover they were dependent still upon tithes paid by their parishioners. Although the Toleration Act of 1689 upheld the compulsory payment of tithes, it seems that in many parishes there was a reluctance to pay by dissenters, who had to maintain their own ministers too. Payment could only be enforced by the minister prosecuting the defaulter in the church courts, which did not improve relations with nonconformists in the parish. Moreover such litigation was risky, since laymen prosecuted by the clergy sought prohibitions to transfer the cases from eccclesiastical to secular jurisdiction. The result was an increase in the poverty and resentment of the Anglican clergy.

On her thirty-ninth birthday, 6 February 1704, Anne sent a message to the House of Commons informing them that she proposed to devote the revenue raised from clerical first fruits and tenths to the augmentation of low stipends. The sums involved, between £16,000 and £17,000 a year, were insignificant to the Crown, but could lift a living worth less than £50 a year above the poverty line when administered by a Trust set up specially for the purpose.[26] Queen Anne's Bounty, as it was known, did much to alleviate clerical poverty and to take the sting out of the tories' charge that the Church was in danger during her reign.

This Act did not, however, prevent the representatives of the inferior clergy in the Lower House of Convocation from attacking the bishops in the upper House. Nor did it stop the tories from pursuing their vendetta against occasional conformists.

Among the peers whom Sunderland listed as being opposed to the occasional conformity bill was George Kidder the bishop of Bath and Wells. His name appears on the first list drawn up, but is missing from the second. This was because the good bishop was unfortunately killed along with his wife as they lay in bed on 26 November 1703 when the 'great storm' blew their chimney down on them. To some tories, Kidder's misfortune was a judgement since Kidder occupied the see by virtue of the fact that Thomas Ken, his much respected predecessor, had been deprived of it after the Revolution through his refusal to take the oaths to the new regime. Ken thus became a leader of those non-juring clergymen who kept up a small but significant schism in the Church of England.

The destruction wrought by the hurricane was also seen as a judgement by those whigs who subscribed to the views of the societies for reformation of manners. These watchdogs of public morality had emerged in various centres, and above all in London, since the Revolution. They argued that the blessing bestowed on England by Providence in that event would be forfeited if it were not accompanied by a moral revolution. So far from mending their manners, however, the English were, in the eyes of the societies, more debauched than ever. The societies drew up black lists of those who indulged in profanity, drunkenness or 'night walking' after prostitutes. Any natural calamity, from harvest failures to outbreaks of smallpox, were pressed into service by the reformers as evidence of divine displeasure with the English. To them the tempest was literally a godsend.

The great storm was indeed the strongest wind to blow across England before the hurricane which wreaked such damage in 1987. On that earlier occasion trees went down like wheat before the scythe. Lead from cathedral roofs was rolled off like sardine tins opened with a key. Many ships, including fifteen warships, sank. Damage was particularly severe in the south-west. The Eddystone lighthouse was swept away. Bristol suffered more than any other town. The wind blew across southern and eastern England, showering London streets with

Figure 3 The Great Wind of 1703 – damage to the Royal Navy.

tiles and stripping the roof from Ely cathedral. Northern England was less affected.

Although Scotland escaped the tempest altogether it experienced some severe political storms in the same year. After the change in the ministry there Anne dissolved the Scottish parliament. The spring elections resulted in a strengthening of the Cavalier party in the new parliament.

When it met on 6 May it was noted that there had never been a more magnificent 'riding', as the opening ceremonies were known. Some twenty Lords who had never attended Williamite parliaments now took the oaths. These peers presumably strengthened the Cavalier party. The cavaliers made difficulties for the commissioner, Queensberry, who wanted two things from the new body: supply, and recognition of the succession of the house of Hanover to the throne of Scotland. He received neither. The Cavaliers wished to keep the Stuart option open. The Country opposition still rankled at Darien and desired satisfactory terms for Scottish trade. Led respectively by the dukes of Hamilton and Argyll the two parties combined in an opportunistic alliance to pass two Acts: the Security Act, and an Act anent peace and war. The Security Act declared that Anne's successor should not be the same as the one due to succeed to the throne of England according to the English Act of Settlement unless two conditions were met. First, 'that in this present session of parliament or any other session of this or any other ensuing parliament during her Majesty's reign there be such conditions of government settled and enacted as may secure the honour and sovereignty of this Crown and Kingdom, the freedom frequency and power of parliaments, the religion liberty and trade of the nation from English or foreign interference'. Secondly, satisfaction had to be obtained from the English parliament for 'a free communication of trade, freedom of navigation and the liberty of the plantations'. The advocate of the first set of conditions was the republican Andrew Fletcher of Saltoun. He wished to go further and spell out limitations on the prerogatives of the Crown, since as he observed this clause was 'general and indefinite'. The Estates, however, rejected his specific proposals, such as a requirement that they grant all offices previously conferred by the Crown. Nevertheless another requirement, that they had to approve declarations of war and peace, or the conclusion of treaties with foreign powers, formed the basis of the Act anent peace and war, which bound a future monarch in Scotland not to make peace or declare war without consent of parliament.[27]

The prospect of Scotland becoming again a separate kingdom on the death of Queen Anne was too nightmarish for the English government to contemplate. It even opened up the possibility of the Pretender succeeding to the northern kingdom on Anne's death, for although a Protestant succession was ensured, a Stuart restoration could occur should he renounce the Catholic faith. Not surprisingly, Godolphin advised Anne not to give the royal assent to the Act.

The Lord Treasurer and Marlborough were even worried that troops might be required to be sent to Scotland from the Low Countries, not as a contingency against separatism, as is sometimes assumed, but to stifle any Jacobite rising which might occur as a result of the so-called 'Scotch plot'. On 17 December the Queen informed parliament 'of very ill practices and designs carried on in Scotland, by emissaries from France; which might have proved extremely dangerous to the peace of these kingdoms . . . by this seasonable discovery I shall be able to give such directions for our security as will effectually prevent any ill consequences from these pernicious designs'. She had herself inadvertently encouraged Jacobite activity in her northern kingdom by issuing a proclamation the previous spring indemnifying Scots who had committed crimes against the Crown since the Revolution. Many emigrés had returned, including some genuine plotters. Ciphered letters from France to one David Lindsay had been intercepted in the office of Secretary Nottingham and passed on to the duke of Queensberry.

Although the cipher was difficult to decode, and appeared like gibberish, the correspondence seemed to contain plans for a rising in Scotland with French help.

Queensberry himself was also informed of a conspiracy, allegedly involving many of the opposition in the Edinburgh parliament, by an anonymous agent who wished his anonymity to be guaranteed by the government. Nottingham obliged to the extent of providing him with a pass to leave the country under a false name. The Secretary did not even know the identity of the informer. It turned out to be Simon Fraser.

Although Queensberry told the queen that Fraser was a man of integrity there was little in his career to justify such a view. On the contrary, Lord Lovat, as he became known after the death of his father in 1699, was one of the greatest rogues of his generation. In William's reign he had tricked the sister of the earl of Tullibardine, Lord High Commissioner of Scotland, into a forced marriage, invading her bedchamber with a clergyman to perform the ceremony and a piper to stifle her protests. Tullibardine had marked him down for destruction for this outrage and had successfully prosecuted Lovat for treason. Though he escaped execution by procuring a pardon from the king through the intercession of the duke of Argyll, he still suffered the confiscation of his estates which he was determined to retrieve. Meanwhile Lovat had found it prudent to withdraw to France where he ingratiated himself with the Jacobite court in exile at St Germains. Following Anne's proclamation pardoning former traitors he made his way back to Scotland pledged to raise a rebellion for the Pretender. Once there, however, he proceeded to inform Queensberry of the alleged Jacobitism of his political enemies. These included Lovat's brother-in-law, the former Lord Tullibardine, now duke of Atholl. Queensberry was delighted to have ostensible evidence of Atholl's treason in the form of a letter from Mary of Modena, the Pretender's mother, which stated 'you may be sure that when my concerns require the help of my friends you are one of the first I have in my view'. It seems certain, however, that this was an 'open' letter which Lovat personally addressed to Atholl.

Lovat's treachery came to the notice of the government and to Atholl in November, just after he had returned to the continent on the pass obtained for him by Nottingham. Two inveterate plotters divulged his double dealing, Sir John Maclean to Nottingham, Robert Ferguson to the duke. Atholl, incensed that Queensberry had been prepared to implicate him in Jacobite intrigue, now turned the accusation against the Scottish commissioner.

The fact that a tory Secretary of State, Lord Nottingham, had allowed a notorious Jacobite to get out of the country was a godsend to the whigs. Two whigs in particular, the dukes of Devonshire and Somerset, both members of the cabinet, appear to have used the incident to extract every ounce of political capital they could from the incident. They were prominent in the debates in the upper House which led to the resolution 'that there had been dangerous plots between some in Scotland and the Courts of France and St Germains.' They also headed the list of peers chosen by the Lords to examine other Jacobite agents apprehended in England.

The attack on Nottingham in the Lords led the tories in the Commons to defend him. After heated exchanges they sufficiently vindicated him to get the House to resolve *nem con* on 21 December 'that the earl of Nottingham . . . hath highly merited the trust her Majesty hath reposed in him.' They also addressed the queen protesting that the Lords had taken the examination of key witnesses out of the hands of the Crown by appointing a committee to interrogate them themselves.

The 'Scotch plot' thus became a political issue between tory and whig and, like so many questions in Anne's first parliament where the tories had a majority in the Commons and the whigs dominated the Lords, a constitutional clash between the two Houses. This ensured that it continued at the top of the parliamentary agenda for the rest of the session. In February the Lords again appointed a secret committee to investigate the plot and went on to blame the government for not prosecuting those involved.

Two other issues also embroiled the Houses during the session of 1703 to 1704. These were: the commissioners of public accounts; and the case of Ashby versus White.

The device of appointing commissioners to investigate the accounts of ministers had been employed by backbenchers in the reign of William III to expose alleged corruption. In the 1690s it had united tories and whigs into a Country alliance against the Court. As in so many political spheres, this had been transformed into a party issue between tory and whig in the last two parliaments held under William. The turning point again was the attempted impeachment of the whig ministers Halifax, Orford and Somers. This was the key issue which marked Williamite politics off from those of his successor. Now tories revived the commission with the avowed purpose of investigating the accounts of ministers they had failed to impeach in 1701. The Commons chose seven high tories as commissioners.[28] Their names were then inserted in the bill for stating public accounts. When this reached the Upper House the Lords removed one commissioner, Robert Byerley, 'as being to account for himself' and added, by ballot, three staunch whigs.[29] Some tories were so angry that they threatened to throw out the bill when it came back to the Commons. In the event cooler counsels prevailed, and instead they simply refused to accept the amendments, though, when a joint conference with the Lords also failed to produce agreement, they did move for a protest to be entered in the Journal of the House, a motion that dropped only through the session ending that very day.[30]

The case of Ashby versus White produced even more friction.[31] It arose following the first general election of 1701 when one Ashby, who had voted in the Buckinghamshire town at previous elections, was not allowed to vote by the Mayor, White. Ashby sued at the county assizes, which upheld his plea that the vote was a legal right he had been denied. White then appealed to the court of Queen's bench on the grounds that the House of Commons alone had jurisdiction over the rights of elections. The four justices of the court were divided. Three found for the plaintiff. But the most distinguished, Lord Chief Justice Holt, gave a different judgement, maintaining that a legal right implied a legal remedy, and that Ashby could have recourse to the common law to uphold his claim to be a qualified voter in Aylesbury. Since the majority went against Ashby he appealed to the House of Lords, which heard the case on a writ of error. The Lords upheld Holt's view of the matter. Inevitably this procedure involved a clash with the Commons who were jealous of their right to be sole judge of electoral matters.

While constitutionally the Lower House was in the right, politically it was not a question of right or wrong so much as a trial of strength between the parties. For Ashby was a whig and had voted in Aylesbury for candidates backed by the Junto whig, Lord Wharton. Indeed without Wharton's financial backing Ashby, described as a cobbler, could not have afforded such protracted litigation. As Sir Edward Seymour put it when the Commons debated the Lords decision on 21 January 1704: 'I do not think there was virtue enough in the cobbler of Aylesbury, nor had he purse enough, if a Lord had not acted that part.' This prompted the whig leader Lord Hartington to protest 'I think the liberty of a cobbler ought to be as much regarded as of anybody else; that is the happiness of our constitution.'[32] The solicitor general, Sir Simon Harcourt, put the case bluntly: 'the question was not whether the Lords had the right to reverse a judgement in Queen's bench on a writ of error but whether or no it be the sole right of the Commons of England to determine their own elections?' The whigs tried to draw a distinction between the right of adjudicating the merits of elections in general and the qualifications of particular voters, but the tories would have none of it: 'if you do not assert that you have the power of determining the qualifications of electors you give up the right of the Commons of England', asserted Sir Christopher Musgrave. The House divided on the issue and upheld its right to judge individual qualifications by 215 to 97. Though the whigs kept up their objections when the debate was renewed on 26 January, the tories prevailed in maintaining the rights of the Lower House against the claims of the upper.[33]

Where the end of the session also ended the dispute about the commissioners of public accounts, and postponed the Aylesbury case until the next meeting of the Houses, the political fall-out from the Scotch Plot led to the removal from the ministry of both Queensberry and Nottingham soon after Anne prorogued parliament. The Scottish commissioner was the first to go, being replaced by the marquess of Tweeddale in March 1704. Nottingham fought stubbornly to avoid the same fate. He went on the offensive, demanding the removal from the cabinet of whig ministers who had led the campaign in the Lords against him. But they had the backing of Godolphin and Marlborough. The Lord Treasurer was aware that Nottingham held him partly responsible for his discomfiture in the upper House. As for the Captain General, he resented the Secretary's depiction of the campaign in the low countries as 'useless', as well as his attempts to deprive that theatre of troops in order to open up the Iberian peninsula to the allies. As he stayed in Harwich en route to the continent on 8 April he wrote to Godolphin, 'I am assured that he [Nottingham] tells his party that the Queen is desirous to do everything that would give them satisfaction, but that she is hindered by you and me; that he is so convinced that we shall in a very short time put all the business into the hands of the whigs, that if he can't get such alterations made in the Cabinet Council as he thinks absolutely necessary for the safety of the Church he would then quit.' Ten days later the treasurer informed Sarah that Nottingham 'was very positive that the Queen could not govern but by one party or the other, and that the keeping the duke of Somerset in the Cabinet Council after what had passed would render her government contemptible'.[34] Godolphin did not demur when the Secretary offered to resign on 20 April. However, Anne was loath to part with the services of the leader of the high church tories, and asked him to consider the matter for a few more days. The Treasurer then pre-empted his final decision by persuading Anne to dismiss the earl of Jersey from the post of Lord Chamberlain and Sir Edward Seymour from that of comptroller of the household. On 22 April Nottingham handed in his seals of office.

4

1704

After the resignation of the earl of Nottingham in April 1704 his place as Secretary of State was taken by Robert Harley, the Speaker of the House of Commons. This was a mark of his close involvement with the duumvirs Marlborough and Godolphin, so close that to contemporaries at this time they formed a triumvirate. Since he came into the ministry on his own terms, while his nominees filled most of the vacancies created by the departure of Nottingham's associates, it also indicated that, for the time being at least, Harley's views on the relationships between the Court and the parliamentary parties was going to prevail. Precisely what those views entailed puzzled contemporaries and has intrigued historians ever since.

The political principles of the most devious politician of the age impressed contemporaries with their subtlety and cunning, earning him the nickname of 'Robin the Trickster.' Once, at a dinner party, he raised a glass to propose the toast of 'Love and Friendship and everlasting Union', and lamented that there was no Tokay to drink it in. This prompted Lord Cowper to comment that clear white Lisbon was more appropriate than the cloudy Hungarian wine, a remark which those present saw was a deliberate reference to:[1]

> that humour of his, which was never to deal clearly or openly, but always with reserve, if not dissimulation or rather simulation; and to love tricks even when not necessary, but from an inward satisfaction he took in applauding his own cunning. If any man was ever born under a necessity of being a knave, he was.

Historians have also found his activities enigmatic. It has been difficult to classify the politics of a man who began his career as a Revolution whig, joined with the tories against the Junto whigs in William's reign, then under Anne first worked with the tory leaders, then against them, and finally with them again. Harley has been seen as advocating non-party and even anti-party rule. In the first view

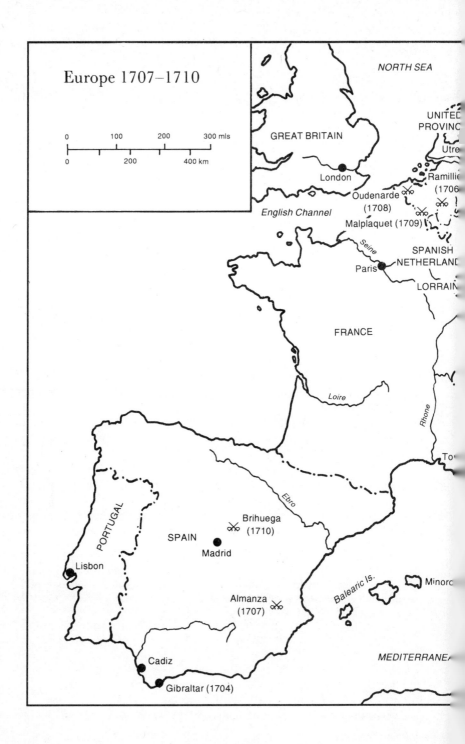

Europe 1707–1710

0   100   200   300 mls

0   200   400 km

NORTH SEA

GREAT BRITAIN

London

UNITED
PROVINC

Utre

Ramillie
(1706

Oudenarde
(1708)

Malplaquet (1709)

English Channel

Seine

SPANISH
NETHERLAND

Paris

LORRAIN

FRANCE

Loire

Rhone

To

Ebro

Brihuega
(1710)

SPAIN

Madrid

Balearic Is.

Minorc

Lisbon

PORTUGAL

Almanza
(1707)

Cadiz

MEDITERRANE/

Gibraltar (1704)

Map 1 Europe, 1707–1710

he sought to balance the parties in the ministry, rather as William
III had done and, as we have seen, Marlborough and Godolphin
did at the accession of Anne. In the second he was a characteristic
'trimmer', working against the prevalent party in order to offset its
influence.

Certainly in Anne's reign he was resolutely opposed to party rule. His
strategy was to prevent any group of party leaders, whether high church
tories or Junto whigs, from engrossing ministerial posts to the point
where they could dictate policy. But the tactics which he employed
to achieve this end changed with circumstances. He recognized that
normally government without parties was impossible, as there were
not enough peers and MPs unattached to the tories or the whigs to
form a stable majority in parliament. In order to obtain parliamentary
stability he accepted that it was absolutely necessary to work with the
party leaders, who commanded the support of the majority of members
of the House of Commons. For the Lower chamber, which alone could
initiate money bills, was the more important during a major war
when supply was crucial to the Court. In this partnership, however,
the party element was to be treated strictly as a junior. This meant
maintaining tight control over ministerial appointments, especially to
the highest policy-making posts which carried with them membership
of the Cabinet. These were to be preserved as much as possible for
men who would support the Court rather than their party if the two
interests conflicted. Party zealots were only to be admitted into the less
influential posts.

The ministerial reshuffle in the spring of 1704 was in accordance
with these views. Up to that time the government since the accession
of Anne had been a partnership between the Court and the high church
tories. But the leaders of the latter, particularly Rochester, Nottingham
and Sir Edward Seymour, had incurred the displeasure of the duumvirs
by attempting to dictate policy. Rochester had been forced out of the
ministry in 1703. In 1704 he was followed by Nottingham, Secretary
of state for the southern department, the earl of Jersey who was
Lord chamberlain and Seymour, the comptroller of the household.
Sir Charles Hedges, Secretary of state for the northern department,
replaced Nottingham and was himself succeeded in May by Harley. The
earl of Kent, who became Lord chamberlain, appears to have obtained
his post through the influence of the duchess of Marlborough. This was
the last time Sarah had any say in the disposal of a major office, and it is
perhaps indicative of her waning influence that, where his predecessor
had sat in Cabinet, Kent did not.[2] All the other changes were due to
Harley's influence. His friend Sir Thomas Mansell succeeded Seymour
as comptroller of the household. Although it was observed that he 'did
not take the abjuration oath till after due consideration' Mansell was

Figure 4 Battle of Blenheim, 1704.

regarded as a moderate tory.[3] Commenting on the changes Charles
Davenant, himself a recent Harleyite convert from the most extreme
toryism, observed "'tis not taken that this is a change from Tories to
Whigs but from Violence to Moderation'.[4]

'Moderation' became a vogue word in 1704. It was made modish
by the queen's urging the members of both Houses in her speech
closing the session of parliament on 3 April to 'go down into your
several countries so disposed to moderation and unity as becomes all
those who are joined together in the same religion and interest'.[5] The
ministerial changes were meant to set an example. They did so not
just by replacing high church with moderate tories but by rewarding
converts from extremism to moderation. The most spectacular conversion was that of Henry St John. Ever since his entry into the Commons
in 1701 he had attached himself to the high church tories and gone
along with their most extreme measures. His being chosen along with
Arthur Annesley and William Bromley, the high-flying representatives
of the Universities of Cambridge and Oxford, to prepare and bring in
the occasional conformity bills of 1702 and 1703 attests to his zeal for
the cause. It also shows that his ambition and ability had taken him a
long way in a short time, though some observers attributed his success
not to his early promise so much as to the patronage of his uncle the
earl of Nottingham.[6] During the winter of 1703 to 1704, however, he
attached himself to Harley's rising star, and in return for dropping his
high church stance was rewarded with the post of Secretary at war. St
John was but the most prominent of '9 or 10 considerable men from
that party [high church tories]' whom the triumvirs won over 'by places,
or promises, or both'.[7] St. John revealed to Sir William Trumbull how
the accommodation of himself and his friends had split the extreme
tories: 'it is plain enough that we are far from being in a whig interest,'
he wrote on 16 May, 'hands have been changed but they have been
such, to speak freely, as struggled not for the Church of England party,
but to vest the power in a cabal that styled themselves so.'[8]

The immediate beneficiary of these ministerial changes was the duke
of Marlborough, whose visible ascendancy in the Cabinet gave him
greater prestige abroad as well as at home and helped to enhance
his authority in the coming campaign. This was as well, for during
the summer of 1704 he embarked on the most hazardous enterprise
of his military career, the march to the Danube which was to end with
his famous victory at Blenheim.

Although the genesis of the march has never been established, its
strategy was dictated by the threat which the Elector of Bavaria posed
to the Holy Roman Emperor after his defection to the French and
successes in the previous campaign. Reinforced by French troops
he was poised to launch an attack on the Empire in 1704. At first

the allies, and especially the Dutch, seem to have considered no more than a diversion up the Mosel to distract French attention from Bavaria. But at some stage, possibly even before he returned to England for a brief visit in February, Marlborough had determined on the more daring plan of advancing up the Rhine and Neckar rivers to intercept the Franco-Bavarian forces on the Danube. His insistence on sole command of the British troops in the allied armies, so that his tactics could not be countermanded, points in this direction. But the first positive commitment to the scheme he outlined in a letter to Godolphin from the Hague on 18 April.[9] 'My intentions are to march all the English to Coblence and to declare that I intend to command on the Moselle,' he informed the Lord Treasurer, 'but when I come there to write to the States that I think itt absolutly necessary for the saving the Empire to march with the troupes under my command to joyne those in Germany that are in her Majesty's pay . . . for the speedy reducing of the Elector of Bavaria.' The duke kept his final destination secret from the Dutch until he had passed Coblenz, fearing that they would object. 'I should not be thus rash in taking al this upon myself,' he informed the duke of Somerset on 3 May, 'were I not confident that if I did not make this march the Empire must be ruined, which would at last prove very fatal to England. If I succeed this expedition will be glorious to the Queen and England; if unlucky I must indure the mallice of my enemys, but shal always have the inward satisfaction of knowing that I have ventured myself for the good of the common cause.'[10]

By then he was at Maastricht, having commenced the great trek from the Hague on 24 April. 'The scarlet caterpillar', as Sir Winston Churchill graphically dubbed the columns of red-coated soldiers, crawled for two months from the Dutch Republic to Bavaria. By 14 May they were at Coblenz where, instead of turning up the Mosel towards Trarbach, as the French expected, they crossed the Rhine over a bridge of boats and marched to Mainz. Ten days later they made a similar crossing over the Neckar, demonstrating that they were not making for Landau, as the French anticipated after they left Coblenz, but for the Danube. On 31 May Marlborough arrived at Gross Heppach, where he was joined by the Imperial generals Eugene of Savoy and the Margrave of Baden. There they agreed that Eugene should lead forces to intercept the French on the Rhine, to prevent them joining with the Elector of Bavaria, whilst the other two jointly commanded the army which proceeded to the Danube. As Marlborough and the Margrave moved towards Donauworth the duke received a message from the Emperor proposing that he be made a prince of the Empire. This was the origin of the principality of Mindelheim which was conferred upon Marlborough, with Anne's blessing, a year later. It showed how much the Emperor was aware that the safety of his Empire depended upon the success of this expedition.

Immediately it was dependent upon the successful taking of the Schellenberg, which Marlborough described as 'a hill that commands the town of Donevert [Donauworth] which passage on the Danube is what would be very advantagious to us'. He ordered the army to storm it on 21 June. The following day he wrote that 'it has pleased God after a very obstinat defence to have given us the victory by which we have ruined the best of the Elector's [of Bavaria] foot'.[11] The 'obstinate defence' had also cost his army dear. Although the allied forces numbered 40,000 while the defenders were only 14,000, the latter were well entrenched at the top of the Schellenberg. An attack uphill inevitably produced many casualties, including at least 1500 English soldiers. The survivors spent the next six weeks wreaking revenge by devastating Bavaria. 'As a result of the ravaging, the fires, and the forced contributions,' the Margrave of Baden informed the Emperor, 'in a short time there may be little of Bavaria left.'[12] They were hoping by thus wasting his electorate to detach the Elector from the French to the allied side. Instead he retreated to Augsburg, where he was joined by substantial French reinforcements commanded by Marshal Tallard. Meanwhile Prince Eugene returned from the Rhine to join Marlborough and the Margrave of Baden. Neither the duke nor the prince trusted the Margrave, and they were not averse to his going to besiege Ingoldstadt, even though this deprived their army of men at the critical juncture of the battle of Blenheim.

On 2 August the forces of Eugene and Marlborough made a surprise attack on the Franco-Bavarian army. The battle raged all day around the village of Blindheim, from which it took its name, Anglicized to Blenheim. The Elector held his own against Eugene, but Tallard's men were routed by Marlborough's while the French marshal himself was captured. By nightfall the victory was complete. Marlborough sent a message to his duchess on the back of a bill of tavern expenses. 'I have not time to say more, but to beg you will give my duty to the Queen, and let her know her army has had a glorious victory. Monsieur Tallard and two other generals are in my coach.' The note and the news were conveyed to England by an *aide de camp*, Daniel Parke, arriving there on 10 August. Queen Anne was so delighted to receive them that she gave their bearer a thousand guineas and, when he requested her picture, a miniature portrait set in diamonds. The queen's joy was shared by all her subjects except the most unreconstructed Jacobites. The *London Gazette* printed the dispatch brought by Colonel Parke, and all the newspapers followed suit, while separate handbills of it were run off the presses. The audience at Drury Lane theatre for Aphra Behn's *Emperor in the Moon* were treated to 'a new prologue occasioned by the good news of the great victory over the French and Bavarians'.[13] Anne proclaimed a public thanksgiving to be held on 7 September, when she herself attended a service in St Paul's Cathedral. Dean Sherlock's sermon on the occasion was promptly published. The service prompted a would-be poet to write *The Royal Triumph*, which contained the lines

> So, whilst Great Marlborough thro' the Danube drives
>   The Armies of our Foes,
>   'Till the choak'd stream the bank o'erflows,
> Our pious QUEEN to Heav'n the Glory gives.

Other poets and versifiers also celebrated the victory in rhyme. Among the former were Matthew Prior and Joseph Addison. Prior's *Letter to Monsieur Boileau Depreaux; occasion'd by the Victory at Blenheim* appeared on 30 September. Its closing couplet drew the familiar Elizabethan parallel:

> Whilst MARLBRO's Arm eternal Lawrel gains
> And in the land where SPENCER sung, a new ELISA reigns.

Addison's *The Campaign* captured the imagination with its vivid image of Marlborough as an avenging angel flying over the battlefield as the great storm had flown over England the previous November:

> So when an angel by divine command
> With rising tempests shakes a guilty land;
> Such as of late o'er pale Britannia past
> Calm and serene he drives the furious blast;
> And, pleas'd the Almighty's orders to perform,
> Rides in the whirlwind and directs the storm.

Among the versifiers was Defoe, whose *Hymn to Victory* contained 1040 lines of doggerel.

Where Addison, Defoe and Prior wrote panegyrics to the battle some jarring notes were struck by others. Tory poets in particular compared Blenheim with the capture of Gibraltar on 23 July and its subsequent defence by Sir George Rooke at the battle of Malaga in mid-August. Thus William Shippen's *Moderation Display'd* contained 104 lines of panegyric on the battle of Blenheim when it first appeared in December, which were omitted when a second edition appeared the following year. Both editions, however, sang the praises of Rooke in the guise of Nereo.[14]

> *Nereo* shall cease t'extend his *Anna*'s Reign
> High as the Stars, unbounded as the Main . . .
> 'Tis he the *Streights Defence* so lately Storm'd
> A Town by Nature Fortified and Arm'd.
> 'Tis he unequal far in Force o'ercame
> A Fleet secure of Conquest and of Fame.

Other tories were even more fulsome in their praise of Rooke's alleged achievement. One, developing the Elizabethan theme, actually claimed that he had surpassed Drake.[15]

Whigs were scathing about the comparison of the battles of Malaga and Blenheim. One poet burlesqued tory acclamations of the first in 'On the greatest victory perhaps that ever was or ever will be'.[16] 'The High Church party look on [Rooke] as their own', Defoe wrote to Harley in September. 'The victory at sea they look upon as their victory over the Moderate party . . . I am obliged with patience to hear . . . the sea victory set up against the land victory; Sir George exalted above the Duke of Marlborough.'[17] An address from the House of Commons coupled the two battles, infuriating the duchess of Marlborough, who was outraged that the duke's 'complete victory at Blenheim' should be 'ridiculously paired with Sir George Rooke's drawn battle with the French at sea'.[18] The House of Lords, by contrast, made no mention of Malaga in their address congratulating the Queen on the success of her rms under the duke of Marlborough. A similar situation arose in Convocation, where the Lower House wished to praise Rooke as well as Marlborough, whereas the bishops did not, so that they could not agree on a joint address to Anne. She openly indicated her preference by granting the manor of Woodstock to Marlborough and arranged at her own expense for Blenheim Palace to be built there. Rooke got nothing from her, never even commanding a fleet again.

Although the capture of Gibraltar, and its defence at the battle of Malaga, could not compare in significance with the complete reversal of French arms and the balance of power which occurred at Blenheim, they were not to be completely dismissed as non-events. The opening up of the Iberian peninsula as a theatre of war, which the alliance with Portugal entailed, had major consequences both in the short and long terms. Immediately it led to the allies asserting the claims of the Habsburg candidate to the throne of Spain. As Charles III he was entertained by Anne in England before sailing to Portugal escorted by Rooke early in 1704.

The allies sought a foothold in Spain so that Charles could at least set foot on the land he claimed to rule. After an abortive landing near Barcelona in May they decided upon Gibraltar. An Anglo-Dutch force besieged it in July, and after three days it surrendered on the 23rd. Again, as at Cadiz in 1702, the English scarcely endeared Charles III to his Spanish subjects by their looting and pillage, during which they sacked nearly every church on the Rock.

When the French learned that the allies had captured Gibraltar they determined to retake it immediately. A fleet under the command of the comte de Toulouse sailed from Toulon and engaged Rooke on 13 August. 'They fought from 10 in the morning till seven at Night when the French bore away.'[19] Both sides claimed victory in the encounter, though Godolphin, admittedly not an unbiased observer, thought it 'a sort of a drawn battle where both sides had enough of it'.[20]

To the Lord Treasurer the news of the battle of Blenheim, if not that of Malaga, was a welcome relief from a rapidly deteriorating political situation at home. In Scotland prospects for the accession of the house of Hanover on Anne's death were more remote than ever. In England it seemed as if the ministerial changes of the spring had not established the ministry on a secure footing. As Lord Stamford put it in June: 'whatever my Lord Marlborough does abroad (which for the sake of Europe I heartily wish may be well) yet his foundation being rotten here and his not increasing his friends, may exasperate his enemies to that height that it may push them on beyond the rules and measures which have been kept hitherto amongst them.'[21]

Failure to secure the succession to the Scottish throne the previous year galled the queen as well as Godolphin. On 5 April she informed the Chancellor of Scotland, Lord Seafield, that she wanted it settled in the house of Hanover and would employ only those Scots committed to it. She also tipped him off that she was prepared to concede some royal prerogatives to the Edinburgh parliament, including the appointment of ministers and judges. These concessions acknowledged the persuasive case Andrew Fletcher had made for similar limitations on the Crown in the previous session. They were presumably offered in a bid to convert him and his supporters to the accession of the house of Hanover to the Scottish throne. It was clear that the English government desperately wanted to get the succession settled in the session of 1704. Since the duke of Queensberry had been discredited by his handling of the Scotch Plot he was replaced as commissioner by the Marquis of Tweeddale. Tweeddale, leader of the country opposition in 1703, now headed what came to be known as the New party. The Queen left him in no doubt what she expected from him, writing to assure him that 'the settling of the succession of the Crown of Scotland in the protestant line will bee a very acceptable service to mee'.[22]

The session of parliament opened in Edinburgh on 11 July 1704. The queen's message was read asking for a settlement of the succession to the throne of Scotland and for supply. Tweeddale indicated that she was prepared to grant concessions in return for these. Led by the duke of Hamilton the opposition proposed a motion requiring not only limitations of the prerogative as a condition of accepting the house of Hanover, but also a treaty with England relating to the commercial concerns of Scotland. The New party failed to defeat this proposal, overwhelmed by a combination of Cavaliers, Country party members and, crucially, followers of the disgraced Queensberry. This alliance was also able to couple supply with a renewed act of security.

Both Acts were to lie on the table until the queen's pleasure was known.

The queen was not at all pleased. But some decision was urgent, for without supply the forces in Scotland would have to be disbanded, which would play into the hands of the Jacobites. Godolphin urged her that there was no alternative, given the grave international situation, but to give her assent to both Acts. The message reached Edinburgh on 5 August, and the commissioner touched both Acts with the sceptre, making them law. Five days later the queen and her English ministers learned that the duke of Marlborough had won the battle of Blenheim. Had they known in time they would never have assented to the Act of Security.

While news of the victory came too late to help the ministry in its handling of the Scottish parliament it made management of the English House of Commons much easier. 'The power of France was broken by it to a great degree, and the liberties and peace of Europe were in a fair way to be established upon firm and lasting foundations', claimed the duchess of Marlborough. 'The less violent part of the tories therefore could not be prevailed with to hazard these great and pleasing hopes, by tacking them to the fortune of the occasional conformity bill. The tack was rejected by the majority of the members, even of this House of commons, so rich in tories and high churchmen.'[23] Sarah was of course partisan, and the defeat of the tack owed as much to Harley's parliamentary management as to her husband's victory at Blenheim.

Shortly after the opening of the session in October 1704 Harley even made an effort to prevent the introduction of an occasional conformity bill. During a short recess between 25 and 31 October he calculated the possibility of throwing out the bill in the Commons. Harley estimated that the Court could defeat the high churchmen if, as he assumed, all the whigs and a considerable number of tories stayed loyal to it.[24] This optimistic estimate was doubtless influenced by the fact that at this time the high church tories still seemed uncertain of their strength. The first move which they had contemplated at the start of the session was the removal of Harley from the Speaker's chair, on the grounds that occupancy of it was incompatible with the secretaryship of state. Although Bromley urged his men to be at the opening debate to make sure of success, which made ministers uneasy enough to whip their own supporters up to town to counter the offensive, in the event the expected attack failed to materialize because 'the party yt intended to throw the Secretary out of the chair found themselves too weak and did not attempt it'.[25]

The failure dispirited the high churchmen who held meetings to take stock of the situation in which they even discussed the possibility of dropping the bill. As for getting it approved by the Upper House, they were divided between delaying supply until it passed the Lords and tacking it to a supply bill to force it through. It took the arrival of Sir Edward Seymour to stiffen their resolve not only to introduce the bill but to tack it to the land tax bill.[26] On 15 November the bill had its first reading in the Commons, where in spite of the Court's efforts it passed by 152 votes to 126. Though Godolphin was annoyed that the placemen had failed to prevent the bill's introduction, they did manage to bring the majority in favour of it below that which it had obtained in the previous session. As Harley pointed out to Marlborough 'it was carried for bringing in the bill by 26 votes, whereas last year it was by 43' which convinced him that 'it will be impossible for them to tack it, if they be mad enough to attempt it'.[27]

They were mad enough. On 18 November Sir Simon Harcourt wrote to Harley that 'Universal madness reigns. The more enquiry I make concerning the occasional bill, the more I am confirmed in my opinion that if much more care than has been be not taken, that bill will be consolidated. I find the utmost endeavours have been used on one side, and little or none on the other. If this be of any moment, you'll think of it.' This letter galvanized Harley into activity. On the back of it he scribbled a list of names of tories who might be persuaded to oppose the tack or at very least to abstain when it was moved.[28] Those approached apparently agreed on condition that no further pressure should be brought to bear on them to oppose the bill itself. Consequently the motion to give the bill a second reading was carried in the Commons on 23 November by 202 to 138, a greater majority than that for its introduction. Next day the ministers held a meeting with canvassed tories to discuss tactics for the defeat of the tack.[29] After it Harley wrote to Marlborough 'we have a party here who are opening their campaign, and seem to fix Tuesday next for the second reading their occasional disturbance, and then to attempt the tacking it. If we are not too secure and negligent I hope they cannot succeed in that point.'[30] The Court certainly was not negligent in the days before the second reading on 28 November. Every effort was made to defeat the projected tack.[31]

The Court's distinction between the merits of the bill and the folly of tacking it to supply became clear in the handling of the long vital debate which took place on 28 November, after the second reading.

> Besides the most obvious argument that the tacking of any acts to money bills takes away the negatives both from the Crown and the House of Lords, gives the Commons the whole legislative power and so tends to destroy the constitution, Mr Secretary Hedges and the Lord Cutts represented to the House: 'That the duke of Marlborough had lately concluded a treaty with the king of Prussia for 8,000 of his men to be employed towards the relief of the Duke of Savoy, who was in

most imminent danger; that those troops were actually on their march, upon the credit of the resolution the House had already taken to make good her Majesty's treaties, and that the obstructing the money bills, which the tacking of the occasional bill would infallibly do, would put an immediate stop to the march of those troops, and thereby occasion the entire ruin of the duke of Savoy.' My Lord Cutts urged 'that the English nation was now in the highest consideration abroad; that all Europe was attentive to the resolutions of this parliament; and that if any divisions should happen between the two Houses, it would cast a damp upon the whole Confederacy, and give the French king almost as great an advantage as we had gained over him at Blenheim.'

The ministerial speakers in the debate thus tacked the tack to the war effort, 'without going into the merits of the occasional conformity bill'.[32]

It was left to the whigs to castigate the bill itself as a persecuting measure. Throughout the crisis nobody in the ministry appears to have thought it necessary to approach the whig leaders. It seems to have been taken for granted that they would oppose the tack. Yet it gave them a glorious opportunity to embarrass the Court. Moreover they were to all intents and purposes in opposition, with hardly any whigs in the government. Nevertheless in the event not one whig voted for it. This can only be attributed to their dislike of penalizing occasional conformists and their fears that the loss of the land tax bill would have a catastrophic impact on the war effort. The Junto's support of the Court was thus based on principle, a point worth stressing since they are often depicted as unscrupulous opportunists at this time, especially by Scottish historians.

That night, after he had sat ten hours in the Speaker's chair, presiding over a debate 'which lasted eight hours and more', Harley wrote to the duke of Marlborough: 'the faction, animated by those your Grace will easily guess, thought partly by surprise and partly by their numbers, they could carry the question to tack the occasional bill to the land tax. They persisted in their opinion of their numbers and majority to the very putting the question. Nothing could persuade them but 251 against 134.'[33] Many tories abstained from the vote, and earned the derisory nickname of sneakers. Others, estimated at over 100, voted against the tack. Harley himself attributed their motive to self-interest, claiming that 'several of the most considerable men of that side having been taken off by the ministers, and gratified with good places, they left their party in the lurch and voted against the tack. And thus this noisy, mischief-making, party-driving, good for nothing bill came to be utterly lost.'[34] Tory placemen who opposed the tack naturally gave more elevated explanations of their behaviour. Edward Brereton, a commissioner of prizes, and a sneaker 'considered that the Lds had formerly published their resolution not to pass any bill that had another

tack'd to it, and that the former misunderstandings between both
Houses was rather increased than diminished, and that it would be
dangerous to try the success of that proposed tack, least the miscarriage
of the land tax bill might bring difficulties upon the nation, and delay
the necessary supplies for the fleet and army . . . now you have the
history of my fanaticism, and I had rather be called a pickpocket than
a whig.'[35]

Whatever motives had prompted over a hundred tories to desert the
high church cause, Seymour and his associates had clearly been guilty of
incredible folly in forcing them to make a choice. They had for the time
being at least completely discredited their claim to lead the tory party.
The tack, so far from exposing the ministry's narrow foundations, had
considerably broadened its basis. As Godolphin put it: 'some measure
should be speedily concerted to continue our present majority to the
end of this parliament which might also lay a foundation of having one
of the same kind in the next.'[36]

Harley was ready with just such a scheme. He was anxious to confirm
the tory converts in their new beliefs by keeping them permanently
attached to the Court. And if at the same time he could similarly
convert the whigs by preaching the doctrine of loyalty to the Queen and
the war, then the false gods of party might be melted down. The breakdown of the two-party pattern which had emerged towards the end
of William's reign would mean that the management of independent
country gentlemen, rather than the manipulation of tories and whigs
would become the prime object of parliamentary management. With
continued military success abroad and careful organization at home
the country gentlemen could be made stalwart supporters of the Court.
And at this kind of management Harley was a past master. He had
shown in the 1690s that he could play on the heart-strings of back-bench
gentry like an accomplished virtuoso. Then he had employed those
talents for the Country party. Now he devoted his energies to keeping
'the gentlemen of England', as he frequently called them in the years
1704 and 1705, devoted to the Court.

Until the Christmas recess Harley felt reasonably satisfied with the
workings of his scheme. A week after the defeat of the tack he wrote
to Marlborough: 'I gave your Grace an account of our success this day
sevennight and by what since hath followed I have further grounds
of assurance that it will prove a very likely conjuncture for her Matie
to unite those who are in earnest to support her Government.'[37] The
Court prudently decided not to overstrain the loyalties of its new
tory friends by attempting to kill the occasional conformity bill in
the Commons, and instead allowed it to pass up to the Lords where
it was promptly rejected on 5 December. But on every other issue
raised before Christmas the tackers made no headway against the

combination of Court tories and whigs. Looking back at the session on Christmas Eve one high church clergyman lamented to another: 'I find our friends very much surprised and disturbed. The party, which some weeks ago found it self so strong, doth now upon all divisions in the House appear so weak, as to be able to carry nothing which they contend for.'[38]

After the recess the tackers tried to create a Country platform against the Court by raising the old canard of placemen sitting in the Commons. Soon after parliament reassembled two 'self-denial bills' were introduced 'which owe their rise to the resentment of some people for the miscarriage of the bill against occasional conformity'.[39] One incapacitated all persons from being members who were entitled by their offices to receive a benefit from annual taxes; the other excluded all persons in any office created since the accession of James II. The first of these bills was lost, albeit by only six votes, on 27 January. 'I wish the bill had pass[ed],' lamented one tory, 'for now the Church of England is checked every little sugar plum is pleasing to her children.'[40] But the alliance of tackers and Country whigs proved strong enough to carry the second bill even to the stage of rejecting some amendments made to it in the Lords.

The incipient realignment of parties into Court and Country, however, was nipped in the bud by the renewal of the partisan battles between the tory-dominated House of Commons and the whiggish House of Lords. These were to close the gaps in the tory ranks opened up by the tack, and to consolidate the unity of the whig party.

The clash between the two Houses over the occasional conformity bills which had sealed their fate in the previous two sessions defeated the third attempt to put it on the statute book. Those tackers who claimed that without tacking it to the land tax bill it would be thrown out in the Lords proved to be correct. On 15 December, the day after it had passed its last hurdle in the Commons by 178 votes to 131, it was refused a second reading in the Lords 'after a Debate of four Hours . . . *Contents*, 33. *Not Contents*, 51. Proxies for the former, 17. for the latter, 20. So 'twas rejected by a Majority (in the whole) of 21.'[41]

According to Burnet 'if it had not been for the queen's being present, there would have been no long debate on that head, for it was scarce possible to say much that had not been formerly said'.[42] Anne attended debates in the House of Lords for the first time this session, being present 'incognito'. This did not mean that she appeared heavily disguized, but only that it was not a formal state visit so she did not have to sit on the throne in her robes. Indeed, finding the chamber chilly she sat on a bench by the fire.

The first debate Anne attended was an inquiry into the affairs of Scotland. Godolphin was aware that he would be criticized for advising her to assent to the Security Act, and got her to be present to give him moral support. As Burnet saw it 'the tories resolved to attack him, and that disposed the whigs to preserve him; and this was so managed by them, that it gave a great turn to all our councils at home'.[43]

The inquiry was set off by what Godolphin himself called 'Lord Haversham's bomb'. John Thompson, Baron Haversham, was a renegade whig turned violent tory whose speciality was annual speeches to the peers on the state of the nation. On 23 November he delivered himself of one which ranged over foreign affairs, the admiralty, a standing army, exports of bullion and the security Act. Their lordships sat still for half an hour after the detonation. Then various means were explored to air the points raised, the Scottish statute being set aside for a full debate on 29 November.

On that day, in the Queen's presence, the 'Lord Treasurer gave the Necessary Reasons for adviseing Her Majesty to Assent to it'. According to the earl of Dartmouth 'he talked nonsense very fast, which was not his usual way, either of matter or manner; but said much as to the necessity of passing the money bill'.[44] Godolphin was rescued from the tory attack by the Junto. It was Somers who gave him a respite by moving for a week's adjournment. 'That is', noted a cynical Scot, 'to have time to treat with the Court about an understanding in English affairs.'[45] The manoeuverings of the whig leaders on this occasion have been criticized as pure opportunism by historians as well as by hostile contemporaries. But they had taken a principled stand over the tack, and there can be no doubt about their commitment to the Protestant succession, which was ultimately at stake in Scotland. There was undoubtedly a price to pay for their continued support of a ministry from which they were excluded. But it was not the abandonment of their principles.[46]

When the debate resumed Somers opened it with proposals which were to develop into the Aliens Act. This would deprive Scots of the right of being subjects of the English Crown, and lay an embargo on Scottish imports of cattle, coal and linen into England after 25 December 1705 if the succession had not been satisfactorily settled in Scotland. One way to settle the succession would be by way of union, and Wharton moved on 11 December that new commissioners should be appointed. A bill incorporating these proposals received its third reading on 20 December. When it went down to the Commons members objected that it contained clauses which placed financial penalties on Scots who transgressed them. Having made a fetish of their right to initiate money bills at the time of the tack, they set aside the Lords bill and introduced another virtually identical with it, except that the appointment of new commissioners for a union was dropped. The Lords accepted the Commons' bill which received the royal assent on 14 March 1705.

On this occasion the Lords refused to be drawn into a constitutional wrangle, since the majority in both Houses now consisted of Court tories and whigs who agreed on the issues involved. Such was not to be the case on those raised by the Aylesbury men. Since the hearing of Ashby's appeal to the House of Lords in the previous session five other whig voters in the borough had sued the tory mayor. These were summoned to the bar of the House of Commons on 5 December 1704, declared guilty of breach of privilege, and imprisoned in Newgate jail. The House of Lords took up their case. Peers of the realm visited the prison or sent presents to the humble prisoners. The Court of Queen's bench was asked to issue writs of habeas corpus for the five. Three of the justices refused on the grounds that they had no right to release people imprisoned by the Commons for breach of privilege, the Lord Chief Justice Holt again dissenting. The Commons, outraged at this interference with their jurisdiction by peers sympathetic to the five Aylesbury men, set up a committee to identify them. On 13 March a free conference between the two Houses broke up in acrimony. The Lords thereupon addressed the Queen for a writ of error to refer the case to their House. This put her on a hook, for she would be damned by the Commons if she did and damned by the Lords if she did not. Anne resolved the dilemma by ending the session. On 14 March she answered the Lords, 'I should have granted the writs of error . . . but finding an absolute necessity of putting an immediate end to this session I am sensible there could be no further proceeding upon that matter.'

5

1705

Although the closing weeks of the last session of Anne's first parliament had seen the tories recovering from the divisions inflicted upon the party by the attempted tack, Harley was still optimistic that with proper management, both of the general election and of the new House of Commons, a majority of them could be kept loyal to the Court rather than to their high church leaders. At the same time he also hoped to divide enough moderate whigs from the Junto to enable the ministry to manage parliament without conceding office to the five whig lords. 'Sir, the whigs are weak, they may be managed and always have been so', Daniel Defoe advised him in November 1704. 'Whatever you do, if possible divide them, and they are easy to be divided. Caress the fools of them most; there are enough of them. Buy them with here and there a place; it may be well bestowed.'[1] Some months before Harley had opened negotiations with the duke of Newcastle, a whig peer whom he hoped to bring into the Court orbit. His overtures came to a successful conclusion in March 1705 when Newcastle replaced the tory duke of Buckingham as Lord privy seal, and as Lord Lieutenant of the North Riding of Yorkshire. Newcastle held a key position in Harley's schemes to influence the elections in such a way as to assist the return of whigs, as well as tories, who would toe the Court rather than a party line. As he told the duke shortly after the tack:[2]

> The late attempt has given a handle and ripened those things which I spoke of to you last summer, so that it is to be hoped the opportunity is very encouraging, and the best care must be to improve it, not only for the present, but that the succeeding parliament may consist of men in the public interest of the nation. Your Grace must be the corner stone of this fabric, and therefore I hope you will let your thoughts descend to particulars as to persons as well as things, how matters should be modelled here, and what is to be done in order to elections.

Harley was confident that the Court could preserve a majority of members of parliament in its interest by using its electoral influence to keep up divisions in the ranks of the tories and whigs. There was a purge of tackers who held offices in the administration, and of their supporters in the localities, to signal the government's hostility to their interests. At the end of April 1705 Harley wrote to the duke of Marlborough, 'everybody are full of preparations for elections; scarce any body stops in town who has any pretence to be in the country upon that affair. I am more concern'd how to deal with them when they are chosen, than under doubt of having a great majority for the Queen and the public good.'[3] Marlborough shared his view, writing to the duchess from the Hague, 'I think at this time it is for the Queen's service, and the good of England, that the choyce might be such as that neither party might have a great majority, so that her Majesty might be able to influence what might be good for the common interest.'[4]

The general election lasted the whole of May and into June. It was fiercely fought, with more constituencies polling than at any previous election since the passing of the Triennial Act. These contests witnessed a swing against the high church tories, but not as sweeping as the ministry had hoped. Of the 134 tackers, as many as 90 were returned to the Commons.

Moreover three where Godolphin and Marlborough were personally involved – Cambridge University, St Albans and Woodstock – were the scenes of clashes between their electoral interests and those of high church tories which left them both disenchanted with Harley's electoral strategy. At Cambridge the Lord Treasurer hoped to bring in his son Francis Godolphin. This was a reasonable hope, since though the University had returned a tacker, Arthur Annesley, in 1702 it had also found a seat for the chancellor of the exchequer, Henry Boyle, a Court whig. In 1702 there had been no contest. On this occasion, however, the University put up two tories, Annesley again and Dixie Windsor, an army officer. Two candidates also appeared on the Court side, the celebrated Sir Isaac Newton standing with Godolphin. Newton was actually knighted by the Queen on a visit to Cambridge in April to help the Court campaign. Yet to the Lord Treasurer's mortification his son was defeated, Annesley and Windsor topping the polls. As Dyer, a tory newswriter gloated, 'notwithstanding there was all the management and delays possible, and the heads of the Houses against the two first, it was carried for them to the unspeakable joy of the helpful and promising part of that University'.[5]

In St Albans it was not so much the duke of Marlborough as his wife who was involved in trying to keep a tacker out of the House. Sarah's family had estates in the town which gave her an electoral interest which had been used to help seat her husband's brother George. She had been unable, however, to prevent the return of

The High-Church Hieroglyphick

Reprefented in the Sign of the

EMBLEME,

Put up at an Inn in *STOKE* by *Naland*, in *Suffolk*.

An EXPLANATION of the EMBLEME.

BEhold the *Church*, which fome Men fay has ftood,
Unmov'd from Times before the mighty Flood :
Its Bafis laid in the Aufpicious Reign
Of that moft Glorious Murdering Monarch *Cain* ;
By Murdering *Levites* then Poffefs'd and Rul'd,
Whofe Progeny, till now, the People Gull'd.

Its vaft Foundation to great Depths they fix,
Down to the very Banks of Sulph'rous *Stix* ;
Whofe Fiery Waves with Hideous Noife do Roar,
Admit no Bounds, but warp away the Shore :
Its Spires above the Clouds they Proudly rear,
Cover'd about by *Demons* of the Air.
This is *High-Church*, as its *Devotes* her call ;
This is the *Church* you fee enclin'd to Fall.

Stay, Paffenger, a while the *EMBLEME* view,
Say, Is't *a Church that's Falfe, or One that's True* ?
If True, fhe's out of Danger of a Fall ;
'Gainft her the Power of *Hell* can ne'er prevail :
If Falfe, as we have by Experience found,
Bleft be the Hands fhall rafe her to the Ground.

Prepoft'rous Sight ! That *Devils* fhou'd Invade,
And Spoil the Work that their own Hands have made.
Yes, Spectator, Prepoft'rous is the *SIGN,*
That thofe who Built the *Church* fhould *UNDERMINE:*
'Tis not *Infernal De'ils*, nor thofe that Fly,
But its own Sins has weigh'd its Spires awry.

Next view its Sons, the *Buttreffes* o'the *Dome*,
How they with Zeal to its Affiftance come ;
With Brawny Shoulders ftrive to underprop,
And keep the vaft declining Fabrick **Up** ;
The *High-Tantivy-Priefts*, the *Tacking-Elves*,
Who would, to Ruin *England*, Damn themfelvs.

See the *Non-Cons*, and *Moderate-Churchmen* Laugh,
To find themfelves, by *High-Church* Fall, more fafe.
Thus *Virtue* thrives when *Vice* is moft fupreft,
And *Hell* reftrain'd, adds Numbers to the Bleft.

Let *High-Church* ftand, or let it tumble down,
Its Peoples Folly in their Motto's fhown,
Who take a *Rifing* for a *Setting Sun*.

LONDON, Printed in the Year 1706.

*Figure 5 The High Church Hieroglyphick – an anti High Church
emblem printed in 1706.*

John Gape in 1702, a tory who voted for the tack. At this election she determined to defeat him and return a whig, Henry Killigrew. In her zeal to oust Gape she announced to the electors that 'it was the Queen's desire that no such men should be chose, for such men would unhinge the Government, and the Papists' horses stood saddled day and night, whipping and spurring' while 'Tackers would be injurious to the Government and were for the French interest'.[6] Despite her efforts Gape beat Killigrew, largely because the mayor allowed freemen admitted by dint of a charter of James II's reign to vote, but refused the votes of those made free by a subsequent charter.[7]

At Woodstock two tackers had been returned in 1702. The duke of Marlborough, anxious to establish his interest in the borough after the grant of Blenheim Palace, put up a comrade in arms, Brigadier General William Cadogan, against two tories, Charles Bertie and Sir John Walter. To his and Godolphin's consternation Cadogan was hard pressed, and every vote had to be called upon. As the Lord Treasurer observed 'this battle at Woodstock vexes me very much. What good will it do us to have Lord Marlborough beat the French abroad if the French at home must beat him.' In the event Cadogan won a seat, leading Dyer to claim that the poll book would be printed 'that it may be seen who they were that poll'd for the Brigadier, whose grandfather was Governor of Trim in Ireland for the Parliament and his grandmother was daughter to the famous Sir Hardress Waller'.[8]

The duumvirs blamed the clergy for the intransigence of the high church tories in the election. Thus Godolphin observed to the duchess of Marlborough that 'the loss of Mr Godolphin's election at Cambridg is no small mortification to mee, and I have now the same occasion to complain myself of the behaviour of the clergy as some of my friends had before'.[9] Certainly the behaviour of the clergy at the polls attracted considerable comment. Dyer noted how they all polled for the tory candidates in Cheshire, where 'the cry of the whig rabble . . . was Down with the Church and the Bishops, and when about 60 of the clergy, headed by the Dean, came to poll, they said Hell was broke loose, and these were the Devil's black Guard . . . and to compleat their outrage, broke the windows of the cathedral and another church'.[10] The success of a tacker against a whig knight of the shire in Suffolk he attributed 'in a great measure to the diligence of the clergy, of which 80 went in one body, and as great singly, being not advertise'd of the design'.[11] The converse of Dyers' eulogy of the role of Anglican clergymen in the election was the rabid anti-clericalism of the whig press. 'A certain parson in Hertfordshire,' reported the *Observator*, 'out of his passionate zeal for High-Church said, "The Devil take me, if it be not a greater sin to poll against Tackers than to murder my own father".'[12] 'Truth and Honesty', an electoral agent for *The London Post*, visited Norwich, where 'he found to his wonder and amazement all the excess of party fury run up to seed; not the people only bent to expose reproach, but the clergy tearing out the throats of their hearers with Jacobitism, tacking and high church raillery'.[13]

The backing of the clergy for tory candidates eroded the distinction which the Court was anxious to make between tackers and moderate tories. Where Court propaganda played on the actions of the 134, 'the Church in danger' became the rallying cry which closed tory ranks. 'I doubt not,' William Shippen prophesied in December 1704, 'but the name of Tacker will be represented at the next Elections . . . as more odious than that of an Atheist.'[14] Certainly such electoral squibs as 'The Oxfordshire Nine' tried to fulfil his prophesy.

> Perusing the list of the Tackers in print,
> And carefully marking what Members were in't
> Some names I observ'd to most Counties did fall:
> But Oxford afforded no fewer than All.
> Nine members, nine tackers. And more had there been,
> And their Number as great as their spirits were keen . . .
> A desperate risque we had presently run
> Of the League being broke and the Nation undone.

High church ripostes to such charges identified the tackers as tory heroes. Thus 'A Health to the Tackers' urged the voters to

> . . . chuse such Parliament men
> As have stuck to their Principles tight,
> And wou'd not their country betray
> In the story of *Ashby* and *White* . . .

This raised another rallying cry. For as we have seen the case of the Aylesbury men began to heal the breach in tory ranks before the end of the parliamentary session. Henry St John acknowledged its healing power when he informed the duke of Marlborough on 18 May, 'most of the changes I hitherto observ'd on the lists are against the Torys; and it is not to be conceiv'd what a prejudice they have done their interest in all places by attempting the Tack. There is nothing checks the tide that runs against 'em, but their opposition to your Lordships proceedings in relation to the Ailesbury business, which is very far from being popular.'[15]

It was certainly unpopular among tories; but it also served to consolidate the whigs, as a series of instructions to successful whig candidates testified. L'Hermitage, the Dutch envoy, noted that there were several boroughs which instructed their new members, charging them principally with three things: to conserve the rights of the people; to vote supplies for the war promptly; and to maintain the Protestant succession.[16] The instructions from Aylesbury not surprisingly also touched on 'some late proceedings relating to this borough'. In addition to requiring their MPs to vote necessary and timely supplies, and to preserve the toleration 'to all such Protestant dissenters as are truly in the interest of her Majesty and the Protestant succession', they also expected them to 'be tender of the rights, liberties and privileges of those you represent, and by whom you are elected'.

The final result of the general election was a hung parliament. A tory majority of 145 had been turned into a narrow lead for the tories of about twenty. Moreover many tories held posts in the administration, leading one observer to calculate that 'by the nearest computation . . . the whigs and tories are equal, so that the placemen will turn the balance'. Marlborough had no doubt which way the balance should be turned. 'I should have been very uneasy in my own mind, if I had not on this occasion beged of the Queen,' he wrote to Godolphin, 'that she would be pleased for her own sake, and the good of her kingdome, to advise early with you what incouragement might be proper to give the Whigs, that they might look upon it as their own concern to beat down and oppose all such proposals as may prove uneasy to her Majesty or government.'[17]

The first encouragement which the Court gave to the whigs after the election was in the choice of a speaker. Harley, not yet persuaded that the party leaders had reasserted their authority, hoped to find a candidate for the chair who would act as a focus for the Court. He was searching for somebody who, in St John's words 'the whigs would have voted for, and who might have reconciled a great many of those people to him, that may cease to be tories, but can never be whigs'.[18] Knowing full well that he was personally unacceptable to both types, Harley gladly surrendered all claims to the speakership in the new parliament. Sir Simon Harcourt, on the other hand, seemed the ideal man to reconcile all but the most inveterate partisans to the Court, and he began to groom him for the role of his successor. He must have been greatly disappointed when Harcourt failed to attract sufficient support.[19] On 29 June he informed Marlborough, 'the first dispute will be to fill the chair, and that will be between Mr Smith and Mr Bromley'.[20]

Since Bromley, the leader of the tackers, was *persona non grata* to the Court, it threw its weight behind the whig Smith. Towards the end of July the ministers held a great meeting of MPs 'where my Ld Treasurer recommended Mr Smith in a very obliging manner as to himself, and in very pressing terms for the Queen's and public's service, to be Speaker of the next parliament'.[21] 'It seems for the public service to fix upon Mr Smith,' Harley informed Marlborough, 'it is of great consequence not only not to be baffled in it, but that it be carried with a very great majority.'[22] Harley hoped to achieve this by presenting Smith as a Court rather than as a whig candidate, which would in his view bring many moderate tories to vote for him, saving the Court from complete dependence upon the whigs. He stressed the importance of substantial tory support for Smith's candidature when canvassing individual tories. 'If our friends will not be stark mad,' he reassured one 'it is easy to place things in the hands of the gentlemen of England without giving themselves up into the hands of that party which may be feared by some, tho' I think without reason, unless those gentlemen who clamour most force people into it.'[23]

Lord Treasurer Godolphin, however, took a rather different view of the arrangements for the forthcoming session. Where Harley regarded the tackers as an irresponsible minority in the tory ranks, Godolphin suspected all tories of being unreliable. His suspicions were confirmed early in July when a vicious attack on the ministry appeared in a high church tract *The Memorial of the Church of England*.[24] This accused the duumvirs of parting with their old friends the tories. 'The duke of Buckingham, the earls of Rochester, Nottingham, Jersey and Winchilsea, Sir Edward Seymour . . . turned out without the least pretence or colour of offence.' They were inexorably moving towards the whigs.

> In spite of sodomy, adultery, pox or prophaneness, Sunderland shall be a saint, and Somers, Wharton and Halifax prophets, martyrs and apostles. In the meantime to fortify themselves against that odium, which they foresaw they must necessarily incur, having all the places in the nation in their hands, they employed 'em to debauch indifferently such of both parties as were members of parliament, and out of them to raise up a third, which should pretend to be neuters, and depend upon them alone, and vote and act by their direction only, without regard to any other engagement or principle.

The reactions of the duumvirs to this attack were remarkably different. Marlborough, although finding it 'impudent and scaralous', told Godolphin that he could not 'forbear lafing, when I think thay would have you and I passe for phanaticks, and the Duke of Buckingham and Lord Jersey for pillars of the Church, the one being a Roman Catholick in King James's reign, and the other would have been a Quaker or any other religion that might have pleased the late King'.[25] The Treasurer, so far from laughing, was nearer to crying. Godolphin had a much thinner skin than either the duke or Harley.

Godolphin was also much more concerned than them to manage the House of Lords. During the previous parliament, where tories had prevailed in the Commons and whigs in the Lords, friction between the two Houses had almost caused parliamentary business to grind to a halt. To obviate any recurrence of this Godolphin regarded a whig scheme in both as being highly desirable if not essential. To him,

therefore, the speakership was the seal on a deal between the Court and
the whigs in the Lower House. In the Upper the deal was clinched by
the appointment of the whig William Cowper as Lord Keeper in place
of the tory Nathan Wright on 11 October, despite Anne's objections
and apparently Harley's.[26] On the very day of Cowper's promotion the
Lord Treasurer asked the duke of Newcastle to intercede with Harley
who was proving refractory.[27] His refractoriness probably stemmed
from the reflection that the disposal of the Great Seal to a prominent
whig a fortnight before parliament was due to meet rather rubbed
the shine off the assurances which he had given the tories that no
whig scheme was intended. Any annoyance which the Secretary felt
on that score proved temporary, however, for he was soon co-operating
with Godolphin again to apply a last-minute polish to the Court's
preparations for the opening debate in the House of Commons on
25 October. On that day Harley's drive to create a massive majority for
Smith was matched by the tories' equal determination to seat Bromley
in the chair.

The outcome fell far short of Harley's hopes. Smith's nomination
was carried by 248 votes to 205, which was nothing like the 'very great
majority' Harley had thought to be of such consequence. Moreover
the number of tories who supported the Court, so far from being
substantial, as he had expected, came to a mere twenty-seven. Indeed
these were almost offset by the unexpectedly high number of tory
placemen – seventeen in all – who disobeyed ministerial instructions
and voted for Bromley. The wound inflicted in the tory flank by the
tack less than a year before, which Harley had hoped would poison the
party system, had almost completely healed.[28]

From that moment on the ministry was almost entirely dependent
upon whig support. Harley, however, could never bring himself to
admit this. On the day after Smith's election he was still holding
out the prospect that a significant number of tories could be enticed
to support the Court. He insisted that 'with care and application
several of the misled gentlemen, who acted not out of malice but
ignorance, will be reduced to a better sense and opinion of the Queen's
government'.[29] Within a few days the opportunity arose to test this
analysis, for on 7 November there was a contest for the chairmanship
of the vital committee of privileges and elections. The Court and the
whigs backed Spencer Compton, and the tories Sir Gilbert Dolben.
Godolphin, clearly unimpressed by the Secretary's pleas on behalf of
the tories, wrote to him the day before this struggle was decided: 'tho'
I have so violent a cold as does not suffer me to hold down my head
2 minutes, yet I can't neglect telling you it will be very necessary
to take a little pains with our friends not to mistake their interest
tomorrow about the chairman of the committee of elections.'[30] Next

day 'Mr Spencer Compton was set up and carried to be chairman of the committee of elections against Sir Gilbert Dolben who was set up by those who opposed the present Speaker. The former carried it upon a division 188 against 172.'[31] Apparently no success had been obtained in winning over those tories who had voted for Bromley, and indeed the bulk of them remained in opposition for the rest of the session, while the whigs continued to support the Court.

The Queen, in her speech at the opening of the new session, dwelled on developments since the last parliament as well as outlining her ministers' intentions and expectations from the present. Thus she singled out the conduct of the duke of Savoy in the summer campaign as being especially commendable, and drew attention to the Act of the Scots parliament which authorized her to appoint commissioners for Union.

Victor Amadeus, duke of Savoy, had joined the Grand Alliance in 1703. His distance from the other allies and proximity to the French frontier made him the most vulnerable to attack from France. In the summer of 1705 a full-scale invasion was launched against him, which achieved such devastating success that by the end of the year he was left with little but his capital Turin: 'the firmness that the duke of Savoy expressed in all these losses was the wonder of all Europe,' wrote Burnet 'he seemed resolved to be driven out of all, rather than to abandon the alliance.'[32]

It was partly to succour Savoy that a fleet was sent to the Mediterranean. Yet when it reached Lisbon the English commander, the earl of Peterborough, was persuaded by the Austrian claimant to the throne of Spain to capture Barcelona instead. When it fell in September he was proclaimed king Charles III there. It was a great boost to the tory strategists who advocated opening up the Iberian peninsula instead of concentrating on northern German and the Low Countries, especially since the campaign there got bogged down.

Towards the end of the previous year's campaign the allied troops under Marlborough had captured Trier. He hoped to use this as a base to advance further up the Moselle in 1705. His plan was to take Thionville and perhaps even Metz, giving him a bridgehead in the heart of the defensive system built up by Louis XIV in eastern France. It has been claimed that this was the preliminary to a direct attack on Paris, but this seems unlikely. It was more to effect the detachment of the duke of Lorraine from France, which would have forced the French to retreat from the Rhine.[33] Unfortunately late in May Marlborough found his way forward from Trier blocked by an army under Villars which dug in at Sierck, and he had to abandon the planned advance. Instead he was obliged to retreat to Liège which was being besieged by Villeroy. At Marlborough's approach the French withdrew, and he even breached their lines in July. But when he sought to follow this up with a full-scale attack the Dutch generals raised objections. The campaign ended in stalemate.

Although Marlborough's sympathizers blamed the timidity of the Dutch for the disappointing campaign, his detractors did not flinch from blaming the duke himself. Lord Haversham launched a fierce attack on him in the House of Lords on 15 November. He even compared the duke with Buckingham in James I's reign, claiming that the latter 'never had half that power and favour that we see some persons now possessed of'.[34]

Haversham also drew attention to the danger from Scotland, which had resolved not to have the Hanoverian successor to the English throne succeed the queen there. To try to undo the damage of the Act of Security the Court had appointed the duke of Argyll as Scottish commissioner the previous April. But Argyll took the post on his own terms. Thus he insisted on the dismissal of Tweeddale and other members of the New party. These had been discredited anyway by their actions over the case of the *Worcester*. This English ship had been seized in the Firth of Forth by agents of the Scottish East India Company in August 1704 and its captain, Thomas Green, accused of piracy. The evidence that he had commandeered one of the company's ships in the Indian Ocean was frail to say the least. Nevertheless he and his crew were brought to trial in the High Court of Admiralty, found guilty and condemned to death in March 1705. Although Anne herself appealed for clemency from the Scottish Privy Council the majority of councillors, fearful of the wrath of an enraged mob, declined to reprieve Green, his first mate and gunner, who were executed on 11 April. The bloodlust of the mob was thereby sated, and the rest of the condemned crew, whose executions had been scheduled for a different day, were then reprieved. Among those who had supported a reprieve for Green was Argyll, who now obtained the removal of the New party councillors whose cowardice had failed to grant one.

Argyll was in a position to dictate not only whom he would not work with, but those who he wanted as his colleagues in the new Scottish ministry. Thus he insisted on Queensberry's appointment as Lord privy seal. Anne objected strongly, saying it was 'a thing I can never consent to, his last tricking behaviour having made him more odious to me than ever'. Argyll persisted, assuring the queen that Queensberry's appointment was essential to give the Court control of the Scottish parliament. Anne gave in with a bad grace. 'It grates my soul,' she protested, 'to take a man into my service that has not only betrayed me but tricked me several times.' It was the first time she agreed to make a ministerial appointment in order to ensure that her business would be carried through a parliament.

That business was to remove the deadlock over the succession, either by getting the Edinburgh parliament to recognize the house of Hanover or to agree to a union. At first Argyll set out to get recognition for the Protestant succession laid down in the English Act of Settlement. But he then realized that for a variety of reasons the majority of members preferred a treaty, whether for a federal or an incorporating union. He adroitly played off one group against another, crucially gaining the support of the New party, whose transfer from opposition to the Court earned them the name of the flying squadron. This enabled Argyll to carry an Act to appoint a commission to negotiate for a union. The opposition still had a card left to play. They wanted the estates to nominate the commissioners, knowing that they would choose those who favoured a federal union. The Court was equally determined that the queen should nominate men who would negotiate an incorporating union. They persuaded the duke of Hamilton to back them in a *volte face* which the opponents of full incorporation regarded as an act of treachery.[35] Having assured his Country followers that no decision would be taken that day, on 1 September, when many of his supporters had left the debate, he concluded a deal with the Court giving the right of nominating commissioners to the Queen, on the clear understanding that he would be one.

An English eyewitness of the debate, Joseph Taylor, left a vivid description of the occasion of Hamilton's 'U-turn'.[36]

> The next great point was, whether the Queen or parliament should have nomination of Commissioners: Fletcher oppos'd the Queen, for says he, you had as good leave it to my Lord G[o]d[olph]in, and we know that our Queen is in England, under the Influences of an English Ministry, and 'tis not to be expected that the Interest of Scotland should be so much considered by her, as the inclinations of an English Parliament . . . H[amilton] contrary to the expectation of his party, voted the Queen to nominate, giving this reason . . . that the Parliament was too much in heats and feuds, and could never agree upon proper persons, but the Queen, who was free from partiality, might doubtless make a good choice . . . ,'Twas carried the Queen should nominate by 4 Voices.

Taylor entertained several of the majority at his lodgings afterwards. They 'seemed mightily pleas'd at what was done; and told us we should now be no more English and Scotch, but Britons. And thus we merrily spent the night, in drinking to the Success of the treaty and happy union.'

In view of this it was hard to see what Haversham was driving at when he deplored developments in Scotland as jeopardizing the Protestant succession. But the point of his rambling speech became clear when he concluded with a motion to invite the successor, the dowager electress of Hanover, to reside in England during the queen's lifetime. Knowing that Anne, who was present for the debate, was utterly opposed to this – she once protested that Sophia's presence would be like having her coffin constantly before her – Haversham objected that her attendance in the Lords inhibited free debate. Another peer offended her by suggesting that the residence of Sophia in England would be desirable in case the queen became senile, a doubly offensive remark since the dowager was 75 at the time while Anne was only forty. But the man who mortified her most was the earl of Nottingham, since he had previously led her to believe that anybody who suggested such an invitation 'did it with a design to depose her'. When he had the nerve to support Haversham's motion she marked him down for destruction. Fortunately for the queen Godolphin had sufficient notice of tory intentions to concert tactics with the Junto to get the Court off the hook. Appreciating that a direct vote against the motion would create difficulties for their own followers, they moved an amendment to set aside another day for a debate on means for better securing the Protestant succession in the house of Hanover, which was carried.

When the day came Lord Wharton opened the debate with a long and witty speech, in which he congratulated the tories on the miracle of their conversion to the Protestant succession. He then proposed that, in the interim between the death of the queen and the arrival of the Hanoverian successor, there should be a regency consisting of the leading ministers of state. This proposal was accepted and a bill drawn up by Somers was introduced to give it effect.

During the debate 'the earl of Rochester moved, that the parliament and the regents should be limited, to pass no act of repeal of any part of the act of uniformity, and in his positive way said, if this was not agreed to, he should still think the church was in danger, notwithstanding what they had heard from the throne, in the beginning of the session'.[37] Anne, in her speech at the opening of parliament, had alluded to the *Memorial of the Church of England* by censuring those who argued in print that the church was in danger under her; 'and therefore we may be certain that they who go about to insinuate things of this nature must be mine and the kingdom's enemies.'[38] Rochester's challenge was taken up in the Lords on 6 December when, with the queen present, her speech was again read to the House. He then 'professed himself of Opinion, *That the Church is in danger*; nor did he think it the less so, for the pains that were taken to stop men's mouthes on that head'.[39] The peers sat in silence for a quarter of an hour waiting for somebody to second Rochester. At last Halifax broke the tension by replying that the cry 'the church in danger' was always raised 'when a certain faction is disregarded'. When Wharton got up he echoed this theme: 'all the danger mentioned in the *Memorial of the Church of England* was that the

D. of B. and E. of R. were not in the Ministry.' Somers too enquired 'whether it was necessary, for the preservation of the Church, that three or four particular lords should be in the ministry? If so, he thought there ought to be a Bill brought in, not onely for the restoring of them, but for the continueing them there for ever, and makeing them Immortal.' The Junto thereby pinned the blame squarely on the duke of Buckingham, the earl of Rochester and other high church tories. These were clearly implicated in the resolution which the Lords agreed by the crushing vote of 61 to 30, 'that whoever insinuates or suggests that the church is in danger under her present Majesty and her administration is an enemy to her Majesty, the Church and the Kingdom'.[40] When the House of Commons was asked to concur with the Lords they obliged by moving an identical resolution which passed by 212 votes to 160. As Burnet noted 'such a concurrence of both Houses had not been seen for some years: and indeed there was in both so great a majority for carrying on all the interests of the government, that the men of ill intentions had no hopes, during the whole session, of embroiling matters.'[41]

The only exception in Burnet's view was the struggle which arose in parliament over the conditions for placemen in the Regency bill.[42] Among the arrangements made by it for the continuity of government on Anne's death was the provision for parliament to convene for up to six months, unless the legitimate successor dissolved it earlier. But this raised the awkward question of what was to become of placemen? By the Act of Settlement no member could hold office under the Crown after Anne's reign. Were this to come into force on her death then the very contingency which the bill was designed to create, a smooth transference of authority to her Hanoverian successor, would be jeopardized. For about 150 office-holders, including Cabinet members, would be deprived of their seats in parliament. The Court was anxious to remove the general exclusion of placemen, but Country members, whigs as well as tories, moved to retain it. The Court prevailed, albeit by the narrow margin of 156 votes to 151.

Country whigs then put forward a clause for insertion in the bill 'explaining, regulating and altering' the provision for placemen. Instead of a blanket exclusion they stipulated a number of posts, some 47 in all, which were eligible for members to hold with their seats in parliament.[43] All other posts would disqualify men from sitting in parliament within ten days after Anne's death. Since those whigs who advocated restricting the number of placemen by this method were known as 'whimsicals', their proposal was dubbed the 'whimsical clause'. Despite strong Court pressure it passed the Commons. The Lords, however, amended the clause. Where the Commons had enumerated offices which members of parliament could hold, they proposed the opposite method of specifying those they could not hold. Thus those appointed to offices in the prize office, and to any 'new' post which might be created, were to be disqualified from sitting in parliament. These amendments were, however, rejected by the Commons on 4 February.

The Court was by now thoroughly alarmed that the wrangles over the issue of placemen would jeopardize the passage of the Regency bill itself. They therefore proposed a series of meetings between the Houses, at which the principle of negative exclusion was upheld, and the ideal of positive inclusion enshrined in the whimsical clause was dropped. But the whimsicals still held out for greater concessions, requiring more offices to be declared incompatible with a seat in parliament than those in the prize office and 'new' posts. The Court conceded a range of minor posts, and agreed that the disqualifications should come into immediate effect and not await the queen's demise. 'Here comes the best', one whimsical whig informed another. 'No man to take any place after being elected a member of parliament but accepting such a place shall make his election void.'[44] Besides the suspicion of the executive which lay behind Country objections to placemen, another criticism they had was that no man could serve both God and Mammon. Members of parliament could not simultaneously fulfill their obligations to their constituents and at the same time do their duty to the Crown as placemen. The clause finally inserted in the Regency bill whereby MPs appointed to offices under the Crown had to vacate their seats, and seek the endorsement of their constituents by standing at by-elections, went some way to reconciling the conflict of interests.[45]

With the exception of the proceedings on the whimsical clause, when the tories got some support from the Country whigs, the tory party found itself on the defensive in both Houses during this session. Consequently when the queen laid before them an address from the Edinburgh parliament for the repeal of the Alien Act 'the tories, upon this occasion, to make themselves popular after they had failed in many attempts, resolved to promote this'.[46] They found, however, that they were knocking on an open door, and the Act was repealed, excepting the clause enabling the queen to appoint English commissioners for a union, in record time in both Houses, the bill drawn up for the purpose receiving three readings in the Lords in one day and the royal assent before the adjournment for Christmas.

Early in the new year commissioners were named by the queen for Scotland. They were all, as one put it 'on the revolution foot' except for the Jacobite George Lockhart. He was recommended by his uncle Lord Wharton. Wharton's choice has baffled historians, some finding it inexplicable. But, apart from family ties, it could well have been a sound move on the Junto whigs' part to have at least a token

Jacobite among the commission to negotiate the Union. Otherwise the rest were old party men led by Queensberry. Argyll failed to be nominated, which seems surprising in view of his key role in the Edinburgh parliament. This has invited speculation. Perhaps his attitude had irritated Anne. She certainly irritated him by declining to nominate the duke of Hamilton, despite the deal in the Edinburgh parliament. Yet his irritation must have been soothed by his promotion to the English peerage as earl of Greenwich. He also planned to take part in the continental campaign that summer along with Marlborough. Maybe his intended absence abroad led him to decline being on a commission he could not attend.[47]

The English commissioners were not named until April. They were more politically mixed than their Scottish colleagues. This was because the ex-officio members of the commission included tories like archbishop Sharp of York, the Secretary of state Sir Charles Hedges, and the attorney general Sir Simon Harcourt. But the individual politicians added to their number were all whigs, including all five Junto Lords.

The role of the Junto, and especially of Somers, has provoked speculation and controversy among historians. According to G. M. Trevelyan, who regarded the negotiation of the union as a supreme act of statesmanship, though 'Anne's prejudices excluded [Somers] from office', his 'great talents were now to be put to their final proof in perhaps the best piece of service that he ever rendered to his country'.[48] Dr Riley, in sharp contrast, sees the whig lords as cynically exploiting their nuisance value for their own ends. They had no real interest in the union except that it could be used to obtain advancement.[49]

The greatest achievement of the decade, the Union, cannot be attributed to the sordid intrigues of venal and corrupt politicians seeking their own advantage. As we shall see in the next chapter, it was far more than a mere episode in the faction fighting at Westminster and Edinburgh.

6

1706

The Union commissioners began their negotiations on 16 April 1706. The English and Scottish members held separate meetings to thrash out the terms of the treaty. Only the arrangements for the representation of 'North Britain' in the parliament of Great Britain roused such contention that they were obliged to meet together. Otherwise minutes were sent from one nation's commission to the other's. Thus on 22 April the English commissioners sent a proposal drawn up by Somers 'that the two kingdoms . . . be for ever united into one kingdom by the name of Great Britain . . . [to] be represented by one and the same parliament'. The Scots reply favoured a federal union 'like that of the united provinces or of the cantons in Switzerland'.[1] When the English commissioners insisted on a full incorporating union the Scots withdrew their federal proposal, and on 15 April the two commissions agreed to a united kingdom with one parliament, the same successor and free trade.

The main point of the union had thus been agreed with remarkable speed. To many Scots, both at the time and since, this was due to the careful choice of Scottish commissioners by the Queen to ensure their subservience to the wishes of the English court. On 29 May, for instance, they sought guarantees for the separate laws and legal system of Scotland in the united kingdom of Great Britain. 'It is eloquent of the nature of the Union,' observes a modern Scottish historian, 'more a take-over than a merger, that it was not thought necessary to state that the laws of England would continue in force.'[2]

It took some more serious wrangling to reach agreement on what basis Scots were to be taxed, the amount to be paid by England to eliminate Scotland's national debt, and the representation of the northern nation in the new state. Scots were to contribute £48,000 to the British land tax at the war time rate of four shillings in the pound, which raised £2,000,000 in England. The Scottish share of the excise

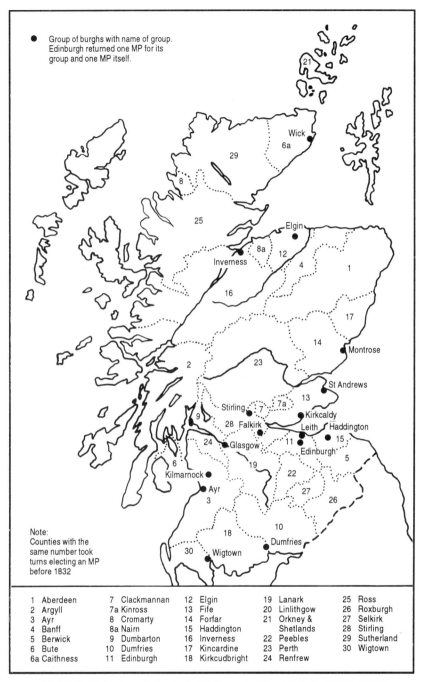

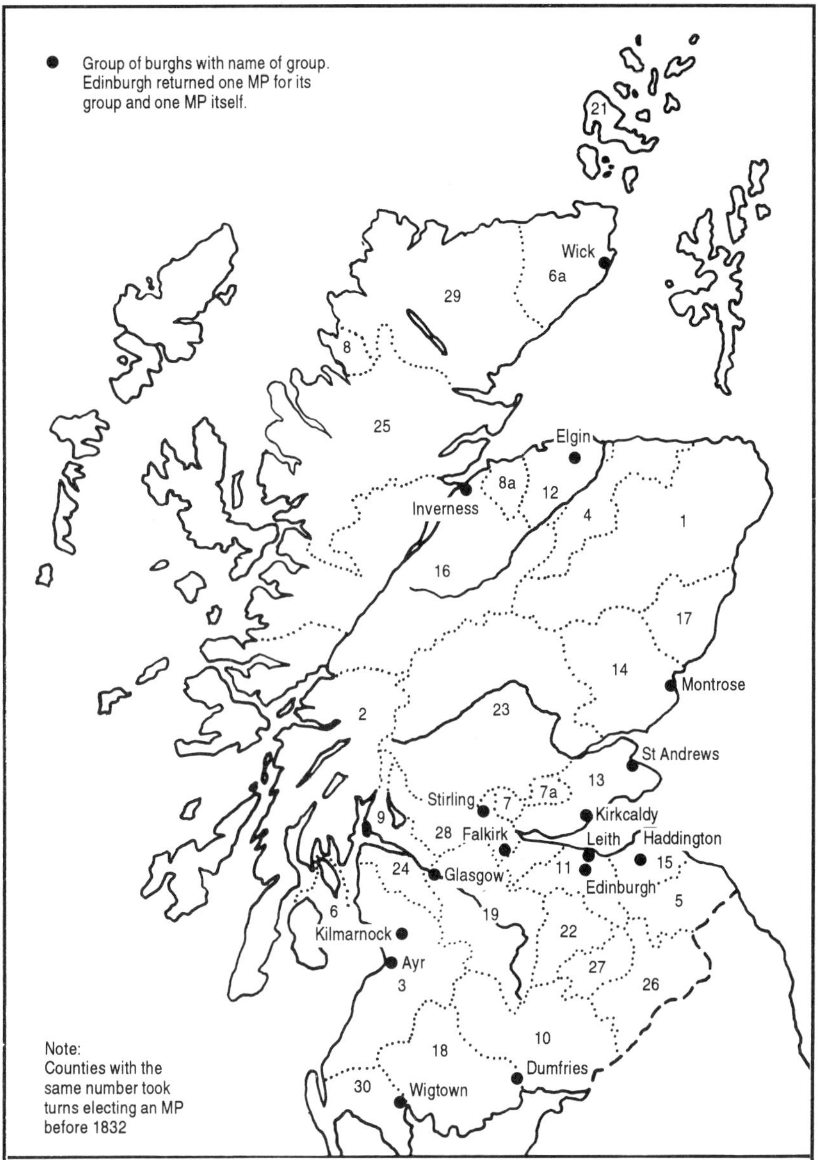
Group of burghs with name of group. Edinburgh returned one MP for its group and one MP itself.
21
Wick
6a
29
8
25
Elgin
8a
12
Inverness
4
1
16
17
14
Montrose
2
23
St Andrews
13
7a
Stirling
7
Kirkcaldy
9
28
Falkirk
Leith
Haddington
15
24
Glasgow
11
Edinburgh
5
6
19
Kilmarnock
22
Ayr
27
3
26
10
18
Dumfries
30
Wigtown
Note:
Counties with the same number took turns electing an MP before 1832

1 Aberdeen	7 Clackmannan	12 Elgin	19 Lanark	25 Ross
2 Argyll	7a Kinross	13 Fife	20 Linlithgow	26 Roxburgh
3 Ayr	8 Cromarty	14 Forfar	21 Orkney & Shetlands	27 Selkirk
4 Banff	8a Nairn	15 Haddington	22 Peebles	28 Stirling
5 Berwick	9 Dumbarton	16 Inverness	23 Perth	29 Sutherland
6 Bute	10 Dumfries	17 Kincardine	24 Renfrew	30 Wigtown
6a Caithness	11 Edinburgh	18 Kirkcudbright		

Map 2 Scottish representation in the Parliament of Great Britain, 1707–1832

was fixed at a ratio of 1 to 36. This was a reasonable recognition of their ability to pay. The sum proposed to pay off the debt, much of it owing to shareholders in the ill-fated Darien company, was fixed at the precise figure of £398,085 10s 0d. Since Scots after the Union were to take over their share of the burden of the national debt this money was known as the Equivalent.

The arrangements made for Scottish representation were to prove the most controversial. There were to be sixteen lords in the Upper House, chosen by their peers in north Britain, and 45 members in the Commons. To some modern observers this under-represented Scotland. Certainly the number of seats seems meagre, since the county of Cornwall alone sent 44 MPs to Westminster. Had there been a system of representation based on individuals then the million or so Scots should have been allocated about 100 seats to offset the 513 for the five million inhabitants of England and Wales. Contemporaries, however, did not base the criteria of representation on population. There was no serious consideration given then to that notion, the principal consideration being the proportion of taxation which an area contributed. As William Seton put it when the allocation came to be debated in the Edinburgh parliament, 'if both nations are to be represented by one parliament there must be members from both nations and their numbers must be adjusted by some rule, which can be no other than that fundamental in the union of all societies whereby suffrages are computed, to wit the proportion each society contributes for the support of the whole'.[3] On this basis Scotland did not do too badly, for its contribution to the British treasury was significantly less than the ratio 45:513. On that basis Scotland would have obtained only 28 seats in the Parliament of Great Britain. The English commissioners originally offered the Scots 38, while the Scottish proposed 50. Forty-five was thus a compromise between the two. When it was finally agreed the terms of the treaty could be presented to the queen. This ceremony took place on 23 July 1706. Lord Keeper Cowper and Chancellor Seafield made speeches on behalf of the commissioners for the two countries, who were thanked by the Queen 'for their unanimous concurrence in a thing so necessary and advantageous to the two nations'.[4] The terms had yet to be ratified by the two parliaments, who were to be rather less unanimous.

Godolphin anticipated trouble from the tories in the English parliament 'in case it passes in the Scots Parliament', informing Marlborough on the day the treaty was signed by both commissions that 'now it begins to bee preached up and down that the *church is in danger*, from this union'. The duke replied, 'care must be taken against the mallice of the angry party, and notwithstanding their mallicious affectation of crying the church may be ruined by the Union, the Union must be supported'.[5]

Marlborough was then in the Low Countries where he had spent the summer campaign. He had not planned on doing so, since he felt that the French would be on the defensive in that theatre and would take the offensive in Italy and Spain. Indeed he had hoped to go to the Italian theatre to help his comrade-in-arms Prince Eugene to stave off the French attack. Unfortunately the imperial forces were defeated by the duke of Vendome at Calcinato before Eugene could get to their relief. He had to re-group the shattered forces and retreat to the Trentino, leaving the duke of Savoy exposed to Vendome's army, which besieged Turin from May to September.

Meanwhile Villars had after all taken the offensive in Germany, forcing allied troops back across the Rhine. Moreover another French army under Villeroy, so far from adopting a defensive posture, threatened the allies in The Netherlands. This led the Dutch to persuade Marlborough to stay in the Low Countries rather than going to the aid of Eugene. They sent some Dutch troops to Italy, and promised the duke a free hand to engage Villeroy in battle should the opportunity present itself.

The chance came early in the campaign when the French general challenged Marlborough at Ramillies on 12 May. At the head of France's finest troops Villeroy felt confident that he could inflict a decisive defeat on the allies. Instead those troops fled from the field as the duke of Marlborough won his greatest victory. Marlborough himself was almost killed in the engagement. Having been thrown from his horse, as he mounted another the aide-de-camp who assisted him had his head blown off by a cannonball which allegedly passed between the duke's legs.

The battle inspired the imagination in England, provoking responses at all levels of society. A medal was struck depicting Anne as Minerva chastizing Louis XIV who lay at her feet. The reverse depicted a biblical scene wherein Abimelech was killed by a stone thrown by a woman. A Latin inscription read, 'The Almighty Lord hath delivered him into the hands of a woman'. This medal was reproduced as the six and seven of clubs in a pack of playing cards, one of which showed the procession to St Paul's on 27 June for a thanksgiving service.[6] It was reported that 'a greater number of the nobility attended than ever was known upon such an occasion'.[7] Similar services were held throughout the country. The clash of arms inspired a battle of the poets as versifiers published odes to celebrate the victory. First into the lists was Defoe who dashed off an 'execrably bad' poem 'wrote like mad' in three hours.[8] Thus he described the duke's fall from his horse:[9]

> Britannia's Fate was touch't in Marl'brough's Fall
> The Horse, crush't with th'unusual pond'rous Weight
> Of rising Glory, fell beneath the Load . . .

As a critic of Defoe's effort noted:

> Some more, below the dignity of Verse
> In short-liv'd Lines wou'd glorious Deeds rehearse.[10]

Among the less fleeting was Matthew Prior's *Ode humbly inscribed to the Queen on the Glorious Success of her Majesty's Arms*. This was 'written in imitation of Spencer's stile', striking a deliberate Elizabethan echo, comparing Anne with Gloriana.[11]

The rout of the French was so complete that they virtually abandoned the Flemish-speaking region of the Spanish Netherlands, retreating to the Mons–Lille–Dunkirk line, from which they could still control much of the Walloon district. Over the summer Marlborough laid siege successfully to Ostend, Menin, Dendermonde and Ath. Most of the towns in the Flemish region meanwhile threw off their allegiance to Philip V and declared for the Habsburg Charles III. Since he was at that moment in Spain and unable to rule his new possessions in person, the English and the Dutch took over the administration of the territories which Marlborough had wrested from Bourbon control. To assert Habsburg rule over them the Emperor offered Marlborough the post of Viceroy of The Netherlands. The duke himself was sorely tempted by the offer, and the English ministry was interested in the proposal. But the Dutch took alarm at what they thought was against their strategic interests. They were particularly anxious to acquire a strong barrier in the southern Netherlands against French aggression. If the English and the Habsburgs did a deal which denied them that protection then they would seek it from France, which was eager to offer them terms which would detach them from the Grand Alliance. Fear that the proposed government of the newly acquired territories would divide the allies led Marlborough to decline the offer. Instead an Anglo-Dutch condominium based in Brussels ruled the Habsburg Netherlands until the end of the war.

Meanwhile the English and Dutch governments began negotiations which were eventually to lead to the Republic agreeing to supply forces to guarantee the Protestant succession in England, in return for the acquisition of a number of barrier towns on each side of the border between France and the Spanish Netherlands to be guaranteed by Britain. Discussions in the summer of 1706 were inconclusive because the English side balked at ceding Dendermonde and Ostend to the Dutch. Moreover as the summer advanced so hopes of concluding a union with Scotland made the conclusion of the barrier and succession treaties less urgent to the English.[12]

The failure of the English government to follow up the victory at Ramillies by seriously negotiating peace with France was to lead to accusations that the duumvirs were deliberately prolonging the war for their own advantage. Certainly they expressed alarm that the Dutch might seek separate terms from the French, and pressed the United Provinces to commit themselves to one more year of hostilities. Yet Marlborough was convinced that 'one campagn more would secure us a good peace'.[13] He was concerned that as things stood in 1706 the Bourbons would retain at least part of Spain, and was determined that Charles III should rule over the whole of that country.

At one time his chances of doing so had seemed excellent. Since his arrival in Catalonia the previous year most of the eastern seaboard of Spain had declared for him. He had survived a five-week siege of Barcelona by the French in the spring. The day it was raised by the arrival of an English fleet witnessed an eclipse of the sun, which was regarded as an ill omen for Louis XIV, 'the Sun King'. An allied army led by the earl of Galway had entered Castile from Portugal and driven Philip V from Madrid in May. It looked as though Charles III would be able to take possession of the Spanish capital. But then discord among the allied generals in the east fatally delayed his journey to the city, and the Bourbon king returned. At the end of the campaign, therefore, Spain was divided between the two claimants, with Philip V enthroned in Castile and Charles III in possession of Catalonia, Aragon and Valencia. The peace terms offered by the Bourbon powers to the allies in 1706 provided for the permanent division of the country along these lines. Marlborough was not prepared to accept the partition of Spain. He had inflicted a tremendous blow to French military prestige in Ramillies in May, and his colleague Prince Eugene delivered another when he relieved Turin in September. The first had expelled the French from the Spanish Netherlands; the second ended the war in Italy. Only the Iberian peninsula remained a Bourbon bastion.

While Marlborough was to be castigated for his intransigence by the tories later, at the time they were if anything even more committed to the Iberian theatre, and the war aim expressed in the slogan 'no peace without Spain', than were the whigs. For their part the Junto gave full backing to the duumvirs in their dealings with the Dutch, the French and the Scots during this summer.

Although the Junto's support for the policies of Godolphin and Marlborough was based on principle they did not expect to support the government without any reward for their services. Yet, although all five lords were commissioners for the treaty, not one was in high office when the commission worked out the terms in the spring. They therefore mounted a campaign to get the earl of Sunderland into the

Cabinet as Secretary of state in place of the tory Sir Charles Hedges. Although both Godolphin and Marlborough backed their efforts they were thwarted for most of the year. Queen Anne conducted a rearguard action with all the obstinacy and stubbornness of her family. She was reinforced in this policy of inertia by the shrill insistence of her erstwhile favourite Sarah duchess of Marlborough that she budge. Anne was also backed by Robert Harley, who resisted the steady encroachment of the whig leaders. This was to split up the triumvirate which had managed parliament so successfully since the tack.

At the end of the session on 19 March 1706 Marlborough expressed the opinion to Anthonie Heinsius, the Pensionary of Holland, that it 'has most certainly been the best that ever was in England'.[14] His praise stemmed from its prompt voting of supplies for the war effort. As soon as he could thereafter he crossed the North Sea to the campaign in the Low Countries, leaving his colleagues Godolphin and Harley to the business of the political campaign in England.

Taking stock of the alignment of parties in the recent session the Lord Treasurer observed to Harley:

> I think as you do in your letter t'other day that the Tories are more numerous in this Parliament than the whigs, and the Queen's servants much the least part of the three. My computation runs thus: of the 450 that chose the Speaker Tories 190, whigs 160, Queen's servants 100, of the last about 15 perhaps joined with Tories in that vote of the Speaker, by which they amounted to 205, and so afterwards more or less in almost every vote. Except in the Place Bill, that is the *clause*, the 160 voted always with the body of the Queen's servants. Now the question in my opinion is, whether it be more likely or more easy to keep the 160 (whigs) which with the Queen's true servants will always be a majority or to get (sic) from the 190 (Tories).

He concluded that it was the Court's business 'to get as many as we can from the 190, without doing anything to lose one of the 160'.[15]

This policy was utterly at variance with Harley's political ideas. It severely restricted the Court's freedom of manoeuvre by making it dependent upon one party; it ran the very great risk of ultimately surrendering power to the leaders of that party; and above all it limited the Queen's prerogative of choosing her own ministers regardless of their party affiliations. To the Secretary, therefore, Godolphin's prescription, so far from being a remedy for current political ills, would only allay the symptoms for a while, eventually bringing on a violent recurrence of the complaint, which would not only debilitate the health of the body politic but imperil the life of the constitution. This diagnosis and his own recommendations for a cure he jotted down on 25 September 1706 in a draft of a letter presumably sent to Godolphin:

Queen began her reign upon the foot of no partys. She has thrived in
it, & had success. Will you set up another? Which shall it be? The least
or the greatest? The Queen would not give herself up to the tories when
they were unreasonable though much the majority. Shall she do that for
the whigs who never can be so? . . . Do the whigs deserve to enjoy all the
Queen's successes? and nobody else?

Harley's conclusion was that 'the foundation of the Church is in the
Queen ,the foundation of liberty is in her! Let her therefore be arbitress
between them'.[16]

Harley wrote these jottings a few days after the queen had attempted
to end the deadlock over the demands that Sunderland be given
Hedges' secretaryship by offering him instead a place in the Cabinet
with a pension but with no office.[17] The Junto, however, declined the
offer. Godolphin found himself between the irresistible force of the
Junto and Sarah on the one hand and the immoveable object of the
queen backed by Harley on the other. Anne's obstinacy was, if anything,
stiffened by the duchess's demands and especially by a letter which
Sarah wrote to her in August. Although she sensibly told the queen
that ''tis certain that your government can't be carried on with a part of
the Tories and the Whigs disobliged', she outraged Anne by expressing
the hope that 'Mr and Mrs Morley may see their errors as to this nation
before it is too late'.[18]

Since neither the duchess of Marlborough nor the Lord Treasurer
could make any headway with Anne they persuaded the duke to use
his considerable influence with her. At the end of September he wrote
to Anne a letter clearly spelling out his own position.[19]

As I am persuaded that the safety of your government, and the quiet
of your life, depends very much upon the resolution you shall take at
this time, I think myself bound in gratitude, duty and conscience, to
let you know my mind freely. And that you may not suspect me of
being partial, I take leave to asure you, in the presence of God, that
I am not for your putting yourself into the hands of either party. But
the behaviour of Lord Rochester and all the hote heads of that party
are so extravagant, that there is no doubt to be made of their exposing
you and the libertys of England to the rage of France, rather then not
be revenged as thay cal itt. This being the case, there is a necessity as
well as justice of your following your inclinations in suporting Lord
Treasurer, or al must go to confusion. As the humour is at present,
he can't be supported but by the Wiggs, for the other seekes his
distruction, which in effect is yours. Now pray consider if he can,
by placing some few about you, gaine such a confidence, as shall
make your business and himself safe, will not this be the sure way
of making him so strong, that he may hinder your being forced into
a party?

Even this plea from the duke of Marlborough failed to change Anne's mind. Godolphin thought that only his presence in England would make the required impact, and urged the Captain General to return before parliament met. 'You will be very much wanted here for severall things which ought necessarily to bee done before the Parliament', he wrote to the duke on 29 October. 'And your being here before their sitting down, must needs have a very great influence toward hastening their preparation for next year.'[20] Marlborough arrived in England on 17 November. On the 20th he had a meeting with Godolphin and Harley in which they persuaded the Secretary that Sunderland must be given Hedges' place. Sunderland's appointment was announced on 31 November. This was just in time for the parliamentary session which began on 3 December.

This was an usually late day for a session to start. It had been delayed so that the outcome of the Scottish parliament's debate on the treaty of union would be known before it was debated by the Houses in England.

The Scottish Estates met for their last session on 3 October.[21] Anne's letter, dated from Windsor on 31 July, was read out by the Lord Clerk Register. 'The Union has been long desired by both nations,' she wrote, 'and we shall esteem it as the greatest glory of our reign to have it now perfected, being fully persuaded that it must prove the greatest happiness of our people.' Then the articles were read, with Lord Annandale laughing at every one.[22] Afterwards the House adjourned for a week so that they could be printed, dispersed and digested.

When the debate resumed the opposition proposed that another week be set aside for the articles and the accompanying minutes of the commissioners to be considered. A vote was therefore pressed to proceed with the discussion of the articles, which was carried by a majority of 66. Such a clear victory for the advocates of union was achieved by the flying squadron's joining with the Court. The Court, ably led by the duke of Queensberry, the Queen's commissioner, included such ministers as the marquis of Montrose, president of the Council, and the earl of Seafield, the Chancellor. They were joined by the duke of Argyll, brought back from the continental campaign specially to reinforce the Court. Allied to them was the 'flying squadron' from the New party, led by Marchmont, Montrose, Roxburgh and Tweeddale. Since the majority was greater than the number voting against proceeding one Court supporter thought they could have carried it without the New party's support.[23] However, there were to be times when the Court needed all the help which the New party could give it. Their alliance held throughout the debates on the articles, in which the opposition could only filibuster.[24] They were divided anyway, between Jacobites like George Lockhart, republicans such as Andrew Fletcher, mavericks like the duke of Hamilton who had his own hereditary claim to the Scottish throne, Country politicians like the duke of Atholl, and staunch Presbyterians like Walter Stewart, member for Linlithgow. Despite their divisions they managed to spin the debates out until 16 January 1707, long after the time that the English ministers had expected the session to be over.

The queen had warned the Estates that the 'enemies' of the union would 'use their utmost endeavours to prevent or delay' it. Defoe observed that 'from article to article they disputed every word, every clause, casting difficulties and doubts in the way of every argument, twisting and turning every question, and continually starting objections to gain time, and if possible to throw some unsurmountable obstacle in the way'. This was done partly with a view to spinning out the discussion of the articles until the English parliament was forced to meet to vote supply, when 'they expected to confound the measures for carrying on the treaty by mutual proposals debates etc.'. It took nine sittings held over two weeks just to read the articles. The Court went along with this leisurely timetable to forestall opposition criticisms that they were rushing so important a business, though of course they incurred the charge anyway. When the reading of the articles was completed, and the discussion of each in turn was proposed, the opposition again attempted to abort the proceedings. Thus they tried to deny the parliament's right to decide on the fate of the nation on the ground that sovereignty resided in the Scottish people. However this was successfully resisted by the Court. Then the opposition attempted further delaying tactics. Thus they argued that the views of the English parliament should be available, a manifest effort at procrastination since that body had been prorogued until 21 November deliberately to let the Scottish Estates debate the articles further. When this failed they sought to postpone debate on the first article, which encapsulated the principle of an incorporating union, until the others, detailing the form it was to take, had been discussed. The Court carried the motion that they proceed article by article from the first to the last, conceding that the parliament was not committed to any until all had been agreed.

On 1 November, therefore, they at last began to debate the first article, that the two kingdoms be united into one with the name of Great Britain. This was the most crucial of all 25 articles. As William Seton put it in the debate on 2 November 'this article is the foundation of the whole treaty, and the approving or rejecting it must determine Union or no Union betwixt both kingdoms'. One of the more celebrated speeches against the union was made by Lord Belhaven in the debate on this day. He saw the loss of Scotland's independence not as the 'end of ane old song' but of two thousand years of history. 'I think I see a free and independent kingdom delivering up that which all the world hath been fighting for since the days of Nimrod; yea, that for which most of all the empires, kingdoms, states, principalities and dukedoms are at this very time engaged in the most bloody and cruel wars that ever were; to wit, a power to manage their own affairs by themselves without the assistance and counsel of any other.' For some reason these unexceptionable sentiments were ridiculed, perhaps because of the melodramatic way in which they were delivered. Thus Defoe dashed off a poem *The Vision* which satirized the speech: 'two hours he talk'd and said nothing at all.'[25] Lord Marchmont 'was of opinion it required a short answer which he gave in these words, "Behold he dreamed, but lo! when he awoke, he found it was a dream".'

Yet, although the first article was approved on 4 November by a majority of 32 votes, one of Belhaven's objections to the union, that it gave no security for the Scottish church, was taken sufficiently seriously for the ministry to offer a separate Act to preserve the presbyterian establishment in Scotland 'in all succeeding generations'. This 'Act for securing the Protestant Religion and Presbyterian Church Government' was rushed through the Estates between 4 and 12 November, in stark contrast to the pace of the debates on the articles. It was then made a part of the treaty.

On 14 November the second article, placing the succession in the House of Hanover, was debated. The opposition tried to defer consideration of the succession, moving that the fourth article be discussed instead. This tactic as chancellor Seafield noted 'coast us one dayes labour'.[26] But the Court carried it for taking the treaty article by article by 26 votes. 'I was afraid that this vote would be narrow' Lord Mar admitted 'yet you see the plurality was not despicable. And now this article is almost over I hope our work shall be much easier after this than if we had left this article last as our opposers would have done.'[27] The Act of Settlement passed in England in 1701 was read. This not only settled the throne on the Hanoverian successor but was for 'the further limitation of the Crown and better securing the rights of the subject'. Limitations had appealed to Scottish commonwealthmen led by Andrew Fletcher previously, and Belhaven now proposed them as 'the best security'. He was backed by Hamilton, who actually moved that the treaty be dropped and an address be made to the queen to accept the Hanoverian succession with limitations. This was clearly the last serious attempt to beat the treaty in parliament and during a very noisy debate the opposition forced two divisions.[28] But Defoe noted that they 'came too late, since the party who were for the succession formerly with limitations, were now come into the Union'. Consequently the second article was approved on 15 November by 58 votes.

On 18 November the third article, that there be one parliament, was read and approved by 31 votes. A proposal that every third year at least the parliament of Great Britain should meet in Scotland was put off until the discussion of the 22nd article, which allocated the number of Scottish representatives to the united legislature.

The first three articles were the most crucial and controversial. Once they were passed the English ministers could cautiously anticipate a successful conclusion to the debates in parliament. Although it took until 23 January 1707 for all the articles to be ratified, this was due as much to the technicalities of the commercial and financial details as to any sustained opposition. Thus the provision for the equivalent in article 15 had to be referred to a committee which co-opted two professors of mathematics to assist with the arithmetic. Criticisms were nonetheless made of the detailed arrangements, since the opponents of the treaty hoped that by carrying amendments to particular articles they would invalidate the whole, arguing that the terms were to be accepted or rejected entirely as the commissioners had negotiated them. When they carried minor changes the Court side anxiously wrote for clarification from London in the form of a memorial. In reply ministers informed them to accept amendments which 'explained' the treaty but did not change it. This was a splendid bureaucratic distinction, but absolutely essential, otherwise the union would have been in jeopardy. For as Defoe informed Robert Harley on 16 December, 'the alterations are numerous and confused, but I take them hitherto to be not very considerable and none of them fatal to the Union in general'.[29] Despite attempts by the opposition to prove that Scotland would be crippled by the tax burden and that her economy would suffer, the majority accepted that the fiscal arrangements were generous. Thus the malt tax was not to be imposed on Scotland for the duration of the war, while it was confidently felt that it would not be levied during peacetime.[30] Moreover it was generally agreed that the economic prospects would be grim if Scottish merchants were not allowed to trade freely with England. Indeed the threat by the English in the Aliens Act to cut off the trade in black cattle, coal and linen concentrated Scottish minds wonderfully on a commercial union. 'That a union will do in the Scottish parliament I think very probable', the earl of Roxburgh prophesied in November 1705. 'The motives will be, trade with most, Hanover with some, ease and security with others.'[31]

All that the opposition could do after 18 November 1706 was to exploit fears outside parliament that the treaty was a betrayal of Scotland's history and culture. These found expression in demonstrations and petitions against the union. 'The mobb is uneasy at the Union in Scotland and has been very unruly', Godolphin informed Marlborough as early as 1 November. 'The majority in Parliament for it is so great, that they begin to find it cannot be resisted but by tumult and open force.'[32]

The first disturbances occurred in Edinburgh on 23 October. The house of Sir Patrick Johnston, one of the commissioners of the union, was attacked by three or four hundred men, who 'broke open his doors, search'd his house for him, but he having narrowly made his escape, prevented his being torn in a thousand pieces'.[33] The guards had to be called out to restore order. The south-west then witnessed popular objections to the union. In Dumfries the articles were publicly burned by Presbyterians, who vowed that they would not be binding on Scotland even if ratified by the parliaments. Glasgow was the scene of riots throughout much of November and early December. 'I am sorry to tell you the war here is begun', Defoe wrote alarmingly to Robert Harley on 30 November. 'The Glasgow men, a hundred only very well armed, are marched and two hundred are to follow; the Stirling men, Hamilton men and Galloway men are to meet them.'[34] They were in fact met by troops, who dispersed them.

The riots in Glasgow were brought about by the refusal of the magistrates to sign an address against the Union. In all some ninety addresses were presented against the union, and none in its favour. Almost every sitting of the Scottish parliament after 4 November began with the reading out of hostile addresses. In December the opponents of the union threatened to convene a demonstration in Edinburgh of those who had signed them. The authorities took this sufficiently seriously to issue a proclamation banning it.

Yet the addresses themselves were not taken seriously. Argyll contemptuously jested that they were only fit to make kites of. Burnet wrote of them:[35]

> Those who opposed the union, finding the majority was against them, studied to raise a storm without doors, to frighten them: a set of addresses against the union were sent round all the countries in which those who opposed it had any interest: there came up many of these, in the name of counties and boroughs and at last from parishes: this made some noise abroad, but was very little considered there, when it was known by whose arts and practices they were procured.

But if there had been strong support for favourable addresses it should not have been beyond the ability of the Court to organize them. As Sir David Nairne observed, 'Why has there not been some pains taken to get counter addresses from some places? I hope there would be as many and as good hands at them as at the other.'[36] Had they been procured Daniel Defoe would not have had to indulge in some tortuous arithmetic to prove that the more affluent Scots did not address.[37] He recorded that:[38]

There were indeed in several places addresses prepared from the gentry of the country, for the encouragement of the treaty, but it was concluded to be needless, since that would have been a kind of telling noses without doors, and the party would have been pleased to have had it past for a sort of polling the nation, in which, they having before dissatisfied and alarmed the common people, they had the most hopes of success; this therefore was laid aside, as a step that would be of no use, and would put the Union upon a trial altogether inconsistent with the constitution and, as it were, debate it a-la-mob.

This is a most revealing admission by Defoe. The fact of the matter is that by any test of public opinion the union was unpopular in Scotland.

Yet the question remains, why, if a majority of their countrymen were passionately opposed to the treaty, did it pass the Estates? Ever since it did there have not been wanting Scots to assert that they were bribed. George Lockhart, the Jacobite commissioner, was convinced that a sum of £20,000 sent by the English treasury to 'sweeten' the pill by paying off debts owed to Scots was a blatant bribe. These charges were reiterated by William Ferguson who described the whole negotiation of the union as a gigantic *job*.[39] English historians on the whole have been sceptical. Trevelyan dismissed Lockhart's claims on the grounds that, although 'it would be idle to pretend that no money passed to ease the passage of the Union' such '*douceurs*' were normal at the time. 'The Treaty was carried, as it was also opposed, for grave public reasons earnestly considered by men who were not indifferent to their country's interests, nor, it may be admitted, to their own.'[40] Riley, while no more inclined than Ferguson to accept Trevelyan's view of the statesmanship of those involved, dismisses the sum as too paltry to account for the behaviour of most beneficiaries.[41] Where the amount owed by the Court to the recipients can be ascertained it was in almost every instance larger than the sum received. Thus Queensberry obtained £12,325 and Tweeddale £1,000, but their recorded arrears were £26,756 and £2,577 respectively. Even when no arrears are known this does not mean that they did not exist, for more than £250,000 was outstanding on the Scottish civil and military lists in 1706. Against this, however, it can be pointed out that the Court seems to have been selective in its payments at this time, the squadrone especially benefitting from them. Moreover rewards were not confined to the £20,000. Many Scots had claims on the Equivalent, which involved relatively massive sums. Former shareholders in the Africa company, who included many squadrone members, were to be compensated from it. So were the creditors of the Scottish government. 'Here was a swinging bribe to buy off the Scots members of parliament from their duty to their country', claimed Lockhart, 'as it accordingly prov'd; for to it we may chiefly ascribe that so many of them agreed to this Union.'[42] Even Trevelyan conceded that 'the arrangement certainly oiled the wheels of the Union Treaty. Most, though not all, who benefited by this clause, were in fact strong supporters of Union.'[43] Inducements to support the Union were not just in cash. Argyll, for instance, obtained a major generalship in the army for himself and a peerage for his brother. It was probably to such 'sweeteners' that Robert Harley was referring with his cynical remark 'we bought them'.[44] Many supporters of the Union in the Scottish parliament were paid, certainly. But it is too facile to say that they were bribed. That is to imply a single, and rather sordid, motive for their support: venality. Yet when we look back closely at the behaviour of these men in the crucial weeks of autumn 1706 and early winter 1707 we cannot give so simple an explanation of it. The situation was far too complex.

Above all, for Unionists it was dangerous. The unpopularity of their stance was brought home to them night after night in the most threatening way. On 23 October, when Sir Patrick Johnston's house was attacked, the rioters threatened to break into the parliament house. 'Had the mob got in,' claimed Lord Mar, a leading Unionist, 'it was too probable that the consequence wou'd have been tragicall.' That night when Hamilton went to dine at the duke of Atholl's, accompanied as usual by a cheering crowd, Mar and some fellow Unionists were the guests of Lord Loudoun, whose town house happened to be situated next door to Atholl's. Loudoun's dinner party expected to be attacked by Hamilton's supporters, and decided to adjourn to the Abbey for safety, a decision which meant running the gauntlet of the hostile Hamiltonians. 'This expedition of ours I confess was as hardy as wise', Mar admitted. 'If one stone had been thrown at us there had been five hundred.' It took great courage to defy an angry and violent mob that way. One of Loudoun's guests, Lord Lothian, not surprisingly left town the next day, and it was noted that a client member of parliament thereafter voted against the Union.

The Unionists had to undergo considerable intimidation for their support of the treaty. So great was their danger that rumours spread that the commissioner and others would be assassinated. Queensberry had frequently to face a barrage of stones as he went to parliament, 'some whereof even enter'd his coach and often wounded his guards and servants; so that often he and his retinue were obliged to go off at a top gallop and in great disorder'.[45] 'We are threatened every day we shall be murdered', Mar informed Sir David Nairne, adding that 'several thousands are coming to town armed who will force parliament to give over this affair'. The anti-Unionists did not make their position any easier by warning of civil war and threatening to bring signers of hostile petitions to Edinburgh to coerce parliament. While not condoning riots, they did object to the use of military force to suppress them, arguing that the rioters were merely expressing 'the true spirit of this country', while the troops cowed parliament.

How great the strain was on the supporters of the treaty was exemplified in the fate of one of their leaders, the earl of Stair. When the 22nd article, allocating Scottish representatives to the parliament of Great Britain, was debated there were apprehensions that the opposition would get support for the proposition that Scotland's share of parliamentary seats was too small. Stair spoke for four hours in its favour 'with such vehemence in disputing with those who opposed it that he died two or three hours afterwards.'[46]

The Queen became 'extreamly concerned' for the Unionists, and asked how she could best support them, as did 'lord treasurer and several about the Court'. Any payments they might have received were not so much bribes as rewards, a kind of danger money for services rendered. These men might not have been high minded idealists. They were too hard-boiled for that. At the same time they were not sordidly venal, selling their birthright for a mess of pottage. They believed in what they were doing sufficiently to risk life and limb every day for three months. 'You have acquired a great deal of reputation to our kingdom of constancy, courage, wisdom and moderation in the conduct of this whole affair', a fellow Scot wrote to Mar when the articles were at last ratified by the Edinburgh parliament on 16 January 1707, 'which God bring to a happy conclusion'.

That could only be achieved by their ratification by the English parliament too. The ministers had intended to delay the meeting of the Houses in London until the treaty had been agreed in Edinburgh, but the debates on the articles had taken so long there that it was felt to be necessary to open the session in England, which had been prorogued until 3 December, in order to get supplies voted for the coming campaign. When the session opened the Queen drew attention in her speech to the fact that the Scottish parliament was still debating the treaty. 'I hope the mutual advantages of an entire union of the two kingdoms will be found so apparent,' she went on, 'that it will not be long before I shall have an opportunity of acquainting you with the success which it has met with there.' Meanwhile she hoped, since their meeting was later than usual, that they would 'give as much dispatch to the public affairs as the nature of them will admit'. They responded by voting all the revenues requisite for the war effort in less than a week. When the bills were presented for Anne's approval on 21 December the Speaker observed that 'this dispatch . . . was like the victory at Ramellies, over before the forces known to be in the field'.[47]

The Houses then marked time until the news reached London that the Edinburgh parliament had ratified the articles of Union. The earl of Nottingham tried to jump the gun on 14 January by asking that the proceedings on the Union might be laid before the House of Lords, but was successfully deflected on the grounds that the time was not ripe. Nottingham's motive was concern that the Act for safeguarding the Church of Scotland had been embodied in the Act for ratifying the articles of Union. He wanted a similar safeguard for the Church of England. So did several clergymen of the Anglican church led by the archbishop of Canterbury. Tenison convened a series of meetings which thrashed out a bill to be presented to parliament when time ripened with the passing of the Union in Scotland.

News finally arrived of this on 20 January 1707. On the 28th Anne formally informed parliament of it, and laid before it the Act of Ratification for its concurrence and approbation. Archbishop Tenison immediately moved for leave to bring in a bill for the security of the Church of England, which 'stun'd many of the other side'.[48] Just as the Scottish Act had been essential to allay Presbyterian fears about the consequences of the Union, so this bill was vital to overcome Anglican objections. Its final wording was thrashed out at a meeting between the bishops and the Junto on 21 January. It was given its first reading in the Lords on the 31st. There was a warm debate on 3 February at its second reading. High church bishops and temporal lords made an effort to insert in the bill a clause to make the Test Act fundamental for the security of Anglicanism, but this was defeated by 60 votes to 33. The bill then went through its remaining stages without difficulty and was sent down to the House of Commons. There high church tories led by Bromley tried the same tactic as their colleagues in the Lords but as Robert Walpole put it 'we would permit no alterations'.[49] The attempt was defeated by 211 to 163.

Meanwhile the Commons had started to discuss the articles of the union. On 4 February, in a committee of the whole House chaired by Spencer Compton, the high church tories led an assault against the treaty. Sir John Pakington said 'that for his part he was absolutely against this incorporating union, which he said was like the marrying a woman against her consent; an union that was carried on by corruption and bribery within doors and by force and violence without'. He failed to see how the Queen could be supreme governor of the Church of England and bound to uphold the Church of Scotland, 'and therefore he thought it proper to consult the Convocation about this critical point'. He was answered by a whig army officer that 'he might, if he thought fit, consult the Convocation, for his own particular instruction; but that it would be derogatory from the rights of the Commons of England to advise on this occasion with an inferior assembly who had

Figure 6 *The Duke of Queensberry & Dover presenting the Act of Union to Queen Anne, 1707.*

no share in the legislature'. In fact Convocation was prorogued during the Union debates in parliament to prevent communication between high church clergy in the Lower House and tories in the Commons.

Some members then tried a tactic which had been attempted by opponents of the treaty in the Edinburgh parliament, moving to postpone discussion of the first article until the rest had been considered. The committee rejected this motion by a great majority, whereupon its supporters seceded from the House. This left the others free to approve the first four articles.[50] On 8 February the rest of the articles were approved, 'so soon, that it was thought they interposed not delay and consideration enough, suitable to the importance of so great a transaction'.[51] Some tories objected to the indecent speed, 'crying out "post haste; post haste".' Sir Thomas Littleton very smartly pursued the allegory and said 'they did not ride post haste, but a good easy trot; and, for his part, as long as the weather was fair, the roads good, and the horses in heart, he was of opinion they ought to jog on, and not take up till it was night'. The House agreed to the committee's resolutions to accept the articles as ratified by the Scottish parliament and ordered a bill to be brought in to give them effect.[52] On 28 February it passed its third reading by 274 votes to 116 and went up the House of Lords.[53]

Their lordships had meanwhile approved the articles. As in the Lower House the tories had tried to postpone discussion of the first, but had been overruled. Haversham had then proposed a federal union. The whigs, scenting victory, forced a vote on this issue which the Court carried by 71 to 20. Although the tories also forced a vote on several of the articles, 'every division of the house was made with so great an inequality, that they were but twenty against fifty that were for the union'.[54] By 24 February all the articles had been approved by the Lords. The Queen had attended many of the debates in the Upper House, showing her support for the Union.

On 1 March the ratification bill came up from the Lower House. This had been drawn up in such a way, with just one enacting clause, 'that it cut off all debates'.[55] The only handle the opposition could use for a vote was the Act for security of the Scottish church, which was appended to the bill. Though the tories pressed two divisions on it they were defeated by 55 to 19 on each occasion.[56] On 6 March the Queen gave the royal assent. 'I make no doubt,' Anne declared when assenting to the Union, 'but it will remembered and spoke of hereafter to the honour of those who have been instrumental in bringing it to a happy conclusion.' And so, until recently, it was.

As the last sessions of the English and Scottish parliaments proceeded to a close their members became preoccupied with the arrangements for the first parliament of Great Britain. Tories in England set great store by the prospect of immediate elections to it, but were thwarted by the Court, which insisted that the current English parliament should survive until an election was due to it under the terms of the Triennial Act. This delayed a dissolution until 1708. In the Scottish parliament, too, the Court and squadrone members combined to defeat a move to have the first representatives from North Britain elected by the peers and voters at large. They rightly feared that this would produce a Country and possibly Jacobite majority. They therefore proposed that the Scottish contingent bound for Westminster should be chosen by the Estates.

The Union was to come into effect on 1 May 1707. Meanwhile a loophole was discovered by some merchants who found they could import into Scotland at the pre-Union low rates, and then bring goods into England without paying duty.[57] A petition was presented to parliament protesting at this. The Court thereupon brought in a bill on 8 April to make those who imported goods from abroad into Scotland liable to the English duties if they conveyed them into England after 1 May. Although the measure tried to exempt merchants resident in Scotland, it nevertheless provoked an outcry from Scottish merchants who claimed that it was a breach of the union. Robert Harley, who had been ill during the discussion of the articles and the ratification bill, returned to the Commons concerned about the unfair advantage this would give some importers. He exacerbated the situation by proposing to make the measure retroactive to 1 February. The Lords took cognizance of this and, led by the Junto, would not agree to it.[58] The Upper House could not alter a money bill so they merely indicated their dislike of the proposal. This unexpected clash between the two Houses was irksome to the Court. 'The close of the best sessions of Parliament that England ever saw,' Godolphin informed Marlborough, 'has been unhappily hindred by a wrangle between the 2 Houses.'[59] The Queen tried to resolve it by a brief prorogation, which technically brought business to an end so that the bill could be reintroduced in what was a new session. Meanwhile the Commons were asked to modify the bill to make it more acceptable to the Scots by dropping the stipulation that it refer back to 1 February. But instead they actually stiffened its provisions. Scottish merchants who were exempt from paying duties were now defined as those who had been born there or who resided there. This excluded naturalized Scots living in England, one of whom at least had moved considerable quantities of tobacco north of the border hoping to make a killing from the rebate on duty he would get when he brought it back into England. This raised grave legal questions, for since the accession of James VI and I the law had been that subjects born in either kingdom were subjects of the Crown in the other and had the same rights. The Lords therefore decided to consult the twelve judges of the courts of common pleas, exchequer and queen's bench for a ruling on the distinctions made in the bill, as well as on the sensitive matter of whether or not the whole measure was a breach of the Union. On 23 April the judges attended the Lords, but refused to offer an opinion on the matters in question, apparently on the grounds that they would prefer a test case to come before the courts. The Lords expressed some impatience with this response, and asked the twelve to retire to consider their position. When they returned they maintained a collective silence. The Lords were so incensed by this that they considered some kind of punishment, but thought better about it and adjourned the debate. Next day the Queen got everybody off the hook by proroguing parliament until 30 April, which left no time for anything to be done about the loophole.[60]

One week later the Union came into effect. There was a magnificent service of celebration in St Paul's attended by the Queen and a great retinue consisting of Scottish nobles, who had accompanied Queensberry from Edinburgh, and members of both Houses of the English parliament. In the evening there were bonfires and fireworks in London and throughout England. It was noted that in Scotland the celebrations were more muted. Bells played the tune, 'why should I be sad on my wedding day?' For one happy couple it was a real and not a symbolic nuptial occasion. White Kennet, dean of Peterborough, 'married a Scots Merchant to an Eng[lish] Lady by a Ring with this Motto *The Happy Union*'.[61]

7

1707

*

During his celebrated speech in the Scottish parliament Lord Belhaven aimed his main shafts not at the English whigs but at the 'triumvirate' of Godolphin, Harley and Marlborough. 'There has got up a kind of aristocracy, something like the famous triumvirate at Rome', he exclaimed.[1]

> They are a kind of undertakers and pragmatic statesmen, who, finding their own power and strength great, and answerable to their designs, will make bargains with our gracious Sovereign. They will serve her faithfully, but upon their own terms: this man must be turned out, and that man put in; and then they'll make her the most glorious Queen in Europe.

Even as he spoke strains had already appeared in their relationship. As we have seen, Harley had stiffened Anne's resolve not to give in to the demands of the Lord Treasurer and Captain General to admit Sunderland into office. For the time being, though, the tension between them remained concealed from the public.

Their private correspondence, however, reveals that the triumvirate broke up as a result of two separate strains. There was the tension caused by the protracted bishoprics crisis, which lasted throughout the year. And there was the shock brought on by Harley's bid to oust Godolphin from the treasury in the winter, which brought about his own sudden fall in February 1708.

The bishoprics crisis began when the bishop of Winchester died in November 1706. The Junto, anxious to obtain ecclesiastical as well as political posts, had reached an understanding with Godolphin and Marlborough that whig clergy would be preferred to vacant livings in the Church. It was unfortunate that the first see to become available was Winchester, the richest in England, for Godolphin had committed himself to translating Sir Jonathan Trelawny, the bishop of Exeter, to it. The whig leaders considered this to be reneging on the agreement, but Godolphin appeased them by undertaking to promote one of their followers to the see of Exeter when Trelawny left it. He also undertook to appoint whig clergymen to the bishopric of Chester and the Regius Chair of divinity at Oxford, which both became vacant through the deaths of their incumbents in January.

Anne regarded these deals as a challenge to her prerogative, an opinion which Harley privately stiffened. She had anyway committed herself to giving the professorship to one of his clerical acquaintances, George Smalridge. When the duumvirs found out about this commitment they began to suspect that the Secretary was primarily responsible for the resulting crisis. In fact, as far as the disposal of the vacant bishoprics was concerned, Anne's chief adviser was John Sharp, the archbishop of York. Sharp recommended two high church friends, Offspring Blackall and Sir William Dawes, to Exeter and Chester respectively. He also probably persuaded the queen to translate the bishop of Norwich to the bishopric of Ely when it too became available with the death of Simon Patrick on 31 May. Anne's denials that Harley's influence was at the bottom of the bishoprics affair were therefore valid.

Nevertheless Godolphin and Marlborough became convinced not only that Harley was behind it, but that it was part of a scheme to remodel the ministry along tory lines. Marlborough was so much of this view that in July he actually wrote to the queen to warn her that 'if anybody near your person is of opinion that the Torrys may be trusted, and at this time made use off, that you would be pleased to order them to put their project in writing, and know if they will charge themselves with the execution, then you will see their sincerity by excusing themselves'.[2] Godolphin decided to keep the bishoprics of Chester, Exeter and Norwich vacant 'till he can have Mr Freeman's assistance in these spirituall affairs', that is until Marlborough returned from the continental campaign.[3] This postponed the final resolution of the crisis until the winter.

Meanwhile, although Godolphin blamed Harley for it at the time, over the summer he became convinced that there was no scheme on foot, and that their difficulties over the bishoprics arose from 'the misfortune . . . that the Queen happens to bee intangled in a promise that is extreamly inconvenient'.[4] It seems that Godolphin was anxious to retain a good opinion of Harley. The duchess of Marlborough later recalled that 'at this time and some time after poor Lord Godolphin would not believe anything to the prejudice of Mr Harley . . . [and] sometimes would snap me up notwithstanding his good breeding when I said anything against Mr Harley'.[5] It also appears that the Secretary managed to conceal the true extent of his intrigues against the duumvirs until the parliamentary session. But it is likely too that at this stage Harley had no specific proposals for reversing the drift to the whigs which had set in since 1705.

One intrigue of Harley's which was definitely kept secret, even from close associates like Henry St John, was his encouragement of the Queen's regard for one of her bedchamber women, his cousin Abigail Hill.[6] Abigail played a key but contentious part in the political machinations of this year.

Ever since the duchess of Marlborough found out that the woman she had herself introduced into Anne's service in 1697 had been secretly married to Colonel Samuel Masham in 1707, Abigail has been ascribed a major role in the breakup of the triumvirate. Sarah was mortified to learn that Abigail Masham, as she had become sometime in the spring, had been given a present of £2000 by the queen. 'I discovered that my cousin was become an absolute favourite', she later recorded, '& I likewise then discovered beyond all dispute Mr. Harley's correspondence and interest at Court by means of this woman.'

The Conduct of the dowager duchess of Marlborough has been a key source for historians of Anne's reign since it was first published in 1742. Sarah's account of how she was ousted in the queen's affection by a mere bedchamber woman has come to be regarded by some as evidence of the importance of such intrigue in the politics of the reign.[7] The relatively recent availability of much more material, especially in the papers of Robert Harley and the archives from Blenheim Palace, has substantially revised opinions of Sarah's reliability. On the one hand, male historians especially have tended to dismiss her version of events as 'petticoat politics'. Thus it has rightly been pointed out that Anne never accepted Abigail as her social equal, as she had done Sarah, while Harley had his own access to the queen and did not need a bedchamber woman's intercession.[8] On the other hand scholarly analysis of the duchess's numerous drafts of the *Conduct* has shown how far her account of the episode was self-serving.[9] It could even have been psychologically necessary for Sarah to blame somebody else for the breach between her and the Queen, for in reality she had nobody to blame but herself. Her volcanic temperament had long since removed the deep regard with which Mrs Morley had held Mrs Freeman. The strain of coping with her uncontrollable temper is sufficient explanation for Anne's turning to the more deferential servant. There are even strange hints of sexual jealousy which the stunningly attractive duchess had for a woman so plain and acned that she was nicknamed 'Carbuncunella'. It is now impossible to substantiate innuendos of lesbianism in the relationship between Anne and Abigail. While it cannot be ruled out, the likelihood seems remote, not least in view of the queen's devotion to her husband, Prince George.[10]

George's influence on Anne has been consistently underestimated.

His political significance still remains shadowy. However, the fact that Samuel Masham was made a groom of his bedchamber in June 1706, while in the spring of 1707 Anne was persuaded to give him Lord Windsor's regiment as a special favour, provide tantalizing clues to another force operating behind the scenes in this year. 'It was said,' Burnet noted, 'that the prince was brought into the concert, and that he was made to apprehend that he had too small a share in the government, and that he was shut out from it by the great power that the duke of Marlborough and the Lord Treasurer had drawn into their hands.'[11] It was also reported in May that the Prince's Council was to be discontinued, and that he would have the earl of Orford as his vice-admiral.[12] These rumours, that the Junto had designs on his running of the Admiralty, may well have persuaded the Prince to take seriously Harley's view that they were encroaching unduly on the Queen's prerogative. Insofar as the Secretary's anxiety on this score, and prescription for remedying the situation, were advanced by Court intrigue, it could be that the intriguers included the Prince as well as the Queen.

This perhaps partly explains why the Prince's Council of the Admiralty became a prime target of the Junto's attack on the Court when parliament met in November. Admittedly, they had plenty of ammunition in the poor performance of the Admiralty in 1707. As Burnet observed:[13]

> France set out no fleet this year, and yet we never had greater losses on that element: the prince's council was very unhappy in the whole conduct of the cruizers and convoys: the merchants made heavy complaints, and not without reason: convoys were sometimes denied them; and when they were granted, they were often delayed beyond the time limited for the merchants to get their ships in readiness . . . many of the convoys, as well as the merchant ships, were taken . . .

The navy itself in fact performed well. Under Sir Cloudesley Shovell a combined Anglo-Dutch fleet efficiently supplied the allied forces led by prince Eugene which besieged Toulon that summer. 'In our history the Navy has sometimes stood by to watch the Army do the work' observed Sir Winston Churchill. 'Here was a case where a navy tried by its exertion and sacrifice to drive forward an army. It did not succeed.'[14] Toulon was meant to be the body blow to France's soft underbelly which would decisively end the war. But the Imperial commitment to the siege, on which all depended, was lukewarm. The Emperor sent troops to occupy Naples and Sicily which would have been invaluable in Provence. Eugene and the duke of Savoy led an army along the south coast of France from Nice to the main naval base of the French Mediterranean fleet. The fleet itself was scuttled to avoid being taken by Shovell's ships. Louis XIV, determined not to lose the base itself, threw in reinforcements to augment the forces which had been digging in ever since the allied plan had been known. Eugene concluded that they were invincible and ordered the raising of the siege. The 'great design' of 1707 had ended in failure.

Indeed so far from the campaign of this year bringing France to her knees, as Marlborough had hoped, it revived French fortunes. In The Netherlands Vendome replaced the incompetent Villeroy with orders to avoid engaging Marlborough in another battle, such as Ramillies, which had been so disastrous to French arms. He skilfully obeyed his instructions, and the two armies did little more than move like chess pieces across the board of Flanders and Brabant. In Germany Villars advanced into Wurtemberg after breaking through the lines of Stolhofen. He took Stuttgart and for much of the summer levied huge taxes from the locality, withdrawing only when his retreat back over the Rhine was threatened.

But the biggest reversal the allies suffered was in Spain. Just as the Emperor had weakened the army sent to Toulon by diverting troops to Naples, so his son 'Charles III' divided the allied army, sending forces into garrisons throughout Catalonia and Aragon. This left a small force of Dutch, English and Portuguese under the earl of Galway and Das Minas to take on the Bourbon army, which was, ironically, led by Marlborough's illegitimate nephew the duke of Berwick. The allied army was outnumbered by about two to one when they encountered their French and Spanish opponents at Almanza on 14/25 April. Before they finished the battle they were only a third the size of the opposing army since the Portuguese fled the field. The result was a rout. After Almanza the allies would never again be in a position to prise Philip V off the throne of Spain by force of arms.

The disastrous campaign ended with the death of Sir Cloudesley Shovell on his return from the Mediterranean. His ship *The Association* ran aground in the Scilly Isles, and while the crew was drowned he was apparently murdered by a woman who robbed his body of valuables. The wreck of the admiral's flagship deepened the gloom of a year which had totally failed to fulfil the promise of its predecessor.

The gloom cast a pall over the meeting of the first parliament of Great Britain in October. *Switch and Spur*, an anonymous tory verse, imagined what Anne would have said to the Houses if she told the truth, instead of retailing what her ministers wanted them to hear.[15] In the actual speech she put as fair a gloss as possible on the defeat at Almanza and the retreat from Toulon.[16] Of the failure to take Toulon she said 'though it had not wholly its desired effect [it] has nevertheless been attended with many great and obvious advantages to the common cause in this year; and has made our way more easy, I hope, to greater in the next'. Although she, or rather her ministers, admitted that 'the French have gained ground upon us in Spain', she pointed out that they had been driven out of Italy so that 'it is become more easy for all the allies to join their assistance next year, for enabling the king of Spain [i.e. the Habsburg claimant] to recover his affairs in that kingdom and to reduce the whole Spanish monarchy to his obedience'. Having painted a rosy picture of prospects in the war she went on to urge the Commons to vote supplies for it. 'The plain necessity of continuing this war,' she insisted, 'the reasonable prospect of putting a good end to it, if we be not wanting to ourselves, and the honour of the first parliament of Great Britain are I make no doubt sufficient arguments to invite you to provide the necessary supplies which I am obliged to desire of you for the ensuing campaign in all parts, and particularly for the timely support of the king of Spain and the making good our treaty with Portugal.'

The poet put it differently: 'Toulon's preserved' he observed, noting ironically that towns taken in Italy were no recompense for the reputed million pounds spent on the attempt, while

> Spain is quite lost; and Portugal in danger
> Unless the last Extremity make her change her
> Resolves, and quit th'Alliance, which once shaken
> Will soon dissolve.

As for the supplies

> Eight Millions Sterling and Ten Thousand Men
> In name (but in reality ten times ten)
> Must be advanc'd forthwith; make no Delay
> But (Switch and Spur) post on . . .
>   Speed the *Supplys*; let nothing Intervene;
> They only can present a happier *Scene*
> Next year than this: If so, We'l ride in Coaches;
> If not, Then with *Sir Cloudesly, Buenos Noches.*

Although it was technically a new parliament there was no general election to it. For different reasons neither Harley nor the duumvirs wished for a dissolution in 1707. The Secretary realized that the tory contingent at Westminster, on which his scheme rested, would probably be diminished at the polls. Godolphin and Marlborough also anticipated whig gains, which would make the Junto more formidable and put them in an even more invidious position between the five lords and the queen. As far as the English members were concerned, therefore, the only adjustment was the disqualification of those in places rendered incompatible with seats in the Commons by the Regency Act.

The Scottish contingent of 16 peers and 45 MPs, however, did mark a major change. As in England so in Scotland there was no general election, the Court fearing that the aggrieved Scots would take their umbrage at the Union out on the government by returning Jacobites. Consequently the representation of the northern nation was made up of nominees of the last Edinburgh parliament. The Court and Squadrone swept the board in the nomination of the 16 peers, with thirteen Courtiers led by Queensberry, together with Montrose, Roxburgh and Tweeddale from the new party. The same combination also virtually monopolized the 45 members of the Lower House, with 29 Courtiers, 13 squadrone or New party supporters, and only three out and out opponents of the Union.[17] These additions on the whole strengthened the Court's position in both Houses, though the squadrone was inclined to vote with the Junto. The alliance of the Court with the majority of Scottish members was demonstrated on the first day of the session when George Booth, an English whig, proposed John Smith as Speaker, 'which was seconded by Mr Montgomery, a Scotch member, which was unanimously agreed by the House'.[18]

The unanimity did not last long, for although Harley confidently prophesied that 'if it be desired it will not be difficult to have it a quiet session' it turned out to be the most contentious of the decade.[19] Three issues were to dominate the first half of the session: the Admiralty; Scottish administration; and the war in Spain. On all three questions the Junto was to ally with the ministry's tory opponents to give it a hard time in both Houses.

In the Lords an obviously pre-arranged attack on the Admiralty was so managed as to give the utmost dramatic impact. On 12 November Wharton ostentatiously brushed aside the usual consideration of the Queen's speech at the start of a session. When Godolphin 'moved that the House would send an address of thanks to the Queen for her speech my Ld Wharton said there was more necessity for redressing than addressing' and drew attention to 'the great decay of trade'. Somers was up immediately to second him, and 'enlarged upon the ill condition and late mismanagements of the navy'.[20] When Stamford tried to persuade the House to turn to the consideration of the Queen's speech the tory leaders Buckingham, Rochester and Guernsey struck in with the Junto and succeeded in putting aside a day for considering the state of the nation instead.

On the appointed day, 19 November, the Junto again displayed their flair for the theatrical by presenting a petition from 154 merchants urging the government to give their ships better naval protection. But when Haversham and Rochester went on to turn the occasion into an attack on the whole ministry the whigs backed off, and eventually Wharton moved for a week's adjournment of the debate. This *volte face* puzzled observers. As one commented, 'whether he did not like his company or what other reason he had, the vulgar are much at a loss to know'.[21] The likeliest explanation is that the aims of the tory and whig lords were different. Rochester and his allies were anxious to use the Admiralty issue as a handle to overturn the whole administration, whereas Wharton and the rest of the Junto wanted only to disgrace the Prince's council, and particularly George Churchill, in order to replace it with Lord Orford. The enquiry into naval mismanagements in the Lords was referred to a select committee, which gathered evidence for several weeks, thus shelving the issue temporarily.

Meanwhile in the Commons a petition from several merchants was presented on 15 November much the same as that which Wharton introduced into the Lords. When it was debated on 20 November, however, it aroused little enthusiasm. According to Burnet 'the complaints were feebly managed at the bar of the House of commons; for it was soon understood, that not only the prince but the queen was likewise concerned herself much in this matter; and both looked on it as a design levelled at their authority.'[22] Some excitement was generated on 1 December when the House asked for a copy of the commission to the Prince's Council and of the oath taken by its members. This, noted James Vernon, 'looks like questioning the conveniency if not the legality of such a constitution, which may be thought the shortest way to put an end to it, without assigning any maladministration'.[23] On 13 December, however, the whole attack petered out 'without passing any censure'.[24] The tories were not keen, while even some whigs were not convinced that those who had provoked the inquiry had sufficient evidence to convict the Admiralty of maladministration.

Although the Court survived the first onslaught over naval affairs relatively unscathed, it fared very badly on the question of Scottish administration. In her speech at the opening of the session the queen had drawn attention to 'several matters expressly made liable by the Articles of the Union to the consideration of the Parliament of Great Britain'. On 29 November the Commons went into a committee to consider these. For two hours the debate was confined to Scottish members. George Baillie, a squadrone supporter, 'spoke first . . . and concluded with a motion that for the future there shall be but one councell in Great Britain'. This was a direct attack on the Court, since the separate Scottish Privy Council gave it a great degree of control over affairs in Scotland. Consequently the ministry strove to keep it while the opposition was determined to abolish it. From the outset the Court appreciated that the Edinburgh Council was so unpopular that it was not a question of whether to abolish it but of when to do so. The ministry was anxious to retain it until after the general election due in the Spring, since the Council had influence over Scottish constituencies. A Scots member in the Court interest therefore moved to consider it at a more appropriate time. Seeing that the Scots were almost equally divided on the question Harley, Harcourt and Walpole intervened and spoke against it, apparently moving for an adjournment. These were bad tactics, because after that 'the southern Tories and a great body of the whigs joining for the question, it was carried by an infinite majority without a division.' One member who was present calculated that if there had been a division the Court would not have mustered twenty votes.[25]

The debate was resumed on 4 December when the opposition, emboldened by their success six days earlier, raised two other Scottish issues. The first, that the militia of Scotland should be on the same basis as that in England, passed without much debate. But the Court intervened successfully against the second, which was that Scottish justices of the peace should have the same powers as English JPs. Lord Coningsby pointed out that this proposal encroached upon the heritable jurisdictions which the Union had guaranteed. The Court, anxious to retain all it could of the administrative machinery of Scotland, partly because it was so amenable to central influence, partly because it did not wish to jeopardize the Union, managed to move an adjournment at this stage.[26] On 9 December, however, the opposition returned to the attack and carried their resolution about the justices. A Court motion to adjourn was this time defeated by eight votes, after which it was resolved that Scottish sheriffs should act as returning officers in parliamentary elections.

Such a narrow defeat for the Court led the managers to pull out all the stops in an endeavour to reverse it. Harley entertained some fifty members who had opposed the motion in the committee the night before they were to be debated in the whole House. When the debate resumed on 11 December it was again dominated by the Scots, with the Scottish peers present in the gallery. When the resolution concerning the equal footing of the Scottish with English justices was debated, a Scot proposed a Court amendment 'as far as it shall be consistent with the articles of the Union'. William Bennet, a Squadrone member, thought the Court was getting the better on this occasion, and went up to the gallery to receive instructions from the duke of Roxburgh, who advised his connection to concede defeat. On his way back to the floor of the House, however, Bennet was intercepted by William Bromley and other leading tories, who urged him to keep up the pressure on the Court, assuring him of tory support.[27] In the division enough whigs 'joining with the Tories were the prevailing party and threw out the amendment by 149 against 113'.[28]

Thereafter the combination of tories and opposition whigs carried all before it. On 20 December Sir James Montague the Solicitor General, cautioned the committee which had been charged with bringing in a bill to enact the resolutions that it would be well advised to compile two, keeping that concerning the militia separate from the others. Otherwise, since it involved money, the Lords could wreck the whole measure by amending what could be regarded as a finance bill. This advice was accordingly taken to avoid constitutional complications. Consequently after the Christmas recess two bills were introduced into the Commons, one for rendering the Union more complete, the other concerning the Scottish militia. On 15 January they passed their second reading.

In the committee on the first bill on 22 January the opposition moved to abolish the Scottish Privy Council on 1 May 1708, 'the auspicious day on which the Union began and was therefore properest for making it secure'. Sir David Dalrymple on behalf of the Court suggested April 1709, but the opposition carried the first of May by 151 votes to 117. Defeated in committee the Court next day made an effort to reverse the decision on the floor of the House, but were outvoted again by 179 to 118.[29] Despite the tremendous setback of an increased majority against them the ministers determined to fight for the preservation of the Edinburgh Council until 1709, and on 28 January 'the Court tugg'd hard at the last reading to get a reprieve for the privy Council to the next April twelve-month but were overborne'.[30]

The struggle was then carried up to the Lords along with the bill. On 5 February in a committee after the second reading the Court peers offered a compromise. Instead of insisting upon the continuance of the Council until April 1709 they now asked only that it should be continued until 1 October 1708. The motive behind this move was patent. As Burnet observed 'it was visible that this was proposed only in order to the managing elections for the next parliament'.[31] As a result 'all the tories and high whigs and all the bishops, save two, joined against the council' to defeat the Court by 50 votes to 45.[32] Godolphin now made frantic efforts to rescue the Council in the last reading scheduled for 7 february. The day before he energetically canvassed peers who had voted against the Court in the previous day's committee trying to persuade them to support it. Thus at the urgent request of Godolphin the earl of Westmorland, deputy warden of the Cinque ports under Prince George, was summoned to the Prince's apartment at Kensington early in the morning to be pressed to support 'a business going to be in Parliament wherein the Queen thinks her service very much concerned'. Westmorland observed that 'by this discourse I found the treasurer who was much for having the Council the better to make parties was the occasion of my journey'.[33] Godolphin spoke five times in the debate, trying to defeat the bill by reviving the argument that the clause concerning justices contravened heritable jurisdictions which were specifically guaranteed by the Act of

Union. Despite all the Lord Treasurer's efforts the bill was carried by seven votes, and received the royal assent on 13 February.

The separate Scottish militia bill passed the Commons on 11 February and the Lords indicated their acceptance of it on the 25th. But it never received the royal assent. It was in fact the last bill ever to be vetoed by the monarch, though this, so far from rousing hostility passed almost without comment.[34]

The government's defeat over the Scottish Privy Council was the biggest setback suffered by the Court in this decade. Yet the potential outcome of the inquiries into the progress of the war in Spain, the third major issue raised in this eventful session, was even more dangerous, for the ministry ran the risk of incurring censure not for something they wished to do, but for something they had done. They were accused of neglecting the Iberian theatre and thus of contributing to the disastrous defeat of the allies at Almanza.

On 19 December the government was urged by the tories in the Lords to take more care of the Spanish theatre. When assurances were given on this score, the Junto chimed in to move resolutions to make these effective by declaring that 'no peace could be safe or honourable till Spain and the West Indies were recovered from the House of Bourbon'. Three days later the Commons concurred with this resolution, which it was hoped 'may prevent, or, at least, abate any peevishness in those enquiries'.[35]

The hopes were not fulfilled, for an inquiry had already been started in the Lower House which was not to end until the government had been charged with gross neglect of the peninsula. It began on 8 December 'in the angry corner', when Colonel James Grahme, a back-bench tory, asked questions which led to a series of resolutions and orders: that the state of the war in Spain should be considered on 13 December; that the House should be informed how many forces were in Spain or had been sent to Spain since 1705, what forces were at the battle of Almanza and what other forces were in the peninsula at the time, and how the £250,000 voted for the war in Spain in 1706 had been spent?[36] On 13 December Henry St John, the Secretary at war, gave the House an account of her Majesty's forces that were at the battle of Almanza, and of such others as were in the peninsula then, as well as giving the actual numbers of troops which had been subsequently sent there, while James Brydges, the paymaster, presented accounts of how the £250,000 had been spent. No debate arose immediately, as Grahme 'now proposed the putting it off til Thursday, so' one Court supporter hoped 'that may keep cold till after the Holydays'.[37] The following Thursday, however, two leading high church tories, William Bromley and Ralph Freeman, moved for further papers relating to the war in Spain. They included demands for an account of what numbers the several regiments consisted of which were in English pay at the time of the battle of Almanza. Then Grahme again moved for postponing the debate, this time until 17 January.[38]

When the debate resumed on 17 January the clerk's table was loaded with a pile of papers containing information about the war in the peninsula since the taking of Barcelona in 1705. Two separate items were however crucial to the course the inquiry took. Henry St John, the Secretary at war, had provided the account of the number of troops in English pay at the time of the battle of Almanza which had been demanded. These came to 8,660 men. James Brydges the Paymaster, had also presented accounts of money paid for troops in Spain and Portugal during the year ending 23 December 1707, from which it appeared that the Exchequer had received £631,213 for the maintenance of 29,395 men in that period. The significance of these documents only emerged after the House had spent three days reading through the mass of information which had been placed before it. On 29 January Sir Thomas Hanmer, a leading tory, made one of those smooth, gentle, deadly speeches for which he was famous. After accusing the government of neglecting Spain, he ended by moving a resolution 'that it appeared to this House that of 29,000 men the Parliament had given money for, the last year, for the war in Spain and Portugal, there were not in either place at the time of the battle of Almanza above 8,660 men'. The papers of Brydges and St John had been compared and drawn up into this devastating proposal, which had the ministry reeling. St John himself put up such a poor defence in attempting to explain the discrepancy that it appeared to some that he 'was not prepared for such a question'. He claimed he had the list from Lord Tyrawly and that it did not contain officers or NCOs, while some of the money voted for the Iberian theatre had been spent in diverse other ways. Thus Charles III had been given £50,000, while two regiments of deserters from Philip V's army had been taken into the service of the allies and paid by the British. Thereupon the whole tory party 'and a few of the country whigs began to grow warm'.[39] 'The question was very much pressed, and there seemed to be another question to follow it of mismanagement and misapplication of money.'[40] The House continued in a ferment until eight o'clock in the evening, when at last the Junto whigs came to the rescue of the Court and got them off the hook by moving an adjournment until 3 February, so that they could be better informed. This was carried by 187 to 172.[41]

Although the Junto whigs rescued the Court on 29 January, when the debate resumed on 3 February they voted with the opposition. After St John had presented another account, which did a little to mitigate the discrepancy, the Commons allowing that the figure 8,660 did not include officers and their servants, the Junto spokesman Sir Joseph Jekyll moved an address 'desiring her Majesty to order an account to be brought to them, how it came to pass there were no more troops in Spain at that time'.[42] Despite a weak attempt to obstruct the address it passed without a division. Harley later attributed the change in tactics by the Junto to a failure of communication between the whig lords and their adherents in the Commons on 29 January.[43] The whig MPs assumed then that 'it was their business to stand by the ministers in everything' on the first occasion. In fact

> the junto wanted at this time so fair an opportunity to bite the ministers, and force them into a compliance with what they had long been bargaining for, and therefore directed their creatures by all means to let the address pass as smart as the tories would have it; so when this debate came on again [3 February] the warriors were grown as tame as lambs, and the address went without any more than a little faint shewish opposition.

What the Junto 'had long been bargaining for' was Harley's removal from office. This came about in the next few days, before Anne answered the address.

The fall of Harley still remains almost as much of a puzzle as it did to the contemporary who wrote that 'the spring of his disgrace at Court . . . has so many intricate pipes which lead up to it, that we must at present lodge it amongst the mysteries of State'.[44] The bishoprics crisis, which had strained relations between him and the duumvirs during the summer, was not part of the complex plumbing, being finally resolved on 6 January. Blackhall and Dawes then became bishops of Chester and Exeter, but at the same time the Junto were assured that future church appointments would go to whig clergymen. Thus immediately Charles Trimnell was promoted to the vacant see of Norwich while White Kennett was made dean of Peterborough.[45] If anything Harley conceded dispensation of patronage to his colleagues since it was Marlborough's nominee, Thomas Potter, and not his own, Smalridge, who obtained the professorship of Divinity at Oxford.

The parliamentary situation was somehow related to the Secretary's downfall, though exactly how is not easy to ascertain. The session had proved a nightmare for the Court ever since it began, with the tories and Junto whigs combining against it on the issues of the Admiralty, the Scottish Privy Council and the Almanza debacle. Lord Somers was 'persuaded the carrying of the Bill for taking away the Scottish Privy Council was no little ingredient towards making the changes' while a whig member of parliament, Thomas Johnson, claimed that 'the grand fault is that they [the Harleyites] did not prevent the House of Commons coming to the resolution they did relating to Spain'.[46]

Something had to be done to retrieve the Court's position in parliament if the slide towards disaster was to be averted. In the middle of December Godolphin and Harley combined for the last time to present a united front against the leaders of both parties. All the power and influence of the Crown was to be mobilized to give this effect. Anne, delighted to find her ministers co-operating in a determined effort to keep the party wolves from her door, unofficially notified her intentions of supporting them some days before they were announced publicly. On 16 December 1707 she informed archbishop Sharp 'that she meant to change her measures, and give no countenance to the whig lords, but that all the tories, if they would, should come in and all the whigs likewise, that would show themselves to be in her interest should have favour'.[47] The occasion of her public announcement was a speech to both Houses of parliament, polished and re-polished by Godolphin, Harley and Lord Chancellor Cowper, which she delivered on 18 December.[48] 'She is for the future firmly resolved to govern upon such principles as will incline her to side with the violence neither of whig or tory,' James Brydges inferred from the queen's speech, 'that she will never make bargains with either party to persuade them to do that which a sense of their duty alone ought to lead them to, but that those shall always be the object of her countenance and favour who without expecting terms come voluntarily into the promoting of her service.'[49]

Unfortunately the Court's problems with parliament actually worsened after the Christmas recess, when in addition to its troubles over the Edinburgh Council and the Spanish theatre, discoveries were made of breaches of security in Harley's office which his opponents could not but exploit. A clerk, William Gregg, was discovered to be communicating correspondence to France. Although it was proof of no more than carelessness on the Secretary's part, he was bound to be implicated by his political enemies, particularly the other Secretary, Sunderland.

Harley began once more to insist that the only solution to the Court's difficulties was an accommodation with the tories. He actually got this proposal onto the agenda of a ministerial meeting at the chancellor of the exchequer's house on 14 January. Among those invited were the treasurer and the moderate whig duke of Devonshire. Judging by an agenda of 'preliminaries' which Harley drew up for the meeting it was to discuss a major realignment with the tories. But Godolphin refused to come in on such a scheme. Harley therefore opened up negotiations with tory leaders like Sir Thomas Hanmer, Sir Henry Bunbury and Peter Shakerley without the treasurer's knowledge but with the queen's approval. He even got round to constructing a 'shadow' Cabinet which brought tories into high office. Thus the treasury was to be put into commission with himself at the head, St John and Lord Pawlet were to be secretaries of state, Harcourt was to be made keeper of the great seal, the duke of Buckingham Lord privy seal and the duke of Beaufort master of the horse.[50]

The implementation of such a scheme would have required the removal of Godolphin, though Harley clearly hoped to retain the services of Marlborough.[51] How realistic such expectations were in 1708 is a matter for conjecture. Two years later he successfully engineered a ministerial revolution which ousted the treasurer yet retained the Captain General. But that was in very different political circumstances. It is possible that Marlborough toyed with the idea even on this occasion, for his correspondence was noticeably less abrasive than Godolphin's on the subject of Harley's machinations until something happened ten days before the Secretary's fall to change his mind.

Sometime in the week ending Saturday 24 January Harley had an interview with Anne and drew her attention to some 'mismanagements' of Godolphin and Marlborough which had just come to his notice. As the Commons spent much of that week reading through the papers relating to Spain, it could be that he had spotted the discrepancy between the number of troops voted for the service there and those actually present at the battle of Almanza. He might even have drawn it to the attention of Hanmer, who was to use it as political dynamite in the debate on 29 January. If this were so, then, so far from being unprepared for the resolution, Harley and St John were in collusion with the tory opposition to discredit the other Secretary, Sunderland, whose office bore responsibility for relations with the Iberian powers, and Godolphin, who would be implicated in the charges of mismanagement and misappropriation of money which were to follow the bombshell dropped by Hanmer. This would account for the pained language of the letter which the treasurer wrote on the subject of Harley's 'treachery'. Godolphin sent Attorney-General Harcourt to inform Harley that he had incurred his displeasure in the evening of the 29th after the Almanza debate. Harley sought out Marlborough the next day and learned the 'particulars' of his offence. He then wrote a letter to justify his behaviour, protesting that he 'never entertained the least thought derogating from your lordship or prejudicial to your interest'. Godolphin replied, 'I have received your letter and am very sorry for what has happened to lose the good opinion I had so much inclination to have of you, but I cannot help seeing and hearing, nor believing my senses. I am very far from having deserved it of you. God forgive you!'[52]

Marlborough, whose conduct was not implicitly censured during the Almanza debate, was more accommodating at first, even though he suspected from the behaviour of St John in parliament that some deal with the tories had been struck.[53] On Saturday 7 February, however, Marlborough wrote to the Queen to offer his resignation 'since all the faithful services I have endeavoured to do you, and the unwearied pains I have taken for these ten days [i.e. since 29 January] to satisfy and convince your Majesty's own mind have not been able to give you any such impression of the false and treacherous proceedings of Mr Secretary Harley to Lord Treasurer and myself.'[54] Anne arranged to give him and Godolphin a final decision the next day at Kensington, where the Cabinet was to meet.

On 8 February Anne received Godolphin and the duke and duchess of Marlborough in a room adjacent to that where the Cabinet was sitting. James Stanhope, who probably got the story from the duke of Somerset, who played a key role in the proceedings, described the encounter.[55]

> First l[or]d Trea[surer] told the Q[ueen] he came to resign the staff, that serving her longer with one so perfidious as Mr H[arley] was impossible. She replied, in respect of his long service she would give him till tomorrow to consider. Then he should do as he pleased, with all she could find enough glad of that staff.
>
> Then came Lady Duchess with great duty and submission, that she had served her ever with affec[tion] and tenderness: her utmost had been her duty and she had been faithful in it. The reply is said to be: 'You shall consider of this till tomorrow, then if you desire it, I shall then advise you to go to your little house in St Albans and there stay till *Blenheim house* is ready for your Grace.
>
> Then entered the duke prepared with his utmost address. He told her he had ever served her with obedience and fidelity, that [he] had used that sword he must now resign to her to her honour and advantage; that he must lament he came in competition with so vile a creature as H[arley]; that his fidelity and duty should continue so long as his breath; that it was his duty to be speedy in resigning his commands that she might put the sword into some other hand immediately, and it was also his duty to tell her he feared the Dutch would immediately on that news make a peace very ruinous for England. 'And then, my Lord', says [she], 'will you resign me your sword. Let me tell you' says [she] 'your service I have regarded to the utmost of my power, and if you do, my lord, resign your sword, let me tell you, you run it through my head.' She went to the council, begging him to follow; he refusing, so the scene ended.

It was a highly symbolic scene. It showed that Anne was a fighter who was prepared to stand up for her prerogative of appointing and dismissing ministers. But it also shows that Marlborough was in a very real sense the prime minister, who could have his way about men as well as measures as long as Anne was committed to the War.

There ensued what must have been one of the more fraught Cabinet meetings. When Harley tried to contribute to the discussion the duke of Somerset stood up and said, 'if her Majesty suffered that fellow (pointing to Harley) to treat affairs of the war without the advice of the General he could not serve her; and so left the Council'.[56] After other matters had been dealt with the earl of Pembroke closed the meeting by expressing the hope 'that all fair means possible might be used to compose these dissentions, before they should come to the ears of the people'.[57]

After the meeting broke up Anne was subjected to pressure from at least four Cabinet ministers to dismiss Harley or they would resign.[58] The parliamentary reaction on the following day left her with little option. Though the Commons had arranged to debate a supply bill on 9 February they let it lie on the table. In the Lords Wharton moved an enquiry into the Gregg affair, and a select committee was chosen by ballot which consisted of seven staunch whigs, including three of the Junto. The implication was clear. Harley was to be at least impeached, while some observers thought that a bill of attainder was a possibility. Anne now admitted that the game was up, and sent for the duke of Marlborough to inform him that she would ask Harley to resign. Next day she saw the Secretary who agreed to 'concur for your sake'. On 11 February he resigned. Three of his close associates left office with him: Sir Simon Harcourt, the attorney general; Thomas Mansell, the comptroller of the household; and Henry St John, the Secretary at war. They did so because they regarded the fall of Harley 'as a full declaration of the ministry's intention to join entirely with the Whigs, which they thought was inconsistent with the declarations they had made to them, and the assurances which by their authority and commission, as also by the Queen's commands, they had given the Tories that no such thing should be done.'[59]

In the ministerial changes necessitated by Harley's fall the 'duumvirs', Marlborough and Godolphin, made no immediate attempt to bring in the Junto. Having forced the Queen to part with Harley they were in no position to go further and demand posts for the whig leaders even if they had been so inclined. In fact they showed no such inclination, and doubtless hoped that the removal of Harley would at least temporarily appease the Junto. Indeed Marlborough wished to keep the changes to a minimum, offering to retain the services of St John for whom he had a particular regard.[60] The vacancies created by the departure of the Harleyites were either filled with so-called 'Lord Treasurer's whigs', or left vacant.[61] Thus Henry Boyle was moved from the Exchequer to replace Harley as Secretary, the Chancellorship was earmarked for the Speaker John Smith, and Robert Walpole took up St John's post as Secretary at war, while the offices of attorney-general and comptroller of the household remained unfilled until after the end of the session.

Harley resigned on 11 February and the session did not end until 1 April. For nearly two months, therefore, the ministry reconstructed on so narrow a basis had to face a parliament which so far had proved almost unmanageable. Moreover the Spanish inquiry had still to be resolved. It was with some anxiety that the duumvirs faced parliament after the fall of Harley. The attitude of the tories was easy to predict, for they received the Harleyites 'with both arms as strayed sheep come into the true fold'.[62] Thus reinforced their opposition would be more intransigent than ever. The key question was, how would the whigs react?

The Junto were unhappy at the changes attendant upon the resignations of the Secretary and his three colleagues. So far from being a move in their direction they were not even consulted about them. Somers, who of all the Junto Lords most expected, and most deserved, a better understanding with the ministry on this occasion, sent the earl of Portland the news of the changes and concluded: 'Your lordship will perceive by my account that I am not let into any secrets.'[63] And Sir John Cropley, one of the 'lord treasurer's whigs', commenting on the Junto's reaction in a letter to his patron the third earl of Shaftesbury, observed 'there is much anger that the present changes have been filled with creatures of the court and not some of theirs'.[64]

The Junto expressed their resentment at the new appointments on 19 February in the House of Lords, where:[65]

> Lord Wharton moved a very vexatious matter, the fresh enquiry of the navy. Lord Rochester seconded the motion saying the errors and mismanagements had been so notorious he blushed to name them considering the person who was at the head of the sea administration, to which my Lord Treasurer replied, he would have hoped he might have blushed in making so severe a reflection on the person now at the head of the administration. Then rose up Lord Somers and said England must be undone if the sea affair stood longer on the present foot, that England could bear it no longer.

This revived attack on the Admiralty surpassed in intensity the onslaught of the previous November. By now the Lords had ample evidence to sustain their charges, and this time they were levelled not at George Churchill but overtly against Prince George. Some observers were led to believe that the outcome would be the replacement of the Prince as Lord Admiral.[66] In fact it ended on 25 February with a blistering address to the Queen. By a patently obvious device the peers pretended to shield her husband from criticism. 'We do not mean,' they hypocritically claimed, 'that anything in this address should in the least reflect upon him.' But his colleagues on the Prince's Council received a tremendous rebuke. 'There cannot be plainer proof that some persons employed by the Lord High Admiral have made the worst use imaginable of the trust he honours them with.' The address ended with a plea 'that the seamen be encouraged, the trade protected, discipline restored, and a new spirit and vigour put into the whole administration of the navy.' Anne's reply was icily ambiguous.

> I will take care to make the most useful observations on the several particulars contained and referred to in your address. It was always my opinion, that the encouragement of trade and seamen, and the good management of the navy, are of the greatest importance to the prosperity of this kingdom. And therefore you may be assured, I will use my utmost endeavours to encourage all those whose duty it is effectually to perform these services.

The Lords felt it would be sufficient merely to have their address and the reply printed.[67]

A revival of the Admiralty controversy only a few days after Harley's fall boded ill for the stability of the reshaped ministry. The test of its viability would come with the parliamentary reaction to the Court's explanation of the discrepancy between the numbers voted for service in Spain and those actually in the peninsula at the time of the battle of Almanza. Anxious hours must have been devoted to the preparation of the answer to the angry address of 3 February.[68] It was presented to the Commons on 18 February. In it the government tried to ward off the threatened censure. First they laid some of the blame on the Harleyites. 'Her Majesty cannot but be very much concerned to find that matter has not been fully stated to the House.' Then they wrung full advantage from the amendment which St John had obtained whereby the House had conceded that officers and their servants were not included in his original estimate of 8,660 men. Claiming that these were a quarter of the establishment, and that the first estimate had been much too low, they increased the numbers present in the peninsula in 1707 to no fewer than 18,307. Finally the discrepancy between this figure and that voted, which was now much smaller than the address alleged, was owing to the formidable difficulties in raising men and keeping the armed forces at full strength in that theatre.[69] 'The Queen yesterday sent us a long answer to our address concerning the last terrible vote of 21,000 absent soldiers', Sir John Cropley informed Lord Shaftesbury. 'You will see it in print. She complains a false account has been laid before the House which was the ground of that vote. Now a mighty ferment will be on Tuesday to affirm the judgment of the House or to join in the Queen's opinion.'[70]

The debate on the answer took place on 24 February. So far from it provoking a mighty ferment at first 'there was a long silence, which looked as if [it] would end without doing more than adjourning, and it was whispered about as if it was intended to pass without censure or approbation.'[71] Eventually a Court supporter broke the silence by claiming that it indicated acceptance of the Queen's reply.[72] This prompted John Ward, a tory lawyer, and Sir Thomas Hanmer to compare the two accounts and deny that the answer had explained away the discrepancy. They concluded with a motion that the deficiencies of English troops in Spain were due to the lack of timely recruits. A debate then ensued on this question. St John 'spoke in his own vindication that the account he brought them did not differ from this above 1400 men'. When it came to the vote, however, the Court carried the division by 230 to 175. This was due to the Junto's support. Harley, who ostentatiously read a book during the debate and said not a word, voted for the motion.[73] He was contemptuous of the whig leadership. Their followers having rescued the ministry in the first Almanza debate on 29 January, and then voted for the address on 3 February, their tactics in this final debate struck him as a cynical example of pure opportunism.[74]

> An answer to the address is trimmed up (in the Queen's name) to palliate as much as possible, but too narrow to hide the miscarriage from any man that was not willing to be blind to it, and the nation is told plainly that one-third of our army has always been allowed for officers' servants; (a fine cheat for whigs to countenance or acquiesce in) however the Junto had gained their point, and now the party in the house were to let this pass for satisfaction, and so the ministers were brought off from this difficulty. Thus the same men who at first set themselves with all their might to defend the ministers in a matter wherein the nation had been notoriously abused, presently when they are bid, leap over the stick the other way, and join in a complaint against the same ministers for the same fault, and then at the word of command leap back again as you were, all's well, nobody is to be blamed.

Looked at from the Junto point of view, this was an impressive display of whig party discipline. One of their adherents, immediately after the vote, 'proposed an address of thanks to her Majesty for the measures she had entered into for the recovery of Spain . . . which was carried without opposition'.[75] 'Thus went the most important day of this session', commented Addison, adding later 'we look upon the debate . . . as that which has fixt all men in their proper parties and thoroughly establisht the present Ministry'.[76]

8

1708

'Yesterday's Dutch post advises that the French are making great preparations at Dunkirk for a descent', reported a newsletter on 17 February 1708, adding 'some say upon Zealand, others upon Scotland'.[1] This was the first public news of the attempted invasion of Scotland by James Edward Stuart, known to Scottish Jacobites as James VIII, and to English Jacobites as James III. To his opponents he had been known as the pretended Prince of Wales, but now he came to be called, even by the queen, simply 'the Pretender'.[2]

The preparations involved a fleet of five battleships, including *The Salisbury*, an English vessel captured in 1703, twenty-four frigates, and some 6,000 soldiers. These forces were put under the command of the Chevalier de Forbin. Jacobites hoped that the duke of Berwick, the victor of Almanza, would be put in charge of the expedition, but Louis XIV was not prepared to hazard so valuable a general in such a risky enterprise. Indeed the French king and his advisers do not seem to have shared the enthusiasm of the Pretender and his Jacobite adherents for the expedition. Where the subjects of James VIII confidently anticipated his accession to the throne of Scotland, Louis appears to have considered his prospects of success to be slender. It would, however, make a worthwhile diversion from the continental campaign, possibly necessitating the transportation of British troops from the Flemish theatre, thereby weakening the allied army. These divergent expectations were to create tensions between the Jacobites and their French allies during the invasion, and recriminations ever afterwards.

The British reaction was directed by Marlborough, who was still in London. He ordered Cadogan to reconnoitre the activity in Dunkirk, and if there was a design on Scotland to make contingent plans to transport troops to Britain. He arranged for what troops there were to be spared in England and Ireland to reinforce Lord Leven's garrison in Edinburgh castle. He also liaised with his brother George Churchill of the Admiralty Council to despatch ships commanded by Sir George Byng to blockade Dunkirk and thus prevent the expeditionary fleet from sailing. The Prince's Council, which had been much criticized in parliament during the current session, rose to the occasion.

Parliament, indeed, was still sitting, and on 4 March responded positively to the threat. Two bills were quickly passed, one making it a criminal offence to refuse the abjuration oath, another suspending Habeas Corpus until October. The Commons voted extraordinary supply to cover any charge the suppression of the invasion might incur. Both Houses addressed the Queen on the subject of the Pretender's project. They proceeded on this occasion in a non partisan spirit, showing a united front against the threat. It was a tory MP who first proposed an address 'to assure her Majesty that they would stand by her with their lives and fortunes, against the pretended Prince of Wales, and all other enemies, both at home and abroad'.[3] The address concluded by assuring Anne that 'no attempts of this kind shall deter us from supporting your majesty in the vigorous prosecution of the present war against France, until the monarchy of Spain be restored to the house of Austria, and your majesty have the glory to complete the recovery of the liberties of Europe'. The address was then hurried up to the Lords for their concurrence, after receiving which it was presented jointly to the Queen.

A later address from the Lords, however, congratulating Anne on the expedition's being aborted, was much more partisan. It pursued the whig vendetta against Harley thus:

> We hope your Majesty will always have a just detestation of those persons who at a time when this hellish attempt was afoot, and so near breaking out, were using their endeavours to misrepresent the actions of your best subjects and create jealousies in your majesty of those who had always served you most eminently and faithfully. And we beseech your majesty not to give so just a cause of uneasiness to your people, as to suffer any such hereafter to have access to your royal person.

This implication of the Harleyites in the address was taken further by some whig lords, who tried to get evidence that the late Secretary was guilty not just of negligence but of treason in the Greg affair. The committee set up to interrogate the spy in the Tower pressed him hard to incriminate Harley, but he protested his employer's innocence. Greg's refusal to involve Harley was the more remarkable since it would have led to his own reprieve. Instead he went to the scaffold on 28 April blaming only the Devil and his own necessities.

Where Harley's family saw this vindication of his innocence as providential, so Queen Anne and her loyal subjects attributed the outcome of the abortive expedition to Providence. Yet initially the Pretender's adherents could take comfort from signs of providential intervention on his side. He recovered from the attack of measles, which had held up the sailing of the French fleet, just at the time when the elements forced Byng to call off the British blockades and thereby allowed his own ships to escape Dunkirk at three o'clock in the morning of 9 March. They sailed up the North Sea with Byng, who had learned of their sailing at 10 o'clock, in pursuit of them. Forbin's fleet was, however, able to sail more swiftly than Byng's, and had he made landfall off the Firth of Forth would have had plenty of time to land his forces near Edinburgh. Unfortunately his pilots miscalculated, and he overshot his target, finding himself off the Scottish coast in the vicinity of Aberdeen. He had therefore to retrace his passage southwards, by which time Byng was bearing down on the Forth. Forbin sailed into the bay on 12 March, but when he gave a prearranged signal there was no reply from the shore. He therefore sailed back out to sea, narrowly avoiding Byng, and headed north again. Byng gave chase, and captured *The Salisbury*, with the Jacobite Lord Griffin on board. Then, deciding that the defence of Edinburgh was more important than pursuing Forbin, he went back to the Forth. Meanwhile the Pretender tried to land near Inverness, but severe weather prevented him. He therefore had little option but to retreat back to Dunkirk round the northern coast of Scotland. Many lives were lost through exposure, perhaps 4,000 of his troops perishing. They shared the same fate as some of the men shipped hurriedly over from Ostend to Tynemouth following Marlborough's instructions to Cadogan.

Ever since the abortive invasion attempt there has been speculation about its prospects. Jacobites like George Lockhart were confident that they were auspicious, and blamed the ineptitude if not worse of the French, especially Forbin, for its failure. Forbin himself was convinced that it never stood a chance. Until recently historians tended to endorse the French admiral's verdict. Of late, however, some have suggested that his attitude caused the abandonment of a venture which stood every chance of success.[4]

That there was seething discontent in Scotland which the Pretender could exploit is undeniable. The demonstrations against the Union had shown that the majority of Scots were opposed to the enactment of the treaty. Their dislike of it had not abated after 1 May 1707. If anything it had grown, stimulated by the introduction of English customs and excise duties in Scotland and with them hordes of unpopular officials to collect them. According to Lockhart these were 'the very scum and canalia' of England, and he recounted a story of a Scot travelling south of the border who became apprehensive of English highwayman, only to be reassured that he was in no danger, for they were all gone north 'to get places'.[5]

The Pretender and the French king showed themselves quite capable of exploiting this situation to their own advantage. Louis XIV dispatched Colonel Nathaniel Hooke to Scotland early in 1707 to investigate potential support for a rising. Hooke was readily convinced by the contacts he made that there was a general willingness to support a bid to reclaim the throne. He even persuaded ten peers to sign a memorial committing themselves to a rebellion. This Memorial claimed that in the event of the Pretender landing 'the whole nation will rise . . . He will become master of Scotland without any opposition, and the present government will be intirely abolished'.[6] Hooke returned to France with this assurance in May. Although dispatch was urged upon the Pretender and his French backers it took ten months to organize the expedition, delay which Lockhart felt adversely affected its chances of success. Nevertheless the secret preparations of the Jacobites and the poor state of the government's defences in Edinburgh, encouraged him to believe that 'all things concurred to render the design successful in Scotland'.[7]

Forbin, by contrast, 'realized clearly that there was no hope of success in that quarter'.[8]

> It is true that Queen Anne had recently brought about the union of England and Scotland under a single Parliament, and that the innovation had caused a good deal of discontent, whence it might appear that those who were opposed to the measure would not fail to rise in favour of James III (sic). But none the less, there seemed very little prospect of a revolution in his favour.

Forbin explained his failure to land the Pretender and the troops in the Firth of Forth by pointing to the lack of an answer to his signal and the proximity of Byng's pursuing fleet. He also justified his not landing them at Inverness, even though the pursuit had been called off, to bad weather. But Lockhart attributed them to 'the French King's secret designs'. He was convinced that Louis XIV was more interested in fomenting civil war in Scotland than in restoring the Pretender to his ancestral throne.[9] As with so many aspects of Jacobitism, one can only speculate. What would have happened had the Pretender landed in 1708 is anybody's guess.[10]

The only Jacobites who did land then were the prisoners from *The Salisbury*. Lord Griffin was brought to trial, sentenced to death, and then reprieved, dying in the Tower in 1710. Others were rounded up at the same time, so that in Lockhart's words 'the castles of Sterling and Edinburgh, and all the prisons in Edinburgh, were crammed full

of nobility and gentry'.[11] Among those taken up, somewhat incongru-
ously, was Andrew Fletcher the Republican. So far from finding his
incarceration intolerable he seems to have enjoyed it, telling Lord Mar
'we are not locked up here at night [in Stirling castle] we drank all
yesternight of the Collonel's good wine'.[12] Another who was apprehended was the duke of Hamilton, although he was taken up in England
where he had gone, so he claimed, to take care of his estates in Lancashire. His personal influence led the Court to drop charges against
most of the Scots who had been taken to London under suspicion.

A motive behind the clemency shown to Scots implicated in the
invasion was that a general election was in the offing. It was partly
with an eye on the electorate that the Lords' address congratulating
the queen on the failure of the expedition contained its indictment
of the Harleyites. It also asked 'that your majesty should principally
depend upon, and encourage, those who have been ever since the
Revolution, most steady and firm to the interest of the late king, and
of your majesty, during your happy reign'. This was blatantly to get her
to endorse the whigs. Anne, who had been thoroughly shaken by the
alarm, now mentioned the Revolution in public speeches.

Such was the immediate background to the general election which
occurred after the dissolution of parliament on 15 April. For the whigs,
as Burnet claimed, 'the just fears and visible dangers to which the
attempt of the invasion had exposed the nation, produced very good
effects: for the elections did for the most part fall on men well affected
to the government, and zealously set against the pretender'.[13] The
whigs certainly cashed in on the abortive invasion. Arthur Mainwaring
and the duchess of Marlborough composed a pamphlet, *Advice to the
Electors of Great Britain; occasioned by the intended invasion from France.*
In it they posed the hypothetical question, which of the two parties 'is
more likely to have invited over the Pretender, or to have given him
reason to depend upon their interest and assistance?'[14] The answer
was, of course, the tories. Enclosing a copy of it in a letter to Lord
Manchester, claiming that it 'has been very much spread among the
freeholders in all parts' Joseph Addison informed his lordship 'it is
believed this intended invasion will have a great influence on the
elections for the ensuing parliament'.[15]

Whether such propaganda influenced the outcome of the first elections to be held for the British parliament in Scotland is to be doubted.
For the constituencies, both for the 16 peers and the 45 MPs, were so
narrow and amenable to patronage, that the outcome was scarcely to be
determined by genuinely independent votes swayed by public opinion.
In the Scottish elections of 1708 the Junto took their quarrel with the
Court as far as giving their full support to Country candidates. Of
these the most prominent was the duke of Hamilton. His release from

detention was effected by the whig leaders, Halifax and Wharton acting as his bail along with the duke of Newcastle.

The Junto were particularly interested in gaining ascendancy among the Scottish peers, and in this, their chief objective, they were remarkably successful. All told five peers peculiar to their list were elected, compared with ten who appeared on the Court list, while one, the earl of Orkney, had the singular merit to feature on both. Considering that the Court's influence over the choice of the 16 was prodigious this was a very impressive achievement for the Junto. Indeed Hamilton regarded it as a victory.

In the election of MPs, too, they made an impression. Here Hamilton and the Squadrone worked together with the Junto, and especially with Sunderland who, although he was Secretary of State, was active in this election on behalf of his party associates and against his ministerial colleagues. This alliance took on a Court which was handicapped by the abolition of the Scottish Privy Council. The result was that in the new parliament the Squadrone and Cavalier members numbered 19 and the Court 26.

Despite the furore raised by the Pretender's attempted invasion of Scotland the number of contested constituencies in England dropped from the 109 of 1705 to 86, the same total as in 1701 and 1702. Their distribution, however, was somewhat different. The drop was relatively slight in the south-east and the south-west, compared with the north and midlands which witnessed the lowest number of polls in the whole decade. The north was particularly devoid of contests, none at all occurring in the border counties of Cumberland, Durham and Northumberland.

This suggests that the abortive invasion did damage the tories so much that they declined to put candidates up in many constituencies which they had contested three years earlier. It struck contemporaries 'that they were so unactive in these elections'.[16] It was perhaps a sign of their being dispirited that when Henry St John had to stand down for his family's seat at Wootton Bassett at his father's request, the tories were unable to secure his return elsewhere. 'After I had taken the resolution of not appearing at my own borough I did all I could to get myself elected in some other place,' he wrote to a fellow tory in July, 'but found it utterly impossible.'[17] St John was out of parliament until the next general election.

The outcome was a victory for the whigs. With most of the results in James Craggs informed General Stanhope 'the computors (sic) say we have gained 28 upon the Torys'.[18] The earl of Sunderland was even more sanguine, assuring the duke of Hamilton that their 'strength in the House of Commons is by this election increast 70' and the duke of Newcastle that 'it is the most Wig Parliament has been since the Revolution'.[19]

To James Craggs, however, 'their has not bin a more tickleish Parliament chosen since the restoration of King Charles ye 2d'.[20] This was because the triumphant whigs were still divided between those who adhered to the Lord Treasurer and those who followed the Junto. Unlike Scotland, where the two fought each other in the election, the Court did not oppose the Junto in England, though it did not actively encourage them either. Sir John Cropley, who usually described the whigs and tories rather quaintly as 'oaks' and 'pines', began in 1708 to use the term 'nimphs' to distinguish the Lord Treasurer's whigs of whom he was one. 'I can certainly tell you the nimphs don't wish an overgrown oak parliament', he told Lord Shaftesbury.[21] Unfortunately for the Court, its wishes were unfulfilled. Thanks to the Junto's efficient electoral machinery and the swing of public opinion in their favour the whigs swept to victory, gaining an overall majority in the Commons for the first and only time in Anne's reign. The Junto's hand had thus been considerably strengthened in their struggle with the Court.

Only the Queen stood between the Junto and their immediate desires, but though Marlborough and Godolphin pleaded, demanded and threatened she remained obdurate throughout the summer. Sunderland's intervention on behalf of Hamilton and Squadrone peers and Commoners in Scotland outraged Anne, and made her more intransigent than ever. She objected very strongly to his double dealing when it was reported to her, even threatening to dismiss him from the Secretaryship for his treachery to the Court.[22] It certainly did not improve her attitude towards Sunderland's Junto colleagues. To Anne it was a question, as she put it, of 'whether I shall submit to the five tyrannizing lords or they to me?'[23] As Anne's resistance hardened so the Junto's demands increased, until it was not just a question of insisting upon the attorney generalship for James Montague and the Presidency of the Council for Somers. In addition, rightly suspecting that Prince George and George Churchill backed the Queen's stand, they demanded the dissolution of the Prince's Council and the appointment of Lord Pembroke as Lord Admiral. This would create a vacancy for Wharton as well as for Somers, since besides being Lord President Pembroke was also Lord Lieutenant of Ireland. These demands foretold an almighty clash between Junto and Court whigs when parliament reassembled. As James Craggs prophesied, 'we shall certainly have a very whimsical sessions if a lulling draught of success does not attend our affairs abroad'.[24]

Success in fact did come to the allies in the campaign of 1708, reversing the setbacks of the previous year. At first it seemed as though those were to be added to when the French took Bruges and Ghent in the opening weeks of the campaign. They were able to gain these towns through the assistance of a fifth column within them which was

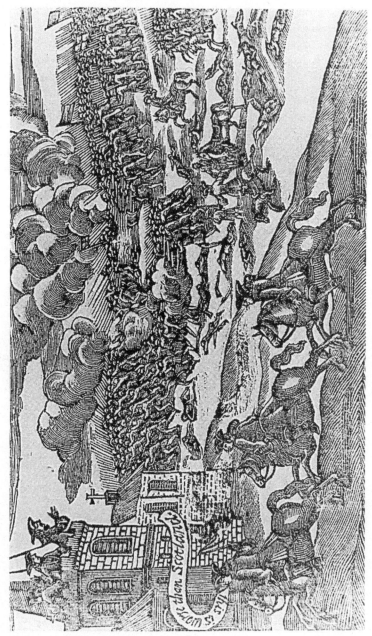

Figure 7 Louis duc de Bourgogne, Charles duc de Berry, and James Francis Edward, the pretended Prince of Wales, observing (and then fleeing from) the battle of Oudenarde, 11 July 1708. An anonymous woodcut.

discontented with their new Dutch magistrates, who were extracting as much revenue from them as they could. As Marlborough put it, 'we have lost the hearts of all the people.'[25]

Fortunately for the allies Prince Eugene linked up with the duke of Marlborough to inflict another crushing defeat on the French at Oudenarde. This was not a set piece battle but a chance encounter between French and British forces on 30 June/11 July, which grew as the day went by into an improvized full-scale engagement. As night fell the French under Vendome acknowledged their defeat, and withdrew from the field, leaving 7,000 casualties and 9,000 prisoners.

The poet William Congreve celebrated the victory in *Jack Frenchman's Defeat*:[26]

> Ye Commons and Peers,
> Pray lend me your Ears,
> I'LL sing you a Song if I can;
> How *Louis le Grand*
> Was put to a Stand,
> By the Arms of our Gracious Queen *Anne*.
>
> How his Army so great
> Had a total Defeat,
> Not far from the River of Dender . . .

Congreve contrasted the conduct of James Edward Stuart, the Pretender, who viewed the battle from a safe distance, and that of the Electoral Prince of Hanover, the future George II, who fought in the allied cavalry. Where the Pretender fled,

> Not so did Behave
> Young *Hannover* Brave
> In this Bloody Field I'll assure ye;
> When his War Horse was shot
> He matter'd it not,
> But Fought it on Foot like a Fury.

The poet concluded that Oudenarde redeemed the loss at Almanza, and predicted that Bruges and Ghent would soon be regained, while Paris itself would fall to the allies.

> From their Dream of Success,
> They'll awaken we Guess
> At the Noise of Great *Marlborough*'s Drums.

Congreve's prophesies, however, were unfulfilled. The French retreated to Ghent, where they regrouped and stayed until the end of the year. As long as they had their base there Marlborough's supply route from the Dutch Republic was jeopardized, making an advance on Paris hazardous. Although he was prepared to risk it, Eugene persuaded him that it was essential first to take the town and citadel of Lille. The siege of Lille lasted from 2/11 August until 11/22 October, while that of the citadel was prolonged until 27 November/8 December. Thus any hope of advancing to Paris had to be postponed until the next campaigning season.

Another hope held out by the battle was also doomed to disappointment. 'Among other fruits which this glorious success is like to be attended,' James Brydges told Marlborough in a letter congratulating the duke on the victory, 'we hope none of the least will be that your Grace will have it now in your power to conquer the dangerous factions of this kingdom, for to subdue monsters and disarm them of all their strength has ever been the work of heroes.'[27]

Marlborough and Godolphin, however, were under no illusions on this score. They knew that unless Anne conceded office to the Junto, the Court would have great difficulties managing parliament. Godolphin began to prepare early for the coming struggle for mastery over the Commons. At the end of May the 'Lord Treasurer's whigs' held a meeting and agreed to put up Sir Richard Onslow for the Speaker's chair.[28] This was a very prudent choice. Onslow was not a 'treasurer's whig', nor a Junto adherent, but an influential Country whig who would appeal to back-benchers. But if Godolphin thought that Onslow's impeccable whiggery would appeal to the Junto too he was destined for disappointment. The Junto objected to what they regarded as a hole in the corner business which could only perpetuate divisions among the whigs. 'It would be much more for the service and honour of his Grace [Marlborough] and ministers to put themselves at the head of the whole party,' observed Wharton 'which would make them strong, and carry them through all the present difficulties; that to think of dividing them again would only increase the troubles of last year.' He also 'thought it would have been much more for the service of the court to have consulted with the whole body of the whigs . . . about so important a point as the choice of a Speaker'.[29]

In retaliation the Junto decided to run their own candidate, and chose Peter King, a choice no less prudent than the treasurer's, for King too was a Country whig almost as influential with back-benchers as Onslow. 'I think he is much the fittest man in the House', Sunderland told the duchess of Marlborough. 'On the other side, if the Court do set anybody upon a whig bottom, as acting in concert with the party, we shall do all we can for them.'[30]

Godolphin tried his best to heal the breech. When Peter King was knighted in September it was given out that he had been thus honoured to reveal that he had Court backing for the Speakership.[31] Then it was strongly reported that Onslow was to be ennobled, that King would drop out of the contest, and a compromise candidate would be agreed.[32] In fact there could be no compromise. The Junto insisted upon getting their way. Not realizing perhaps that the main obstacle to their advancement was the Queen's obstinacy, and that the Treasurer was doing all he could to remove it, they seem to have blamed him for their disappointments. Sunderland even broached the idea of demanding his removal from the Treasurership.[33] The appointment of Sir James Montague as Solicitor General on 19 October so far from appeasing them, merely convinced them that a concerted effort would finally cause the Court's resistance to collapse.[34] Under their relentless pressure the 'Lord Treasurer's whigs' disintegrated. About the time of Montague's promotion the dukes of Devonshire and Newcastle along with Lord Townshend and Robert Walpole threw in their lot with the Junto. Godolphin, after failing to persuade the Queen either to treat with the Junto or accept his resignation, washed his hands of all further responsibility and went off to hold private talks with the whig lords at Ely.[35] Marlborough too wearied of the negotiations with Anne, and told her he wished to be addressed as her general and not as a minister.

The duke was at the time engaged still in the siege of Lille. This had brought the war onto French soil, and before the greatest of Vauban's fortifications, reinforced by an army of about 15,000 men under Marshal Boufflers. The feat itself was an incredible affront to French pride. That Marlborough and Eugene brought it off was one of the most audacious accomplishments of their generalship. The Prince undertook the work of laying siege to the city while the duke protected his troops from attack. Supplying the allied forces across territory held by the French was particularly problematic. At first supplies were conveyed by road from Brussels, but when that route was cut off Marlborough arranged to be equipped directly from England by way of Ostend. The hinterland of the Flemish port was held by troops under General Thomas Erle, who had been expecting to use them for a descent on France itself. Instead he arranged for a convoy of 800 wagons to be conveyed from Ostend to Lille. This route too was threatened by a French force under General La Motte. On 17/28 September, however, General John Richmond Webb repelled it at Wynendael. Since Webb was outnumbered more than three to one, although he was a tory even the whig historian Burnet conceded that the battle 'was looked on as the most extraordinary thing that had happened during the whole war'. Webb indeed was to dine out on it for the rest of his life, until he became a notorious bore. On one occasion the duke of Argyle, who had heard him recount the episode twenty times before, interrupted at the point where the victorious general boasted that he had received four wounds to express the wish that he had got one more, in his tongue; 'for then every body else would have talked of your action'.[36] Immediately after the battle of Wynandael the tories talked incessantly about it, for the *Gazette* at first attributed the victory to Marlborough's aide-de-campe Cadogan, and though this was quickly corrected they made a party point of it when parliament met.

They also queried another success of the 1708 campaign – the capture of Minorca. The island formed part of the inheritance claimed by Charles III, the Habsburg candidate to the Spanish possessions backed by the allies. He urged them to take it for him, and the English obliged. Marlborough himself pointed out to General Stanhope the desirability of taking it, not only for Charles but also so that Port Mahon could be used by the royal navy. It was a better base for naval operations in the Mediterranean than Gibraltar. Stanhope was the commander of the armed forces in a joint expedition with an Anglo-Dutch fleet. They landed on the island on 3/14 September and immediately took Mahon. Ten days later they besieged the more formidable obstacle of Fort St. Philip. Here, as at Lille, there was not only a garrisoned town to take but also a citadel. After a week's siege, however, they both capitulated.

Meanwhile the siege of Lille continued. In a desperate attempt to force the allies to raise it the French flooded the land around Ostend, cutting off further supplies. The besiegers however hung on grimly, supplying themselves by armed raids into the countryside. It was a relief, nevertheless, when Boufflers surrendered the city and retreated into the citadel.

Between the fall of the town and surrender of the citadel of Lille the political crisis which had been festering all year in Britain came to a head. Queen Anne had stood alone against the whigs to the bitter end. For her it was a struggle literally to the death – the death of her husband Prince George. Ever since her efforts to keep Harley the previous winter she had fought stubbornly and fiercely against the cajolery, threats and blackmail not only of the Junto but of the duumvirs. Though physically far from well herself, her spirit had refused to be broken by the pitiless determination with which they had pursued their objectives. But now when she was ready to defy the whole world her powers of resistance were suddenly undermined by the mortal collapse of her husband's frail health. About 20 October the Prince's chronic asthma developed complications. This took all the fight out of Anne. On 22 October she gave Godolphin an interview in which she desired him to give her full details of the Junto's demands. That night the Lord Treasurer wrote to Marlborough: 'the queen is at last brought to allow me to make such condescensions which, if done in time, would have been sufficient to have eased most of our difficulties; and would yet do it, in great measure, if the whigs will be but tolerably reasonable.'

Whatever concessions Anne offered the Junto were not announced immediately, doubtless on account of the uncertainty caused by the Prince's illness. On 28 October, however, George died. Anne was 'under the utmost concern and agonies of grief that can possibly be imagined' according to a sympathetic Courtier. 'She could not be persuaded to leave him till he was quite dead but continued by him to the very moment he expired.'[37] The Junto were callously unsympathetic. 'You will hear by this post the news of the Prince's death', Sunderland informed Admiral Byng, adding insensitively, 'it opens an easy way to have everything put upon a right foot, and I do really believe it will be so and that we shall effectually get rid of George Churchill's dominion'.[38] They did, although it took a month to persuade the earl of Pembroke to move to the now vacant post of Lord Admiral. He relaized that he was little more than a stalking horse for the Junto's preferred candidate, the earl of Orford, and wanted to take out insurance in the event of his being replaced by the whig peer. Thus he insisted on a pension of £2000 a year and the post of teller of the exchequer for his son. These were conceded and on 25 November Pembroke took over as Lord High Admiral. This created two vacancies, the Lord Presidency of the Council, which went to Somers, and the Lord Lieutenancy of Ireland, which was bestowed on Wharton. These appointments put the seal, temporarily at least, on the pact between the Court and the Junto.[39]

Prospects for the Court and the Junto in the new parliament had previously depended on the attitude of the tories. Though their numbers had diminished after the general election, they could still be decisive if the whigs remained divided. The question was, which way would they go? Would they support King's candidature for the Speakership, and thus align with the Junto to harass the Court as they had done so often in the previous parliament? Or would they put up their own candidate in hopes of getting the crucial speaker's chair for their own united party? In the event, on 3 September they held a meeting at Sir Thomas Mansell's house in Wales where they agreed to set up an independent candidate against both King and Onslow.[40] On this occasion they could not agree on a nominee, some being for William Bromley, while others were for Harley or Sir Simon Harcourt.[41] At another meeting held near the end of September, several of Bromley's friends urged him to get Harcourt and Harley to drop their pretensions and to give him their support.[42] When Bromley solicited their help early in October, Harley 'returned an answer that after what had passed by discourse and also letters I could not think there was any room left to doubt of my serving him heartily'.[43] The tory leaders had united. Meanwhile circular letters pressing their supporters to be present at the opening debate were distributed throughout the kingdom. Tories in the northern counties and in Scotland, on the Welsh borders and in Wales, in the Midlands and the West Country, were urged to be at Westminster for the opening of parliament on 16 November.[44]

Unfortunately for the tories the Speakership of the Commons was settled between the Court and the Junto as part of their reconciliation. On the day after the Prince's death James Craggs predicted that the contest between King and Onslow would 'end in a cup of mild and stale'.[45] Though some bitterness remained the parliamentary clash was averted. 'Sir P[eter] King had the chair in his power,' claimed Sir John Cropley, 'but was prevailed upon by Lord Somers to let Sir Dickey have it, for the Court had pitched on him as this new settlement.'[46] The tories for their part 'thought it prudence, not being able to make a majority, unanimously to strike in with the rest'.[47]

At the opening of parliament on 16 November, therefore, Sir Richard Onslow was chosen without opposition, though when his name was proposed a Junto spokesman created a minor diversion which alluded to the recent divisions among the whigs. After Lord William Powlett had moved that the Commons should choose Onslow as its Speaker, and had been seconded by Sir William Strickland, Major General Mordaunt jestingly proposed that they should choose instead Paul Joddrell, the clerk of the House, 'he having been assistant to good speakers, to indifferent ones, and to the worst'.[48]

Instead of presenting the new Speaker to the Queen, as was customary, the Commons presented Onslow to a commission of lords representing Anne, who was too overcome by her husband's death to attend the ceremony. The Lord Chancellor gave a speech on her behalf, expressing the hope that they had the same zeal for prosecuting the war as formerly, and in particular that they would agree to considerable sums being spent on the navy. He also drew attention to the successes of the campaign, in the Mediterranean as well as in Flanders. When the Commons drew up an address of thanks for the speech for some reason the tories raised questions about the passage referring to Minorca, but 'the whigs being in their honey moon of returning their court and acknowledgments for the good harmony that's now betwixt them and Court it was dropt'.[49] 'Matters in parliament go on very smooth and easy, and we have a prospect of a quiet and peaceable sessions', observed the paymaster of the forces. 'The measures that the Court have fallen into have given them so clear a majority that there is no expectation for the opposites to carry any one point.'[50]

Abroad, too, the campaign ended on a high note for the government. Early in December the citadel of Lille finally capitulated. The French withdrew from Ghent and held a line between Nieuport and Bruges against the allies. Their departure led the magistrates of Ghent to petition Marlborough not to besiege the town. The duke went ahead with his preparations for a siege until, at the eleventh hour, the town surrendered to him. Once Ghent was in allied hands the French lines were too exposed, leading them to withdraw from Bruges. On learning this Marlborough wrote to Godolphin on 23 December/3 January 'this campagne is now ended to my own heart's desire'.[51]

It was as well that the troops could get into winter quarters then, for the winter of 1709 was one of the coldest anybody who lived through it either remembered or encountered again. It began to freeze on 26 December, and snow fell every day until 6 January. Early in the New Year the Thames froze over thick enough for a 'frost fair' to be held on it. There was a slight thaw in the middle of the month, but then the temperature fell below freezing again for most of February and into March, while there were more heavy snowfalls. Life was hard to endure even in the houses of the gentry, where it was so icy that ink froze. People in humbler homes perished. Travel was exceedingly difficult. It took the Duke of Somerset's steward thirty days to journey from London to Cockermouth, through deep snow most of the way. Post boys died of the cold, and rode frozen to their horses. The peers and commoners who attended parliament when it resumed its session on 10 January after the Christmas recess had to travel through a country caught in the grip of an arctic winter.

When they got there they renewed the party conflict with vigour. This was particularly noticeable in the decisions upon controverted elections. At the best of times these were no more than partisan victories masquerading as judicial verdicts. The committee of privileges and elections, where they were usually heard, was notorious as 'the most corrupt court in Christendom'.[52] In the session of 1708-9, however, the whigs dropped all pretence at impartiality and tried them at the bar of the House of Commons. 'The business of parliament is extremely tedious and vexatious this session', one tory complained. 'We try our elections at the bar and generally sit upon them till one or two in the morning and then we cannot convince people that thirty are more than three.'[53] One of the more flagrant episodes involved the ejection of Sir Simon Harcourt from the House in favour of a whig petitioner, William Hucks. Hucks had stood against Harcourt at Abingdon, and claimed that the franchise was in the inhabitants paying scot and lot and not receiving alms or charity, whereas his opponent had polled the illegal votes of the inhabitants at large. On 18 January the Commons decided the franchise in favour of Hucks. Two days later, at about 2.30 a.m. they voted him duly elected. 'I had yesterday the hardest service I ever saw in Parliament,' Robert Walpole informed Marlborough, 'the House sitting till past two of the clock in the morning upon Sir Simon Harcourt's election for Abingdon, which was at last carried against him by a majority of 47 and the petitioner voted in. It was much the fullest House that has been this Parliament and the whole affair carried on with greater heat and warmth on both sides than usual.'[54] Harcourt was furious and delivered himself of a scathing speech which was later printed. He insisted that his version of the franchise had held for over 150 years. 'Any opposition may give a handle to a petition,' he protested, 'no matter for the justice of it, power will maintain it.'[55] The whigs certainly used and abused their power to boost their majority. Even Burnet was ashamed of their proceedings, admitting that[56]

> all elections were judged in favour of whigs and courtiers, but with so much partiality that those who had formerly made loud complaints of the injustice of the tories in determining elections, when they were a majority, were not so much as out of countenance when they were reproached for the same thing: they pretended they were in a state of war with the tories, so that it was reasonable to retaliate this to them on the account of their former proceedings; but this did not satisfy just and upright men, who would not do to others that which they had complained of, when it was done to them or their friends.

For the first time election petitions were heard in the Upper House too. They came from Scottish peers who objected to the returns of four of the sixteen representative Lords for Scotland. Votes had been refused from some of the lords who had been arrested and confined in Edinburgh castle on the occasion of the Pretender's attempted invasion, though they had taken oaths there to qualify themselves. It was held that the oaths were invalid, a point which the Lords debated in January. The outcome was that the oaths were accepted, but only one Scottish peer, the marquis of Lothian, was declared not duly elected, and was replaced by the marquis of Annandale. This nevertheless established that the House of Lords was to judge disputed elections of Scottish peers.[57]

The aftermath of the Jacobite fiasco was indeed to occupy much of the remainder of the session. 'The Torys have lately set a foot a furious enquiry into the conduct of the ministry in relation to last year's invasion', Sir John Cropley wrote to General Stanhope on 15 March.[58] It was headed off by a resolution, passed by 186 votes to 76, 'that timely and effectual care was taken by those under her majestie at the time of the intended invasion'.[59] At the same time as the Commons were reassuring the Queen about the measures taken to suppress the rebellion, in the Lords her ministers were pushing a bill to ensure more effective methods for dealing with rebels would be at their disposal in the event of a repeated attempt by the Pretender. Some gentlemen in Stirlingshire had been more forward than others in their zeal for his cause, and had imprudently been 'out' in anticipation of his landing. These were brought to trial in Scottish courts, where the charges against them were found to be 'not proven'. In whig eyes this flagrant miscarriage of justice was due to the defectiveness of the Scottish treason laws. The government decided to pass legislation to make them uniform with those of England, and a bill to this effect had actually been introduced into the Commons before Christmas, but had been defeated in committee after objections from the Scots MPs. However, when the Lords came to take into consideration the abortive rebellion it was revived in the Upper House. On 11 March a bill for the 'improvement' of the Union was introduced there.

The Treason bill, as it was called, ran into choppy waters in committee. Bishop Burnet, who chaired some of its sessions, but was replaced after 'blundering', observed that 'the Scotch lords opposed every branch of this act'.[60] They particularly objected to the changes in procedure in treason trials which the bill introduced into Scotland. Previously the accused there had been allowed some privileges denied their English counterparts. For example, the names of witnesses who were to testify against them had to be made known to them fifteen days before the trial began. Such safeguards were thought to favour the guilty too much by whig lawyers, who held them responsible for the acquittal of the Stirlingshire Jacobites the previous year. The bill, which brought the Scottish laws into line with the English, would have denied those accused any such notice of the witnesses against them. An amendment was proposed to give them five days' notice. This passed by 37 votes to 31. 'The cucumber thus cooked' as the bishop of Carlisle put it, the ministry 'earnestly moved for the throwing out the whole clause, as makeing a Dangerous Change (at this Juncture) in the Laws of England. Whereupon a Second Question threw it out accordingly by 44 against 27.'[61] Those who had advocated the amendment made another effort to get a period of five days' notice incorporated in the bill on 26 March. On that day, 'upon a division of the house on this question, the votes were equal; so by the rule of the house, that in such a case the negative prevails, it was lost'.[62] Undeterred, the proponents of the measure made yet another effort to get it passed at the last meeting of the committee on 28 March, when they were defeated by 40 to 25.[63]

The bill also introduced into Scotland the confiscation of property which the traitor, and thereby his family, incurred in England. Upon this, Burnet observed 'the debates grew still warmer'. The Scottish peers opposed it to a man, and were joined by the tories. Burnet, a Scot himself, was also 'against all forfeitures but *personal*', and actually moved that they should not include real estate. He nevertheless suspected tory motives, claiming that they were 'disposed to oppose the court in every thing, and to make treason as little to be dreaded as possible'.[64]

This combination of Scots and tories opposed the bill when it went down to the Commons. They divided the House on its first and second readings on 29 and 31 March, on each occasion being outnumbered by only eight votes. Another division on 5 April found the government with a majority of only six.[65] With 'every man' of the Scots in the Lower House 'against the Bill' the Court was experiencing difficulties.[66] This was despite the overall whig majority in the general election of 1708 and its 'improvement' by the decisions upon controverted elections. The alliance against the measure actually carried amendments which had been lost in the Lords. 'In the committee upon the Scotch Treason Bill,' Walpole informed Marlborough on 8 April 'we went through the bill without any amendments but at the end two clauses were added, one for confining all forfeitures to the life of the forfeiting person, the other for giving in the names of the witnesses upon trials of treason ten days before the trials, and these clauses were carried by a majority of 51. A very unexpected turn to this sessions.'[67] The third reading was approved on 9 April by nearly two to one, 'notwithstanding Lord Coningsby's Remark, that noe Traytour could now forfeit either Life or Estate'![68] The Scots members were reluctantly prepared to accept it as amended. 'They have forct upon the Scots all our laws relating to high treason,' James Lowther observed 'to the great dissatisfaction of every L[or]d and Commoner that represents that part of the kingdom, and this is carried at the end of a session in a thin House by a very small majority.'[69]

The amendments were debated in the House of Lords on 14 April. Halifax moved that they should not take effect until after the death of the Pretender, since he had threatened one invasion and was threatening another. A Scottish peer, Seafield, thought that the threat was only serious in war-time, and moved that they should be shelved until there was peace. After a debate Halifax's proposal was accepted, despite the opposition of all the Scots present, and then the amendments passed.[70] When the Commons came to debate this clause to delay the implementation of their amendments on 18 April 'both parties mustered up their strength, and many, who had gone into the country, were brought up on this occasion'.[71] The opposition, consisting of Scots tories and some country whigs, managed to change the timing from the death of the Pretender to three years after the accession of the House of Hanover. Otherwise 'the bill, with all the amendments and provisos, was carried by a small majority' of the Court and Junto who 'were very diligent'.[72] 'They assembled all their forces, the lame and the blind and all,' Robert Harley's sister informed their aunt, doubtless passing on information from him, 'and yet it was carried but by six.'[73] Next day in the Lords the clause delaying the enactment of the amendments until 'three years after the Queen's death' was 'agreed to without Division on the Question: notwithstanding some faint Opposition'.[74] The bill then received the royal assent on 21 April, the last day of the session.

The Court ran into difficulties over the Treason bill because it roused the sensibilities of the Scots. They regarded it not as an 'improvement' so much as an infringement of the Union. Their ruffled feathers had to be smoothed by an Act of Indemnity pardoning all treasons committed before 19 April, except by those who accompanied the Pretender at sea. This was rushed onto the statute book to receive the royal assent at the same time as the so-called 'Union of the Two Kingdoms Improvement (Treason) Act.' Scotland was also given its own secretaryship of state, the first incumbent of the new office being the duke of Queensberry. This step too appears to have been contrived to appease the Scots.

On every other issue that arose in the session the Court and the whigs comfortably carried all before them. One measure introduced in January 1709 illustrated that when a party issue was raised the tories could make no headway. This was a bill for the general naturalization of foreign Protestants. According to Burnet it 'was much desired, and had often been attempted, but had been laid aside in so many former parliaments, that there was scarce any hopes to encourage a new attempt'.[75] The whig majority achieved at the polls in 1708, however, provided the opportunity. For the whigs had been sympathetic to the plight of the refugees who had fled to England from foreign persecution ever since the Huguenot exodus from France associated with the Revocation of the Edict of Nantes in 1685. Tories by contrast were suspicious of their influx, not least because they 'scarce ever knew a foreigner settl'd in England,' as Francis Atterbury put it, 'but became a Whig in a little time after his mixing with us.'[76] It was therefore not surprisingly that a whig MP, Edward Wortley Montagu, introduced a bill to naturalize foreign protestants upon their attending a communion service in any Protestant church. And it was even less surprising that a tory, Henry Campion, proposed an amendment that 'there should be a clause inserted in it for obliging such foreigners as should be willing to enjoy the benefit of it, to receive the sacrament according to the usage of the Church of England'.[77] 'But it was thought best to cast the door as wide open as possible for encouraging strangers', claimed the biased Burnet, adding 'this was carried in the House of commons with a great majority'.[78]

When it was debated in the House of Lords it also sailed through all its stages comfortably, even though some bishops tried to restrict its benefits to foreigners who communicated with the Anglican church. Most of these were themselves in the high church party. Thus the archbishop of York lobbied against it, while the bishop of Chester proposed an amendment similar to that which Campion had moved in the Commons. He was seconded, however, by the bishop of Carlisle, who, though he had inclined to the high church position, usually voted with the whigs. They even received the support of three other moderate whig bishops on this occasion. The low church bishops, however, including the archbishop of Canterbury and Burnet of Salisbury, opposed the bishop of Chester's amendment.[79] 'All those who appeared for this large and comprehensive way were reproached for their coldness and indifference in the concerns of the church,' noted Burnet 'and in that I had a large share.'[80] ''Twas thought the Act of General Naturalization would have met with great opposition', one tory opined after its third reading in the Lords, adding that it 'past with hardly any at all'.[81]

Soon after the passing of the Act there was an influx of refugees from the Palatinate. Over the summer at least 10,000 destitute 'poor Palatines' arrived in London. They became a bone of contention between the parties. Whigs contributed generously to their relief, while tories conspicuously declined to relieve their distress. They claimed that as Calvinists, Catholics and Lutherans they posed a threat to the Anglican church. They also insisted that they were attracted to England by the prospect of becoming naturalized subjects under the Act passed by the whigs. This seems unlikely, however, for they were after all escaping the ravages of war.[82]

The plight of foreign refugees would therefore have been eased even more effectively if the hostile powers could have agreed on peace. And at that very moment the first serious negotiations to that end had started at the Hague. So promising did the outlook appear that the whigs concerted an address of both Houses to the Queen. It was first mooted in the Lords, who addressed her to take care that her own title to the crown and that of the house of Hanover should be recognized by France, and that the Pretender should be expelled from French territory. The Commons agreed with these terms and added their own, that the fortifications and harbour of Dunkirk should be demolished. This was incorporated in the joint address which the Queen answered favourably, assuring the Houses that 'no care shal be wanting on my part to attain the end they have desired'.[83] It seemed as though all parties were making a serious effort to end the war.

The Hague peace negotiations were to disappoint those who hoped they would conclude in a treaty between the allies and the Bourbon powers. The English Dutch and Imperial representatives considered that the French king was so desperate for peace that he would agree to his grandson, Philip of Anjou, renouncing all his claims to the territories of Charles II in favour of the Habsburg claimant, the archduke Charles. Certainly French resources had been stretched by her military exertions, while the severe winter made them even scarcer. The allies hoped to make them scarcer still by imposing a naval blockade to prevent corn entering French ports. However, they were not exhausted to the point where Louis XIV would settle for peace at any price. More important was the fact that he could no longer speak for his grandson.[1] Philip V was well entrenched on the throne of Spain, while Charles III had only a foothold in Catalonia. There was no way the Bourbon king would give up his kingdom to the Habsburg without a struggle. When this became clear to the allies they added to the preliminaries the notorious article which committed Louis to helping them remove Philip from Spain. This proved the sticking point. Louis withdrew his representative, the marquis of Torcy, from the Hague.

News that the negotiations had collapsed caused the price of stock on the London market to fall 14 per cent, just as the hopes of their being successful had led them to rise by 20 per cent. The state of public credit was critical to the financing of the war effort, for as Lord Treasurer Godolphin informed Marlborough in July 'unless our credit bee not only supported, but even augmented by success abroad, our provision in Parliament for the expence of the present year will fall short before the end of it by at least twelve hundred thousand pounds sterling'.[2] France was not the only country feeling the economic strain of the war in 1709.

Louis XIV published the reasons for his rejecting the preliminaries to the world. When they were widely known they were held to be outrageous. It was considered unnatural to expect a grandfather to fight his own grandson. The allies, and especially the English who most insisted on 'no peace without Spain', were accused of being warmongers, deliberately prolonging hostilities by making unrealistic and unacceptable demands. Yet the logic of the allied war aims led to their insistence on French assistance to realize them. Had they made peace with France and continued the war in Spain, Louis would have had time to recover his military strength while the allies exhausted theirs in the peninsula. No guarantees that he would not re-enter the war would have been worth the paper they were written on. For the French king had shown time and again that he would not keep any international undertaking he had solemnly signed. Thus in 1697 he had repudiated the exiled Stuarts' claim to the English throne and recognized William III as lawful king, only to recognize James II's son in 1701. It was therefore not the clause requiring him to help expel his grandson from Spain that was unrealistic but the war aim itself. Yet that had been endorsed most enthusiastically by all parties in England, especially the tories, as recently as December 1707.

Now the tories took up the charge that the duumvirs and the whigs were deliberately prolonging the war for their own ends. War weariness had been noticeable among tory backbenchers for some time. In May 1708 Marlborough had written to his wife about an MP who was taken for a whig, though the duke suspected otherwise. 'When you see him,' he wrote 'you may speak as your not doubting of his being for the carrying on of the warr, til a safe peace can be had, by which you will see his inclination.'[3] A disgruntled tory observed early in 1709 that 'every time we give the K[ing] of France a blow we think we have knockt him down, but he still rises again and so he's like to do. However, it may be policy to amuse the people with yearly hopes of peace . . . They have been too long deluded and find that war is intended to be a trade.'[4] Robert Harley accused his former colleagues of perpetuating the war in 'Plain English', a pamphlet he wrote in the summer of 1708, though he did not publish it. 'As long as these rule,' he asserted ' victorys obtained are employd for their private advantage and profit, and not to the end designd for obtaining a safe and honourable peace, but to aggrandize themselves and to prolong that war by which they get such vast wealth, and secure to themselves to[o] much power.'[5] Similar points were made in another Harleyite tract *An Account of a Dream at Harwich. In a letter to a member of parliament about the camisars.* Although it was dated 21 September 1708 it appeared on 15 January 1709. 'I hear the *Dream* was made use of as an argument for the motion of giving thanks to his Grace', observed Edward Harley, referring to the resolution agreed *nem con* by the Commons on 22 January to give the thanks of the House to the duke of Marlborough 'for his signal services the last campagne, as also the indefatigable zeal he perseveres in for the good of the common cause'.[6]

Tory charges that the duke sought to aggrandize his family at the public expense would have been even more telling had it been known that Marlborough had asked the Queen to make him Captain General for life. Later when they did find out they lambasted him as 'King John'. Anne was taken aback by the request. She sought the advice of Somers, who cautioned her not to set such a dangerous precedent. This advice reconciled the Queen to the leader of the Junto, whom previously she had regarded as beyond the pale.[7]

Marlborough apparently first opened the topic when he returned briefly to England to concert the Cabinet's approach in the peace negotiations. On his return to the Hague at the end of March he persuaded the Dutch to reject French overtures for peace, offering them English guarantees for a barrier of fortresses in the Habsburg Netherlands to be held by forces from the United Provinces as security against French aggression. In May the duke was joined by Lord Townshend, who negotiated the final form of the Barrier Treaty with the Dutch. These negotiations were to take up most of the year.

Meanwhile discussions over peace prospects, together with the prolonged winter and a late spring, delayed the start of the campaign until June. Then the allies took the offensive by besieging Tournai. Marlborough supervised the siege, while Prince Eugene commanded the forces guarding the besiegers. The work was hindered by water, partly from the heavy rains of that summer, partly from the ability of the defenders to divert streams into the allied trenches. It took a month to get the town to surrender. The citadel had still to be taken. Where water had held up the besiegers of the town, earth delayed their capture of the citadel. For it was notoriously one of the more impregnable of defence works, and could only be successfully attacked by tunnelling. The French attempted to prevent the digging of tunnels with mines, which buried many men when they exploded. It took another month to get the citadel to surrender. 'The country longs for peace,' observed one disgruntled tory, 'and thinks Tournay and its citadel are a dear bargain for six millions a year.'[8]

By then it was late August in England, early September on the continent. The only other objective for the allies before the campaigning season ended was Mons. Villars and Boufflers, the marshals who led the French army in the Low Countries, moved to intercept the allied army en route from Tournai to Mons at Malplaquet. There on 31 August/11 September was fought the bloodiest battle of the war. Casualties on both sides were high – 15,000 on the French, 24,000 on the allied. Among the allies the Dutch under the prince of Orange incurred the highest, charging the enemy twice and even regrouping for a third until Marlborough stopped it. 'I have not seen the dead bodies lie so thick as they were in some places,' recorded a British officer 'particularly . . . where the Dutch Guards attacked. The Dutch have suffered most in the battle of any.'[9] Villars was wounded during the battle, so it was left to Boufflers to organize the French retreat. This was accomplished so well that very few prisoners were taken. That night Marlborough wrote to his wife, 'we have had this day a very bloody battaile. The first part of the day we beat their foot, and afterwards their horse. God almighty be praised, it is now in our powers to have what peace wee please, and I may be pretty well assured of never being in another battel.'[10]

The duke's prophecy was correct in one respect. He would never again be engaged in another major set piece battle with the French. But in every other respect it could not have been more inaccurate. The fact was that the battle of Malplaquet paradoxically restored French morale. They had survived the heaviest attack the allies could inflict on them, and though they had been beaten in the field they had withdrawn without being pursued. Their frontiers were still for the most part intact. So far from opening the road to Paris the victory had not weakened the defences of France sufficiently to make an allied invasion feasible. The war ceased to be one of rapid movement and became bogged down, as the previous one had done, in a series of sieges. Thus Villars retired to Valenciennes which he fortified strongly against attack, while Marlborough continued the siege of Mons, which was taken at the end of October. The campaign then ended early, as it had begun late.

'Nothing of importance passed on the sea', recorded Bishop Burnet in his *History*, adding that:[11]

> Towards the end of the year, the earl of Pembroke found the care of the fleet a load too heavy for him to bear, and that he could not discharge it as it ought to be done; so he desired leave to lay it down. It was offered to the earl of Orford; but though he was willing to serve at the head of a commission, he refused to accept of it singly; so it was put in commission, in which he was the first.

This was to say the least disingenuous, since the historian knew that the replacement of Pembroke by Orford was the culmination of a sustained drive by the Junto, which the Queen had resisted with all the stubbornness she had shown against whig demands for high office the previous year. Her main objection to employing Orford, indeed, was for his 'crimes in attacking the wise management of the Prince's Council'.[12] The struggle had ground Godolphin once again between the millstones of Anne's inertia and the pressure exerted by the 'Junctonians', as James Craggs dubbed them in a letter to Marlborough written on 20 May. Craggs explained why the whigs were so adamant at getting Orford to be in charge of the Admiralty.[13]

> They urge the next sessions cannot be carryed on without it, for as the majority are in the Whigg interest, they will not be easy without being of a peice . . . Whereas to have a good majority to wind up all the bottomes of the warre quietly and honourably, would make this reigne perfectly happy for the future; and they make all these things to depend upon the good settlement of the Admiralty affaires, as the onely loose hole for faction to practice upon.

It took six months before the dispute was resolved. Orford was offered the place of Lord Admiral on 30 October. He then made a point of declining it, expressing a preference to be first lord of a commission. A new Admiralty commission, with Orford at its head, was therefore appointed on 8 November.

Orford's appointment meant that four of the five Junto lords were in high office. Only Halifax was left outside the cabinet. Tories took alarm at this, seeing the whigs monopolizing the government. On learning of Orford's obtaining the first lordship of the Admiralty Robert Harley wrote to a tory: 'now the faction has gotten this additional power entirely in their hands perhaps they may according to their custom attempt to engross the whole and the white staff [Treasury] and the Generalship cannot long be suffered by them to stay in the hands they are [Godolphin and Marlborough].'[14]

During the days when Orford and his colleagues in the Admiralty commission were kissing the Queen's hands at Windsor an event took place in the City of London which was to lead to the downfall of the whigs and the government. On 5 November the Reverend Doctor Henry Sacheverell, at the invitation of the Lord Mayor, delivered a sermon to the 'aldermen and citizens of London' at St. Paul's cathedral.[15] The day was conventionally set aside for reflections on the providential failure of the Gunpowder plot, and Sacheverell paid perfunctory attention to it in his opening remarks. But he had not been invited by Sir Samuel Garrard, the high tory mayor of the predominantly whig City, to lambast Papists. Sacheverell was well known for his intemperance on the subject of dissent, and had distinguished himself on that score during the summer in a sermon preached at the Derby Assizes on 'the communication of sin'. This consisted primarily of an attack upon what he called 'mungril institutions', the societies for reformation of manners. The text itself was par for the course for a preacher who had threatened to hang out 'the bloody flag and banner of defiance' against dissenters. But the preface to the printed version, which appeared on 27 October, contained allusions to others who 'shamefully betrayed and run down' the principles and interests of the Church of England. These were to be identified in the St Paul's sermon as 'false brethren'.

False brethren rather than professed enemies were responsible, in the preacher's view, for the current deplorable state of the established Church.[16]

> Her Holy Communion has been rent, and divided by factious and schismatical imposters; her pure doctrin has been corrupted and defil'd; her primitive worship and discipline prophan'd and abus'd; her sacred orders deny'd and vilify'd; her priests and professors (like St Paul) calumniated, misrepresented, and ridicul'd; her altars and sacraments prostituted to hypocrites, deists, socininans and atheists.

There were three kinds of false brethren. First, with respect to the Church, were those who modified its doctrines, discipline and worship. Amongst these the Doctor alluded plainly to bishop Burnet, who had been condemned by the Lower House of Convocation in 1701 for his *Exposition of the Thirty-Nine Articles*. Second were those with relation to the state, government or society who advocated resistance to the supreme power. Those who cited the Revolution of 1688 as justifying resistance misrepresented it, for there had been none then. Invective and vituperation being more characteristic of the Doctor's florid style than logical exposition he jumped from this proposition to inveigh against

> These False Brethren in our Government [who] are suffer'd to combine into bodies, and seminaries, wherein Atheism, Deism, Tritheism, Socinianism, with all the Hellish principles of fanaticism, regicide, and anarchy are openly profess'd and taught to corrupt and debauch the youth of the nation . . . Certainly the Toleration was never intended to indulge and cherish such monsters and vipers in our bosom, that scatter their pestilence at noon-day, and will rend, distract and confound the firmest and best-settl'd Constitution in the World.

Having warned his reader that he would return to 'our political false brethren', he dealt briefly with the third sort, 'namely those who in their private capacities are false either in their friendship, correspondence or dealing'.

Sacheverell then proceeded to delineate the damage inflicted on Church and State by false brethren to both. 'What could not be gain'd by Comprehension and Toleration must be brought about by Moderation and Occasional Conformity', he claimed of the dangers to the Church. 'That is, what they could not do by open violence they will not fail by secret treachery to accomplish.' As for the state, it was in danger 'from miscreants, begot in rebellion, born in sedition and nurs'd up in faction'.

Finally he 'set forth the heinous malignity, enormous guilt and folly of this prodigious sin of false brotherhood'. In doing so he included among their number none less than the Lord Treasurer, virtually naming Godolphin when he mentioned 'the crafty insidiousness of such wily Volpones', since he was widely known as 'Volpone'.

His peroration was a call to arms against such wickedness in high places. 'If we shew the same courage and indefatigable zeal and labour to defend as our adversaries to reproach, divide and ruine our Church,' he urged, 'neither their united malice, nor power, nor all the plots and machinations of Rome nor the very gates of Hell it self shall ever be able to prevaile against her.'

It was customary for the court of aldermen to approve the printing of any sermon preached to them on a solemn state occasion, especially if the preacher had been invited by the Lord Mayor. When the court met on 8 November, however, the Recorder, Peter King, and the Governor of the Bank of England, Sir Gilbert Heathcote, both staunch whigs, strenuously opposed Garrard's recommendation that Sacheverell's sermon be printed.[17] They managed to persuade their whig colleagues on the aldermanic bench to refuse their permission. Sacheverell nevertheless went ahead and printed it, claiming the Lord Mayor's command, even though Garrard denied he had given it. The sermon was a best-seller. Henry Clements, the printer who published it, ran off about 40,000 copies. Pirated versions swelled the total to something like 100,000, ensuring that it was read by at least 250,000 people. There can scarcely have been a voter in England who was not familiar with the gist of Sacheverell's intemperate tirade against the whig government.

The ministers therefore could scarcely ignore the sermon. To do so would be to encourage other high flyers to preach similar sermons, giving utterance to thoughts they had felt it prudent to keep to themselves. As a Court tory put it: 'I am clearly of opinion if there is not a stop put to the liberty some gentlemen of his coat take in their pulpits "twill be in vain to think either the Queen can sit safe on the throne or the members meet in peace and quietness in either House of Parliament'.[18] The problem was, however, what to do about it and its preacher? When all other courses had been explored, from simply having the sermon burned by the common hangman to prosecuting its author for seditious libel, they were dismissed as inadequate or inappropriate; and it was agreed to proceed by a full parliamentary impeachment of the Doctor for high crimes and misdemeanours. He was therefore to be prosecuted by the House of Commons and tried by the House of Lords. On 13 December John Dolben, a whig MP, rose in the Commons, holding copies of the Derby and St Paul's sermons in his hands, and, moving that the House took them into consideration, placed them on the Speaker's table. While the tories were clearly taken aback by this resolution, the whigs equally clearly had concerted their measures. The upshot was that Sacheverell was ordered to appear at the bar of the House the following day. The whigs then formally moved his impeachment. As one put it, they were going to 'roast a parson'. A committee was consequently appointed to draw up articles of impeachment. This duly reported on 9 January, when four articles were exhibited against the Doctor. The first, and as it was to turn out by far the most important, alleged that in his sermon he did 'suggest and maintain that the necessary means used to bring about the . . . Revolution were odious and unjustifiable . . . and that to impute resistance to the said Revolution is to cast black and odious colours upon his late Majesty and the said Revolution.' The second accused him of maintaining that the Toleration 'is unreasonable and the allowance of it unwarrantable. And asserts that he is a false brother with relation to God, religion or the Church who defends Toleration and liberty of conscience.' The third charged him with suggesting and asserting 'that the Church of England is in a condition of great peril and adversity under her Majesty's administration' in opposition to the resolutions of both Houses in 1705 that 'whoever goes about to suggest and insinuate that the Church is in danger under her Majesty's administration is an enemy to the Queen the Church and the kingdom'. The fourth maintained that he did 'falsely and maliciously suggest that her Majesty's administration, both in ecclesiastical and civil affairs, tends to the destruction of the constitution'. They concluded by praying that Sacheverell 'may be put to answer to all and every the premises; and that such proceeding, examination, trial, judgment and exemplary punishment may be thereupon had and executed, as is agreeable to law and justice'.

Sacheverell had arrived for his arraignment on 14 December in the coach of the Vice-Chancellor of Oxford University. The high church party was beginning to rally round the embattled Doctor. When he was detained in the lodgings of the Commons' Messenger his sympathizers made sure that he would want for nothing. The duke of Beaufort sent some bottles of claret and 50 guineas, perhaps a present from the tory Board of Brothers of which he was President.[19] The lower clergy rallied to the Doctor in such numbers that the duke of Marlborough got cold feet, and, fearing that they had carried things too far, asked Wharton 'what they should do? or how far they should proceed? . . . To which the Lord Wharton answered in a very rough manner: "Do with him, my Lord? Quash him and damn him".'

Had the proceedings been so perfunctory the case might not have aroused the passions it did, and from the whig point of view might not have got out of control. Unfortunately for the government the trial was

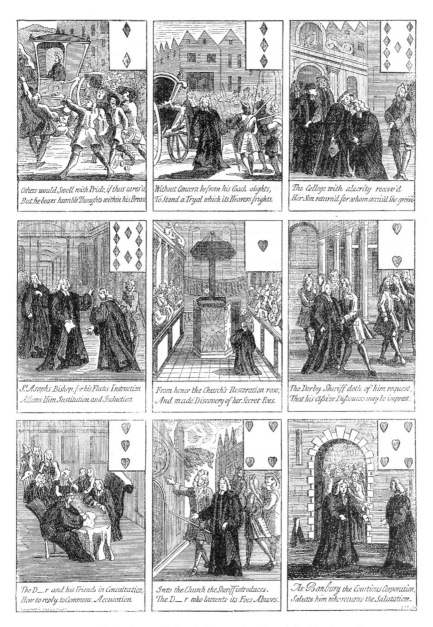

Figure 8 'Sacheverell' Cards illustrating the trial of Sacheverell.

dragged out for over a month. The first delay occurred when the House of Lords allowed Sacheverell until 28 January to answer the articles of impeachment.

The answer was as intemperate as the sermon. Thus the Doctor stoutly upheld his views on the illegality of resistance on any pretext whatsoever, and on the limitations of the 'indulgence' to dissenters granted by the so-called Toleration Act in 1689. So uncompromising was his response to the charges against him that two of his counsel resigned. But he was left with Sir Simon Harcourt, the ablest tory lawyer in England, whose services were available because he had been unseated in the notorious decision on the Abingdon election petition. Otherwise as a member of the House of Commons, in whose name the prosecution was brought against Sacheverell, he could not have been employed by the defence.

The groundswell of sympathy and support for the Doctor became clearer each day that passed. Numerous pamphlets were published in his favour, prayers were offered for him in churches, more ominously still crowds appeared in the streets on his behalf. The government began to realize that time was not on its side, and tried to get the trial over with quickly. But the opposition seized a chance to delay the proceedings, and give them maximum publicity, by successfully moving that the entire House of Commons should be accommodated in Westminster hall for the trial. To convert the hall into an auditorium which could seat both Houses of parliament and over a thousand spectators, including the Queen, required a workforce of carpenters directed by Sir Christopher Wren to labour night and day for most of February. The opening day of the trial was thus delayed until the 27th. This postponement was to prove fatal to the whigs.

They were anyway divided at this crucial time. For the Junto was at odds with the duumvirs. Partly this was due to the struggle for power. It was widely believed that the whig lords would press for Halifax to be appointed, and that one way to accommodate him would be to oust Godolphin from the treasurership. But they were also at loggerheads over the status of the duke of Marlborough. Earlier in 1709 Somers had resisted his attempt to be made Captain General for life. Now another crisis arose involving the duke's constitutional relationship with the Queen in which the Junto leader apparently played an equivocal role. As Captain General, Marlborough had insisted on responsibility for all commissions in the army. This was precisely the kind of usurpation of the royal prerogative which Harley had criticized in 'Plain English'. In January 1710 a chance had arisen for him to persuade the Queen to stand up to Marlborough on this very issue. The earl of Essex, who held the posts of constable of the Tower and colonel of a regiment, died on the 10th after a drinking bout. Backed by Harley, Anne gave the post of constable to Earl Rivers and the regiment to Abigail Masham's brother, Jack Hill, without even informing the duke. Marlborough was outraged. There was little he could do to protest against the appointment of Rivers, since he had indicated his prior approval, even though he privately intended to bestow the office of constable on another. But the promotion of Abigail's brother was a calculated affront, and he objected vehemently to what he termed 'the malice of a bedchamber woman'. After failing to get the Queen to back down, he tried to organize a protest by the whigs against the influence of Abigail. Some responded favourably, raising the issue with the Queen in private audiences. Somers, though, allegedly advised her to stand firm, while protesting to the duke that he had interceded on his behalf. Others, however, were even prepared to go as far as moving an address from the Commons to her Majesty to dismiss Abigail from her service. 'It is children's play, for any men to hold the first posts in a government, & not have it in their power to remove such a slut as that' one of them told Sarah who, incandescent with fury, was exploiting the incident for more than it was worth.[20]

Many of the whig leaders, besides Somers, were lukewarm on the issue, and when Anne made a spirited stand against the proposed address they backed off. She sent a message to the Commons by Vice-Chamberlain Thomas Coke 'that any such address would be very disagreeable to her'.[21] 'It was impossible for any man of sense, honour or honesty to come into an Address to remove a dresser from the Queen' observed another whig 'only to gratify my Lady Marlborough's passions'.[22] The Queen then indicated a willingness to compromise by rescinding the promotion of Hill, although she consoled Abigail's brother with a pension of £1000. This apparent climb down procured an outward reconciliation between Anne and Marlborough. He had an audience with her in which he denied that he had had anything to do with the address to remove Abigail. It was however widely believed that he was lying through his teeth, or as a fellow officer coarsely put it, 'pist backwards' when he said so.[23] As a poem on the incident, with the title 'The Civil War', put it:[24]

> Madam, where I have been with mighty care,
> Health to preserve by taking Windsor air,
> An odd report (as false as God is true)
> Has reach'd my ears (of which I never knew),
> That by Address I had contriv'd that she
> Whom you do love shou'd ever from you be;
> Which cruel consequence I did lament
> And hasten'd quick this Mischief to prevent.
> For surely, Madam, None could ever say
> I cross'd your Inclination any way.

The Sovereign smil'd within herself to hear
Such Lies delivered with so good an air,
But thenceforth bid him seek for no excuse;
Such treachery ne'er should cover such abuse.

The duke was mortified, and anxious to go to the continent as soon as possible. He therefore arranged for a parliamentary address asking the Queen to ensure his presence at the peace conference which was about to start at Geertruidenberg.[25] She was as keen for him to quit the realm as he was, and he left for Holland on 18 February, thereby missing the opening of the trial of Dr Sacheverell.

On the first day the Commons made it clear that it was not just Sacheverell who was on trial, but 'some other of his brethren' who had been 'lately practising in diverse parts of the kingdom'. The prosecution was intended to 'put an end to such sort of seditious proceedings'. The point was emphasized by Walpole on the second day when he hoped that the judgment of the Lords 'will convince the world that every seditious, discontented, hot-headed, ungifted, unedifying preacher . . . who had no hopes of distinguishing himself in the world but by a matchless indiscretion, may not advance with impunity doctrines destructive of the peace and quiet of her Majesty's government'.

Walpole was speaking to the first and most important of the articles of impeachment. He and his fellow whig managers insisted that there had been resistance in 1688 as clear as the sun at noonday, and that it had been justified by the right of the people to resist a monarch who broke the trust between him and his subjects.

It was Peter King, the Recorder of London, who spoke most effectively to the second article. He quoted the passage from the sermon in which Sacheverell had claimed that 'what could not be gained by Comprehension and Toleration must be brought about by moderation and occasional conformity; that is, what they could not do by open violence, they will not fail by secret treachery to accomplish'. King then pointed out that this implied 'the toleration' was 'open violence'; 'that it was an attempt made to destroy the Church, though the Church itself came into and settled this Toleration.'

It was not difficult to demonstrate that Sacheverell's sermon asserted that the Church was in danger. In demonstrating it, however, one of the managers went too far in associating others with the Doctor's viewpoint. John Dolben referred to 'such false brethren as are at your Lordships' bar', an unfortunate expression which he had publicly to repudiate. By everybody's admission, however, Sir Thomas Parker made one of the best speeches in the trial when he spoke to the charge levelled against Sacheverell in the fourth article. He effectively proved that the sermon was consistent with nothing but Jacobitism.

The fourth article had also accused Sacheverell of inciting violence in defence of high church principles. On 28 February, the night after the managers had finished the case for the prosecution, this charge seemed to be prophetic. For a Presbyterian meeting house was attacked and had its windows smashed. The house of its minister, Daniel Burgess, was also damaged. The disturbances on that evening were nothing, however, in comparison with the rioting that broke out the following night. Then there was a pre-concerted attack on Burgess's meeting house which was systematically demolished, and its contents burned in a huge bonfire. The mob then moved on to attack five other dissenting meeting houses, four of which suffered the same fate as Burgess's. They were about to attack the Bank and other targets in the City, including the town houses of Dolben and Wharton, when horse and foot guards sent from St James's on the direct orders of the Queen arrived to disperse them. The timely intervention of the troops saved meeting houses from destruction, for according to a tory newswriter 'there had not been one left standing in the City and suburbs by the morning if the Guards had not prevented'.[26]

The spectacle of a mob demonstrating for a high church cause struck many observers as curious. 'We are now come to fresh paradoxical circumstances,' observed a staunch tory, 'that while the rabble are pulling down houses out of zeal for passive obedience the vile tools of the most arbitrary ministry that ever nation groaned under are rending their throats in defence of forcible resistance.'[27] Another tory was moved to express it in rhyme:[28]

> Invidious *Whigs* since you have made your Boast,
> That you a *Church of England* Priest would roast,
> Blame not the Mob, for having a Desire
> With *Presbyterian* Tubs to light the Fire.

To a whig like Arthur Mainwaring, Sacheverell had 'debauched the very principles of the mob, which used formerly not to be much in the wrong. They rose then against some publick grievance, but never till now against the law & constitution.'[29]

This was, however, a very unusual mob, at least as far as the evidence of those apprehended by the authorities goes.[30] It was not a spontaneous uprising by the labouring poor, but a carefully organized operation by craftsmen directed by some members of the professions and perhaps even concerted by the London tories.[31]

The 'night of fire' provided an interlude between the case for the prosecution and that for the defence. Sir Simon Harcourt handled his brief for the Doctor brilliantly. By all accounts his speech on the first article was spellbinding. He got Sacheverell off the hook of denying that there had been resistance in 1688 by defining the supreme power which, in traditional Anglican doctrine, could not be resisted as the king, lords and commons, and not the king alone. This was to put a construction on the words of the sermon which strained them, for there can be little doubt that the preacher had meant by supreme power only the crown. However there was enough doubt to take the edge off the charge. The other four counsel retained by Sacheverell were undistinguished by comparison with Harcourt, but they had to bear the burden of replying to the remaining three articles. Sir Simon's return to parliament in a by-election for Cardiff had been effected for nearly two weeks before it was formally communicated to parliament. The deliberate delay had enabled him to plead for the preacher on 3 March. Thereafter as a member of the Commons he was debarred from defending him further.

His colleagues were not as convincing in their replies to the remaining charges. Thus one argument used to rebut the second article was that the Toleration Act was only so-called in conventional usage, and did not have that name in law, so that it was not inappropriate to deny that there was a legal toleration. The reply to the accusation that he claimed the Church to be in danger largely took the form of reading out passages from works which criticized the establishment. Finally Sacheverell himself made a speech in his own defence. It had however been prepared for him by such advisers as Francis Atterbury, who ensured that it was much more moderate in tone than his fiery sermons. It took up the point made at the outset of the trial that he alone was not arraigned but stood in for the high flyers in general. 'The avowed design of my impeachment,' he asserted, 'is . . . to procure an eternal and indelible brand of infamy to be fixed in a parliamentary way on all those who maintain the doctrine of non-resistance.' He then maintained his innocence and loyalty in words chosen and delivered so skilfully to win over his hearers that many, hardened politicians as well as sympathetic ladies, openly wept to hear him. The proceedings were then adjourned for two days.

When they recommenced on 9 March the managers replied to the case for the defence. They rehearsed the arguments on each of the articles afresh, claiming that many had not even been addressed, much less refuted by Sacheverell and his counsel. In conclusion Sir Thomas Parker conceded that the Doctor was a representative of a type of clergyman whose views were unacceptable to the prosecution. 'What we expect from your Lordships' justice,' he declared, 'is the supporting our Establishment . . . and I hope the clergy will be instructed not to preach the doctrine of submission in such a way as to prepare the way for rebellion.'

The drama now shifted from the MPs and the lawyers to the Lords, who had to reach a verdict. The first real test of the disposition of the peers came when Nottingham raised a technical point which, if upheld, would have invalidated the whole trial. This was that express words from the sermon should have been specified in the indictment. Although Nottingham had a good point in law, the prosecution managed to uphold the validity of the articles exhibited against Sacheverell on 14 March by 65 votes to 47. This seemed to augur well for the whigs, and to foreshadow a severe punishment for Sacheverell. The next vote came at the end of a long debate on the first article. Although it was on a procedural point of whether the question, that the Commons had proved the first article against the Doctor, should be put in Westminster Hall or the House of Lords, the outcome was another whig victory of 68 against 51. The majority against Sacheverell was so far holding firm. The following day the remaining articles were approved without any division. It seemed as though the tories had conceded the trial to their opponents. When the lords stood in their places to give their individual verdicts on 20 March the outcome was predictable. Sacheverell was found guilty by 69 votes to 52.

The following day's decisions on the sentence, however, were unexpected. The Court wanted him to be incapacitated from preaching, fined and imprisoned. Nothing less, in their view, would deter likeminded incendiaries from delivering seditious sermons. Some of the more zealous whigs would have gone further, to have him pilloried and 'whipped in a cart from the Royal Exchange to Charing Cross'. Sensing that the wind was shifting against an 'exemplary punishment', the ministry in the event proposed a minimal sentence compatible with their insistence upon deterring the high-flying clergy from echoing the Doctor's views. They therefore proposed that he should be barred from preaching for seven years, during which time he should not be given any preferment in the Church, and provide securities for his good behaviour. He was also to be imprisoned for three months, and his sermon was to be burned by the common hangman. An amendment was proposed, however, even to the first proposal, reducing the period of incapacity to twelve months. The ministers managed to obtain a compromise of three years, though even this was carried by a mere six votes. The second recommendation, to deprive him of preferment, was actually defeated by 60 votes to 59. The proposal to imprison the Doctor had then to be abandoned altogether. It was cold comfort to the Court that the burning of the sermon by the common hangman went by on the nod. 'So all this bustle and fatigue,' Godolphin informed Marlborough, 'ends in no more but a suspension for 3 years from the pulpit and burning his sermons at the old Exchange.'[32]

How had this result, so disastrous from the government's viewpoint, so promising from that of the tories, been reached? The apparently rock solid Court whig majority in the Upper House had been broken down by crucial defections. Even the result of the vote on the verdict struck Marlborough as surprisingly slim. 'Out of the list sent of the devission in the House of Lords', he wrote to Sarah, he could not understand 'how these 9 Lords were influenced to be for Sacheverall: Duke of Northumberland, Duke Hamilton, Earl of Pembrook, Earl Suffolk, Bishop of Chichister, Lord Berkley, Earl Northask, Earl Weems, Lord Lexington. I should have thought all these would have been on the other side.' The only two whigs he named, however, Suffolk and the bishop of Chichester, were listed in error. The other seven were Court tories whose defections were at least explicable.[33] What led the Court to lose its majority on 21 March was the defection of eight whigs, including the duke of Somerset who had been absent the day before claiming illness, though Godolphin fancied ''t'was only profound wisdome that kept him away from the House'.[34] Earlier Marlborough had expressed the opinion that 'his behaviour in this matter will be a treu weathercock of [the Queen]'.[35]

Anne's attitude was indeed vital. At first she told Burnet that 'it was a bad sermon, and that he deserved well to be punished for it'.[36] On 27 February, however, she told her physician Sir David Hamilton 'that there ought to be a punishment but a mild one'.[37] Later the marquis of Kent discovered that 'she thought the Commons had reason to be satisfied that they had made their allegations good, and the mildest punishment inflicted upon the Doctor she thought the best'.[38]

It seems that the queen's views moderated over the months which elapsed between the decision to impeach Sacheverell and the final outcome of the trial. Hamilton attributed her inclination to a mild punishment to her fear of the mob getting out of hand if the Doctor were to be dealt with harshly. It seems however that he was not privy to the influence being brought to bear upon her by Robert Harley. Although the duumvirs suspected that he was secretly working on Anne's susceptibilities from the day of his disgrace in 1708, in fact the former Secretary had lain low, rarely contacting her. He did not even arrive in London from his home in Herefordshire for the start of the parliamentary session, but got there early in January 1710. Once in town, however, he quickly picked up the political vibrations emanating from Court. He was aware of the divisions in the ranks of the whigs not only over the Sacheverell affair but also over the Regiments crisis, and was determined to exploit them for his own advantage. It was Harley who won over Somerset to the policy of using the growing concern about the wisdom of prosecuting Sacheverell to wrong foot the government. By working on dissidents in the whigs' own ranks he was also able to convince the Queen that her days of thraldom to the duumvirs could soon be over. He stiffened her resolve to stand up to the duke of Marlborough on the issue of the disposal of Lord

Essex's military posts, in defiance of the Captain General's claims that he should have the last word in the issue of commissions. Above all he determined to exploit the surprising outcome of the Sacheverell trial to effect a change in the ministry, and to succeed in 1710 where he had failed in 1708.

10

1710

The ending of the parliamentary session on 5 April 1710 came as a great relief to the ministers. It offered a breathing space in which they could recover from the humiliations of the Sacheverell trial. There was, after all, over a year to go before a general election would be required under the terms of the Triennial Act, which gave them plenty of time to recover from the setback, especially if the peace negotiations at Geertruidenberg concluded in a successful treaty. As they left London, many of them heading towards Newmarket along with the Lord Treasurer, they can scarcely have suspected that the current parliament would never meet again, that a ministerial revolution would occur over the summer, and that new elections would be held in the autumn which would transform a whig into a tory majority in the House of Commons.

Yet to some onlookers the writing was clearly on the wall. It was obvious that the ministry had lost the support of the Queen. Although according to Burnet her speech ending the session 'seemed to look a different way from the whispers that had been set about', it did not deceive an observant tory poet:[1]

> So represented have I seen
> On Puppet-Stage, a mimick Queen;
> The manag'd Engin seem'd to speak
> With Voice unfeign'd, and Movements make,
> But 'tis thro' an ambiguous Light,
> The lifeless Image cheats the Sight,
> Whilst secret Wire and hidden Spring
> Directs the artificial Thing.
> The Royal Eccho thus rebounds,
> Words not her own, in borrow'd Sounds.

In her speech Anne expressed the wish that 'men would study to be quiet, rather than busy themselves in disputes which must be with an ill intention, since it only tends to foment and not heal our divisions'.[2] Yet sentiments sympathetic to Sacheverell and antagonistic to his prosecutors were already forming the substance of loyal addresses. The first was drawn up on 18 March in Gloucestershire, and 'presented to the queen by Mr Bathurst, member for Cirencester, introduced by the duke of Beaufort'. By the time of the prorogation of parliament it had been followed by others from Cornwall, Devon, Herefordshire, Monmouthshire, Northamptonshire and Warwickshire. These heralded an addressing campaign which produced about 100 tory addresses over the next five months, compared with only 15 whig efforts.[3] Fairly typical of the effusions from the tories was the 'humble address of the county of Stafford assembled at the Assizes', which expressed the concern of its signatories 'for your sacred person prerogative and government, our holy church its doctrine and ordinances in the defence of which we are willing to make a cheerful oblation of our selves and fortunes against all republican schismatical treacherous and inward enemies, as well as against all outward and declar'd ones'. They also declared their intention to 'choose such only to represent us in succeeding parliaments as are true and approv'd sons of the Church, dutiful and loyal subjects of the Crown, and faithful to the succession as by law established'.[4]

At first Anne did not countenance the addresses publicly. Thus when the Gloucester address was presented to her it was noted that 'her majestie took little notice of it'.[5] However, as the trickle became a spate she began openly to show her approval of them and by implication the views they expressed, even though they patently kept up the divisions and animosities among her subjects.

Indeed the groundswell of public opinion in favour of the tories must have encouraged her to embark on the reconstruction of the ministry which Harley urged her to undertake. For it meant that, if the present ministers protested at the changes, she could always hold out the threat of a dissolution which would inevitably procure a tory majority in the Commons and at a stroke remove their main hold over her. The possibility of fresh elections a whole year before they were necessary was at first used only as a weapon to regain her prerogative of appointing and dismissing ministers which in Anne's view, which was endorsed by Harley, she had surrendered to the duumvirs in recent years. That in the end she did appoint a predominantly tory ministry and dissolve parliament does not mean that she intended that outcome from the start. Discussions of the ministerial revolution of 1710 have too often been handicapped by a hindsight which makes the methodological error of deducing intentions from results.[6]

One consequence has been to attribute the changes of the year to the machiavellian cunning of Robert Harley. While he indeed played a major role in them he was by no means in sole control of their course. Others also exercised influence over them, not least the queen. Indeed her part in the alterations has been consistently underestimated by historians.

Anne probably intended in the spring of 1710 only to rid herself of the influence of 'the family', by which she meant the Marlboroughs and Sunderland, to whom Harley added Godolphin though the queen, as we shall see, was reluctant to include him. Marlborough had quarrelled with her during the Regiments crisis in the winter, and while they had been superficially reconciled before he went prematurely to Holland, the resentment against the Churchills still simmered.[7] Sarah brought it to the boil the day after the prorogation of parliament when she had a searing last interview with Anne in which both were reduced to impotent tears. Anne, all too aware of the duchess's scalding temper, tried to restrict conversation by refusing to answer Sarah's impertinent questions, insisting that she put them in writing. This merely served to provoke even more outrageous responses culminating in the curse 'that God would punish her [Anne] either in this world or in the next for what she had done to her this day'.[8] There the interview ended. 'Mrs Freeman' never met 'Mrs Morley again.'

Just over a week later, on 15 April, the queen surprised the political world by dismissing the marquess of Kent from the post of Lord Chamberlain and replacing him with the duke of Shrewsbury. The choice of Kent was possibly revenge on the duchess of Marlborough since she had been instrumental in his obtaining the post. At all events Godolphin, who received the news at Newmarket, 'beleiv'd it was owing to the Queens Estrangement from the Duchess'. While the sacking of 'the Bug', as the malodorous Kent was known, was almost certainly the Queen's doing, the choice of his successor owed much to the machinations of Harley. Shrewsbury had played a prominent part in the politics of the Revolution and William's reign before deciding to go on an extended visit to Italy. After his return to England in 1707 he had rather stayed out of the political world, though his entry was solicited by both Marlborough and Harley. Harley's attentions had clearly borne fruit by the time of the Sacheverell trial when the duke, though regarded as a whig, voted for the Doctor.

The fact that Shrewsbury was a whig has been seen as a feint on the part of Harley, to divert attention from his plan to replace the whigs with moderates from both parties. Thus, despite not being consulted, Godolphin could assure Sir David Hamilton that 'he should not give [the Queen] any disquiet about the Duke of Shrewsbury' unaware that it was the thin end of a wedge to overthrow his ministry.[9] Yet at this stage Anne was intent only on asserting her prerogative and removing the earl of Sunderland, who 'always treated her with great rudeness and neglect, and chose to reflect in a very injurious manner upon all princes, before her, as a proper entertainment for her'.[10] While Harley hoped to persuade her to remove Godolphin too, even he did not wish to go much further, intending 'only the removal of the treasurer and his immediate dependants, with some few others, to make room for his own friends, and then to have continued the parliament and the war with the duke of Marlborough in the command of it'.[11]

The corollary of this was that both the Queen and Harley were prepared to work with the Junto. This seems implausible at first sight, given that both had striven hard to prevent the five 'tyrannizing lords' gaining office in the first place. But time had lessened the strain between them and Anne at least. Somers' charm had worked on her, and she had welcomed his advice during the Regiments crisis. Even Wharton proved less of a bugbear in office then he had in opposition, while his absence in Ireland as Lord Lieutenant, though it did not make her heart grow fonder, helped to reconcile them more. Anne had grown to prefer the whig leaders to high church tories such as the earls of Rochester and Nottingham. Rochester had strained her patience in the first year of her reign because he opposed her grant of a pension to Marlborough, but as we shall see she now took a rather different view of her uncle's opposition to her previous generosity to the duke. Though Rochester was no longer *persona non grata*, Nottingham had rendered himself so obnoxious to her that she refused to take him back into the ministry at any price. Given the choice, and Harley knew that they had to rely on one set of party leaders or the other, it is not altogether surprising that she would have preferred the whigs at this time. Two days before she dismissed Sunderland she confided in Somers that she was 'well aware that your lordship will be very much concerned at this resolution' and assured him that she did 'not intend to make any farther resolutions'.[12]

As for Harley, he was not merely aiming to replace the duumvirs in power as had been the case two years earlier. He now was committed to negotiating peace with France. Yet he did not want a peace at any price. On the contrary, he wished to negotiate from a position of strength. From this point of view the fact that Louis XIV was to call off the peace negotiations shortly after Sunderland's removal was ominous. It indicated that the French king expected better terms from a reconstructed English ministry than he could get from the Dutch. To make too many changes, above all to take in too many tories, would jeopardize Harley's scheme. He too therefore was prepared to work with the whigs.

The Junto for their part were no longer totally averse to dealing with 'Robin the Trickster' as they had been in 1708. Indeed as early as July 1709 Marlborough had been of the opinion that 'the greatest part of

the whigs will join with Harley and Mrs Masham'.[13] They had to be
persuaded to accept the dismissal of Sunderland, one of their number.
This would have been more difficult for Anne and her accomplices
to effect earlier in the reign, when the Junto had shown remarkable
solidarity in pressuring her to take Sunderland into office. However,
the admission of three others, Orford, Somers and Wharton, into the
Cabinet, and the exclusion of Halifax, had rather weakened their unity.
Wharton was still the most strident advocate of collective action, but
he was at a disadvantage in Dublin in trying to persuade his Junto
colleagues to stick together. Halifax was so desperate for office that
he began to intrigue with Harley behind the scenes soon after the
Sacheverell trial. Given assurances that the changes would be restricted
to Sunderland the Junto were ready to acquiesce, as Walpole observed,
the Secretary was 'by none endeavoured to be saved'.[14]

Although Sunderland's dismissal had been agreed soon after Shrewsbury's appointment, it was delayed until 14 June. This delay was due
to disagreements about his successor. The earl of Dartmouth, who
was eventually appointed to the vacant Secretaryship, explained that
Sunderland[15]

> was kept a month longer than was designed, upon a dispute who should
> succeed him; the queen would not hear of Lord Nottingham, nor the
> whigs of Lord Anglesea ... At last the queen proposed me, as one she
> had known long, and believed she could live easily with herself, and
> asked Lord Somers if he thought the whigs could do so too; he told her
> she could not have pitched upon a properer person; for though I was
> looked upon as a tory, I was known to be no zealous party man; and he
> was sure the whigs would live very well with me, and would understand
> it to be her own choice, and think themselves well come off, after the
> alarm Lord Anglesea had given them.

This information from one most closely involved deserves the closest
scrutiny. It is clear from it that Anne took the leading part. It is also
apparent that deals were being struck with the Junto. It was possibly the
whig lords who proposed the otherwise unlikely name of Nottingham
as Sunderland's replacement. Harley had apparently suggested his close
friend Lord Poulet, but he had declined, which was another cause of
the delay in dismissing the Secretary.[16] Obviously the Queen wanted
a tory in the post, and Nottingham at least was a staunch advocate of
'no peace without Spain' to which the whigs were committed. As for the
earl of Anglesey, he was too high church for their liking. Dartmouth, as
he himself acknowledged, was the queen's own choice.[17]

Anne almost certainly wanted to go no further than this. When
Sunderland's fall provoked a deputation from the Bank anxious about
the effects of ministerial changes on the stock market she assured them

that she had 'no thoughts of making any further alterations'. She also informed the Dutch that it was her 'intention not to make any other change, and to support the Allys and carry on the warr with the same vigor as ever'.[18] Two months were to elapse before the next alteration, the dismissal of Godolphin. Where the delay in getting rid of Sunderland was due to the disagreements over his successor, this was caused by Anne's reluctance to part with the treasurer who had served her so long. 'Mr Montgomery' had a special place in her affections, and was not as closely identified with 'the family' as the former Secretary. Indeed if he could have been persuaded to repudiate Sarah, which the queen begged him to do, he might have survived in office. As she told Sir David Hamilton often 'O that my Lord Godolphin would be parted from the Duchess of Marlborough I should be very happy'.[19] Harley was exasperated with her indecision, writing a memorandum before an audience on 3 July: 'you must preserve your character and spirit and speak to Lord Treasurer. Get quit of him.'[20] It took her another month to do so. Anne even attempted to reconcile Godolphin and Harley.[21] What possible accommodation the two could have come to is very hard to see. Given the circumstances in which they had parted company in 1708, when Harley's actions were denounced by Godolphin as unforgiveable, this could scarcely have worked out satisfactorily. Yet Anne must have intended some kind of working partnership between them.[22]

She finally grasped the nettle on 8 August. That day she wrote to the Lord Treasurer:[23]

> The uneasiness which you have showed for some time has given me very much trouble, though I have borne it; and had your behaviour continued the same it was for a few years after my coming to the crown, I could have no dispute with myself what to do. But the many unkind returns I have received since, especially what you said to me personally before the Lords, makes it impossible for me to continue you any longer in my service; but I will give you a pension of four thousand a year, and I desire that, instead of bringing the staff to me, you will break it, which I believe will be easier to us both.

There is a mixture of an accumulation of dissatisfaction hinted at here, together with an immediate cause of irritation – 'what you said to me personally before the Lords.' This must be a reference to something Godolphin had said in Cabinet. The most recent meeting of the ministers presided over by the Queen had been held on 30 July, when they had discussed the question of the dissolution of parliament. Godolphin had been concerned for several weeks about the growing rumours that Anne's secret advisers were pressing for a general election. On 29 June he had informed Marlborough that he had 'told the Queen very plainly that to think of parting with parliament was present ruine and distraction, and therfore it was never possible for him to consent to it, but in that case, he must begg his dismission before that resolution came to bee declared'.[24] Anne was particularly sensitive on the subject, perhaps because it so nearly concerned her prerogative which she was currently concerned to assert against a ministry she felt was bent on usurping it. When, at the instigation of the Junto and the Lord Treasurer, the States general of the Dutch republic sent her a memorial expressing anxiety at the dismissal of Sunderland, and requesting reassurances not only that there would be no more changes but that she would not dissolve parliament, she had been outraged. At a Cabinet meeting held on 2 July where the memorial had been discussed she icily rebuked the States for interfering in British affairs, informing them that 'as it was the first of this kind she hoped it would be the last'.[25] 'The answer that was returned' crowed the tory leader William Bromley, 'I am told was worthy of Q. Eliz. It was given in the Cabinet without consultation upon it, & in such a manner that there was not a word offered against it.'[26]

Besides wishing to retain the prerogative of dissolving parliament on principle, Anne was also using the threat of a dissolution as a weapon against the ministers if they failed to fall into line with the changes she and Harley wished to make. They used the uncertainty which this created to turn the threat against her. Thus they drew attention to the adverse effects it was having on the stock market. 'The credit continues to sink and the difficulties to increase,' Godolphin informed Marlborough on 18 July 'and unless there bee a speedy remedy, the government will bee very soon in the greatest extremitys. All possible pains has been taken to make the Queen sensible of this.'[27] Ministers also claimed that the political situation in England, with its prospects of changes in favour of French interests, led Louis XIV to call off the peace negotiations, publishing his reasons in a manifesto. At a Cabinet held probably on 23 July 'Lord Somers gave his opinion very strongly for the continuation of the war, till the restitution of Spain and the West Indies; and intimated that nothing could have encouraged the French ministers to hold that insolent language in their manifesto, but the intrigues that were carrying on at home.'[28] The day after the meeting Godolphin, who apparently had not been present at it, wrote to inform Marlborough that 'the madness continues as fierce as ever against parliament, and most people that I talk with think that extremity is now very near. Whenever it does come, I am of opinion it must necessarily oblige Godolphin, Somers and Cowper etc. to show their dislike of it in the most publick manner.'[29] It was presumably this intransigent attitude that he adopted at the next Cabinet meeting, which did discuss the rumours of a pending dissolution, and which

Anne had in mind when she sent him the letter of dismissal. Godolphin apparently had the nerve to refer again to the Dutch memorial when the question of the dissolution came up in Cabinet. Commenting on his fall Halifax referred to a report that the 'Lord T[reasurer] let fall some words in the debate about the resolution of the States which gave offence to the Queen personally'.[30] When Godolphin was served notice of his dismissal, allegedly by a groom, he broke his staff of office in the presence of John Smith, Chancellor of the Exchequer, throwing the pieces into the fire place. Smith then reported to Anne that the treasurer had obeyed her commands.[31]

Immediately after Godolphin's dismissal Harley, who up till then had operated behind the scenes, came out into the open. The treasury was put into commission, and though Poulet was nominally first Lord Harley was the effective leader. The other members were Robert Benson, Sir Thomas Mansel and Henry Paget. This was a peculiarly Harleyite body. All were moderate tories, Benson indeed being so 'very moderate' that Addison referred to him as a 'reputed whig'.[32] The commission therefore, as Godolphin guessed, was 'such a one as will utterly distast the Tories'.[33] Harley even offered a place on the commission to the whig Richard Hampden, but he refused when no assurance was forthcoming that parliament would not be dissolved.[34]

Harley was still aiming at a scheme which would remove the influence of 'the family' and replace it with himself and his own nominees, and would then retain as many whigs and make as few concessions to the tories as possible. But the experience with Hampden revealed that there was a price to pay for whig support which he would not, and perhaps could not, pay: a guarantee that there would be no dissolution of parliament that year. Although the whole political world acted after Godolphin's fall on the assumption that a general election was imminent, the final decision on that point rested with the Queen. And she kept people guessing throughout August and most of September. On 1 August she had prorogued the Houses until 26 September. A decision either for another prorogation or a dissolution could therefore not be postponed beyond that date. Yet Anne waited until 21 September before summoning a meeting of the privy council to announce that parliament was dissolved.

Anne's own role in these weeks cannot now be completely separated from Harley's. Yet that she retained some initiative in the changes which occurred before the announcement of the dissolution is apparent. Thus on 13 August the earl of Anglesey and Robert Harley were admitted to the Cabinet 'as a particular favour of the queens'.[35] Anglesey, to the consternation of the whigs, after they had virtually vetoed his appointment as Secretary of State, had replaced Lord Coningsby as Vice Treasurer of Ireland early in July. His promotion to the Cabinet

was unique, no other holder of that office ever having that honour.[36]
While it cannot be proved, it is at least possible that the choice of the
high church Anglesey for Cabinet office came from Anne's predilection
for that wing of the tory party, coupled with a prejudice against its
acknowledged leader, the earl of Nottingham.

The ministerial changes indeed were to go further in favour of
the tories than Harley originally wished, let alone intended. In part
this was because the whigs he approached by and large insisted like
Hampden on a commitment to retain the existing parliament. Thus
Henry Boyle, the Secretary of state who moved from the northern to
the southern department on Sunderland's fall, and Lord Chancellor
Cowper both resisted his blandishments. Boyle resigned on 20 September.[37] Although Harley tried to assure Cowper that 'a whig game' was
'intended at bottom', and even sent Robert Monckton, a moderate whig
MP to camp on Cowper's doorstep for three days, it was without avail.[38]
On 21 September at the privy council meeting chosen to announce the
dissolution of parliament the Lord Chancellor rose to object, but Anne
brought the proceedings to an abrupt end. Two days later, even though
the Queen 'press'd his staying in' he resigned.[39] Harley thought that
Cowper's resignation 'was concerted'.[40] It was accompanied by those
of Orford and Wharton. Wharton, who arrived from Ireland on 8
September, apparently stiffened whig resistance to Harley's overtures.
He had

> a detestation of having anything to do with Harley, of whom he talked
> with the utmost indignation and scorn, saying, he could do no business,
> would soon break his own neck, and that all things would be in such
> confusion as to force the queen back again into the hands of the whigs.
> That this was the situation of power they ought to be in, and not to have
> it in such a motley ministry with such a r[at] as Harley at the head of
> it, who perhaps meant now only to cheat them into an assistance he
> wanted from them for his present purpose. This was strong, and it had
> its effect.

Since Devonshire and Somers had both been dismissed before the
Privy Council met on the 21st the net result of these removals and
accompanying appointments struck Burnet as 'so sudden and so entire
a change of the ministry [as] is scarce to be found in our history'.[41]

The new appointees were tories. Boyle was replaced by Henry St
John, Cowper by a tory commission for the great seal, Devonshire by
the duke of Buckingham, Orford and other whig commissioners of the
admiralty by a tory board headed by Sir John Leake, Somers by the earl
of Rochester and Wharton, eventually, by the duke of Ormonde. Again
it seems that Anne was more inclined towards the tory party than was
Harley at this time. He had not originally planned to bring even his old

colleague St John into the Cabinet. Instead he had been earmarked for his former post of Secretary at war, which he resented as not being a promotion at all. While his eventual appointment as Secretary of state was Harley's doing, the replacement of Devonshire as Lord steward by Buckingham and of Somers as Lord president of the council by Rochester seems to have been more the Queen's. At the time that she made Anglesey Vice Treasurer of Ireland she reportedly 'sent for' Rochester to come to court.[42] Once there he asserted 'that he never was nor ever would be concerned' with Harley.[43] On 18 August he was said to be 'highly disgusted against Mr Harley' because 'he, Buckingham and Nottingham' were 'left out of this new scheme'. There was even a saying attributed to him that 'before the winter was over he did not question but he shou'd see the Duke of Shrewsbury go sick into the country, and Harley glad to get over into France in a cock boat'.[44] By 1 September, however, Rochester was meeting and conferring with them both.[45]

While there is no hard evidence to substantiate it, the circumstances strongly suggest that Anne brought her uncle and her favourite together by the beginning of September. Their discussions involved some hard bargaining. Rochester was offered Somers's post of Lord President of the council, but held out until Harley agreed to take in some tories whom he had wished to exclude.[46] Thus high church tories who had hitherto been kept in the dark now found themselves let into Harley's 'great scheme'. As one of their leaders, William Bromley, wrote to James Grahme:[47]

> The scene being opened I have had repeated assurances that no interest will be considered but the Church's. They are willing to make their bottom as wide as they can, and to receive those who are of distinction, and have no blemish, provided they will come in on the same interest. Some who have been very instrumental in bringing about this great work must be taken care of, and we must not grudge and envy them any advantage, such as E[arl] R[ivers], Arg[yll] and his brother. This is the language to me.

Bromley was referring to the group of whigs in whom Harley had confided ever since the Sacheverell trial, and which some called 'the Juntilla'. Until recently they had included the duke of Somerset, who delighted in the twilight world of intrigue which Harley created around his scheme, but who drew back after Godolphin's dismissal and opposed any hint of a dissolution. According to Bromley 'the delays . . . are imputed to the D of S——t, who has been very serviceable, but of late intolerable . . . They have been unwilling to break with him, bec[ause] a certain person [the Queen] has a kindness to him and therefore all means have been tried to make him easy.' Anne had a regard for the proud duke on account of his wife, who had been a lady of the bedchamber since 1702 and who had replaced the duchess of Marlborough as her confidante.[48]

The Queen's personal predilections had very much to be taken into consideration by her intimate advisers at this time. She was still trying to retain her new found independence from the parties, informing archbishop Sharp 'that she would neither be in the hands of the Whigs nor of the Tories'.[49] Yet the refusal of more than a handful of moderate whigs to stay in office if parliament were to be dissolved, and the necessity to come to terms with Rochester and the high church tories now that they had obliged Harley to make concessions to them, made a dissolution imperative.[50] Still Anne refused to accept the logic of the situation. 'If the Queen wil reforme her cabinet,' Harley wrote on 12 September, 'the rest wil be easier after.'[51] The initiative lay with her, and it was with evident relief that Harley informed the duke of Newcastle on 14 September that she had at last agreed to a dissolution 'it being resolved in her own breast'.[52]

The Proclamation dissolving parliament drew attention to the addresses which had been pouring in ever since the Spring.[53] One in particular had been especially welcome to Anne. This was from the bishop of London and the clergy of London and Westminster, assuring her Majesty that their acknowledgement of her hereditary title did not mean that they were Jacobites. It was presented by bishop Compton accompanied by over 150 clergymen on 22 August, and received very kindly by the Queen.[54] They claimed to represent 'the unanimous sense and resolution of the clergy, not only of these Cities, but of the whole Kingdom'. Their studied moderation and regard for the Protestant succession was exactly the antidote Anne and her new ministers wanted to the fireraising antics of Sacheverell, who had been electioneering in the Midlands and Welsh border counties during the summer. The Queen herself said on the very day that the address was presented that '*Sacheverel* was a foolish man, for going into the country'.[55] During his progress he encouraged addresses to the Queen for a new parliament, their tone becoming 'increasingly shrill, frequently hysterical'.[56] The address from the clergy of London and Westminster seemed to indicate that the high church hysteria which Sacheverell had whipped up was at last dying down, and that more moderate views were beginning to prevail. Hence the Queen's public acknowledgement of her approval of its sentiments.

Certainly Anne and Harley were anxious not to encourage tory extremism during the election campaign. On the contrary it was noted that the ministerial changes were checked, as Swift observed, because 'the new ministry are afraid of too great a majority of their own side in the House of Commons.'[57] They wished to convey the image of being 'something of a mixture'.[58] This was particularly true of local

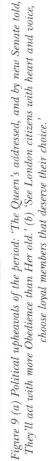

Figure 9 (a) Political upheavals of the period: 'The Queen's addressed, and by new Senate told, / They'll act with more Obedience than Her old.' (b) 'See London citizens with heart and voice, / choose loyal members that deserve their choice.'

offices, which had a significant influence on elections, and which were not changed to anything like the same extent as central posts. In only two counties, Cornwall and Hampshire, were whig Lords Lieutenant replaced by tories. The duke of Beaufort was made Governor of the Isle of Wight and the earl of Berkeley chancellor of the Duchy of Lancaster.[59] Otherwise nothing was done by the Crown in the localities to influence the elections. Indeed local officials in the customs and excise, post and salt offices were given specific instructions from the Treasury commission 'to be very sure that they do not unduly meddle in elections contrary to law'.[60]

The general election of 1710 witnessed more contests than any other during the decade, at least 127 constituencies going to the polls in England and Wales. As usual the south-east accounted for most, though this was to some extent owing to the fact that, uniquely, all the Cinque Ports but Dover were contested. Here Harley must have taken some comfort from the fact that the results of these contests did not indicate a marked swing to the tories. The sixteen seats had been held by fourteen whigs, one tory and the archetypal Court placeman William Lowndes, Secretary to the Treasury, on the eve of the polls. Immediately after the polling only two more tories had been returned. This indicated the success of the prime minister's strategy of not using the influence of the Court on behalf of tory candidates. Lord Weymouth had written to him in late July to inform him that 'we understrappers are as busy as if the writs were sealed, and hope for good success could we see a reformation of the Excise and Custom House officers, whose influence on boroughs is greater than can be imagined. The Cinque Ports are much guided by the Lord Warden . . . '.[61] Yet there had been no purge of the revenue officials, while the whig earl of Dorset was retained as Warden. Ominously, however, there were petitions from three unsuccessful tory candidates against whigs returned for Hythe and Winchilsea. Their fate depended on the national results of the election. An overall tory majority would give them a sympathetic hearing and alter the ratio of tories to whigs representing the Cinque Ports.

And nationally the results began to run in favour of the tories more than Harley wished. The Huguenot journalist Abel Boyer noted that the first results indicated an even number of tories and whigs, which 'answered the expectation and desires of those who having gained their chief aim . . . and having now the principal management of affairs, designed to carry things fair and even between both parties'. However, 'it soon appeared that they were mistaken in their computations . . . and that the new members of the Church party far outnumbered those of the contrary side'.[62] The tendency was already clear by the end of the first week. 'In a list I saw yesterday of about twenty,' Swift observed

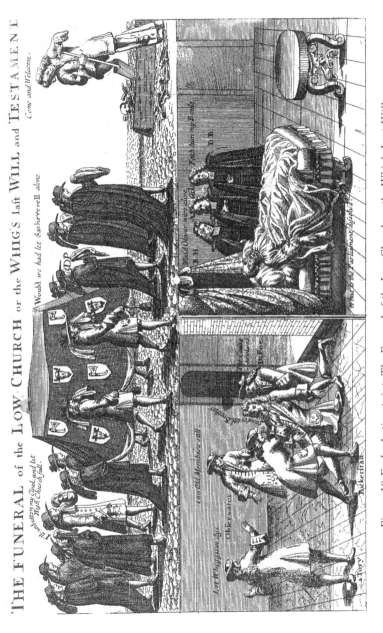

Figure 10 Early election print: *The Funeral of the Low Church or the Whig's Last Will and Testament 'Would we had let Sacheverell alone'*, 1710.

on 6 October, 'there are seven or eight more tories than in the last parliament.' Four days later the trend was even more marked, 'for of thirty new members', he informed archbishop King, 'about twenty six are Tories'.[63] By the time almost half the results were published James Brydges wrote to inform a tory friend in his own constituency 'my calculation is 178 Tories, 61 Whigs & 14 doubtfull, as I take them from the Gazettes & I believe I am pretty exact'.[64] The tory newsletter writer Dyer was jubilant, his reports on the results from the first on 5 October to the last on 9 November being ecstatic commentaries on the success of 'the Church party' in the open constituencies.[65] 'Since my last,' he wrote on 19 October, 'we have had an account of divers other elections, some of which have gone for the Church, other for the whigs, but the latter are still considerable losers in the main.' 'The elections since my last,' he crowed on 31 October, 'have gone as well as heart could desire.'

Commenting on the Westminster election Dyer claimed that the whigs used the cry 'no Pretender' while the tories riposted with 'no managers, but for the Queen and Church' which slogan, he predicted 'is like to carry it thro the Kingdom'. The Westminster result came relatively early, on 9 October, and was a pointer to the outcome of contests in populous constituencies. The candidates were two tories, Thomas Medlycott one of the members in the late parliament, and Thomas Crosse, a local brewer; and two whigs, Sir Henry Dutton Colt and General James Stanhope, who at the time was absent on military duty in Spain, where he had just been conspicuous in the removal of the Bourbon Court from Madrid. The main contest was held to be between the whig general and the tory brewer. Stanhope was supported by a galaxy of whig peers, including no fewer than five dukes; Bedford, Devonshire, Montague, Newcastle and Somerset. Some whigs were sanguine that Stanhope would succeed. 'It pleases me very much that I think his election is beyond a dispute', Robert Walpole told another General on 16 September.[66] Others were less optimistic. James Lowther was convinced from the outset that:[67]

> The elections are like to go just as I expected, that is always as the Courtiers please, especially at the change of a ministry, when peoples malice, revenge, hopes, fears etc. all help to gett a present majority . . . Westminster [will go] for any body that is countenanced by the Court, Gen[era]ll Stanhops great services in Spain, his integrity and great abilitys, now the Court sun does not shine upon him, can make nothing of it against a brewer.

The contest sparked off a literary battle. On 28 September Arthur Mainwaring published in *The Whig Examiner* an election speech for Stanhope in the *persona* of Alcibiades. 'Let it not avail my competitor that he has been tapping his Liquors while I have been spilling my Blood; that he has been gathering Hopps for you, while I have been reaping Laurels.'[68] Jonathan Swift entered the fray with 'A Dialogue between Captain Tom and Sir Henry Dutton Colt', a 'ballad full of puns on the Westminster election that cost me half an hour' as he told Stella.[69] In the event Stanhope lost, Dyer reporting that 'the Church party were above 200 voices more than the whigs'.

This presaged the rout of the whigs in the larger constituencies. The counties especially went for the tories. Of the 78 English knights of the shires, 43 had been whigs in 1708, while only eleven were returned in 1710. Such a massive change simply cannot be attributed to the Court, especially when it had done next to nothing to indicate to the forty shilling freeholders that it wished them to vote tory. Such a huge swing can only have been due to the impact of issues. As a defeated whig candidate in Lincolnshire observed, 'the bent of the nation is against us'.[70] Thus a canvasser in Wensleydale recorded the influence of the Sacheverell affair in that remote Yorkshire valley, noting of Middleham 'all the town are Sacheverellians and value themselves mightily upon it'.[71] Any whig who had opposed the Doctor was a target for the tories, especially if, like Stanhope, they had been managers at the trial.[72]

The influence of the clergy was felt to be particularly potent in this election. Dyer noted again and again how the clergy polled in a body for the Church candidates.[73] A similar claim in the *Postboy* for Bedfordshire was challenged by a clergyman in that county who claimed that nearly forty of his colleagues voted for the whig candidates.[74] There is no way of checking these claims and counter claims except by examining poll books recording votes cast by the clergy. Those that have survived by and large support tory claims that the clergy were overwhelmingly on their side.[75] In this respect the tory party truly was the Church party in 1710.

By the same token the whigs could claim the support of the dissenters. ''Tis observed,' wrote Dyer on 28 October, 'that the Quakers all England over have polled with the dissenters against the Church.' Again this claim can be checked from poll books, since the Quakers were allowed by law to affirm rather than to swear the freeholders' oath.[76] These confirm that most Quakers polled for whig candidates at general elections in Anne's reign.[77] In 1710 it was hoped that they might support tory candidates since their leader Penn was known to Harley.[78] In the event, however, it was generally agreed in tory circles that 'they all voted against the Church this election'.[79]

The general election of 1710 thus polarized the English electorate along religious lines. So strong was the high church tide that there was nothing the whigs and little the Court could do to stop it. As the results came in Walpole's earlier optimism evaporated. 'The infatuation is so

general in the kingdom that we are beaten everywhere in our elections'
he admitted to Marlborough 'and I believe the highest complement of
whigs in this parliament will not exceed two hundred'.[80] By contrast
the tories were buoyant. 'We have certainly got a noble parliament,'
gloated one individual, 'two thirds at least for the church, besides what
will be made by petitions and also those placemen or officers who will
come over.'[81] The final outcome in England and Wales was to return
332 tories and 181 whigs to Westminster.[82]

Scotland had not been similarly affected by the Sacheverellite fever.
Scottish elections were anyway very different, for party alignments did
not coincide exactly with the English and Welsh whigs and tories,
while the electorates in the 45 constituencies were narrow and far
less influenced by public opinion. A breakdown of the 45 MPs made
on 11 November 1710 placed them into three categories: Episcopal
tories, Court tories, and whigs. A handful of results had still to be
determined, but it was nevertheless clear that the Episcopal tories had
won, there being 21 returned compared with only 11 Court tories and
six whigs.[83]

If the whigs could find no solace in the results then there was little
in them for Harley. Far from it, too many tories had been returned for
his comfort. The problems posed by a large majority of tories, many of
them high church men, were to plague his ministry for the next three
years.

Conclusion

The ministerial revolution of 1710 ended not only the decade but the duumvirate of Godolphin and Marlborough. Although the duke remained as Captain General until January 1712, after his colleague's departure from the Treasury it was very much as a lame-duck commander. The tories who returned triumphantly to parliament in the general election of 1710 were for the most part desperate for peace. To pave the way towards the Treaty of Utrecht they accused the duumvirs of having deliberately prolonged the war for their own advantage. As 'The Duumvirate', a Jacobite poem, put it:[1]

> Mightier than Kings this ruling paire is grown
> For they the Purse and Sword command alone . . .
> Our Mony and our Blood are spilt abroad
> Two Monsters at home with wealth to load

Suspicions that there was a conspiracy between the monied and military men to wax fat at the expense of the landed gentry were fed by propagandists for the new ministry headed by Harley. His 'chef de propagande' was Jonathan Swift, who attacked the alleged Treasury–Military nexus mercilessly in *The Examiner* and *The Conduct of the Allies*.[2]

Although in fact there was no sinister conspiracy, nevertheless there was a close connection between the Court and the City which brought into being the 'fiscal–military state'.[3] This state was established in William's reign but came to be personified in Anne's by the Lord Treasurer and the Captain General. In their hey-day between 1704 and 1708 they seemed to be the saviours of British and of European liberties. The completion of the Union with Scotland and the duke's greatest victories against France were achieved in these years. They also saw the triumph of 'moderation' in politics between the ascendancy of the high church tories and the Junto whigs. 'Moderation' indeed became a kind of catch word at this time. William Shippen grudgingly acknowledged its potency in his poem *Moderation Display'd*.[4] The 'new race of moderate men' identified themselves with the duke of Marlborough, regarding him as 'the rising sun'.[5] But if moderation owed its appeal to the duke's victories abroad, its success at home was in no small measure owing to the political abilities of Robert Harley. For a while he was so influential that men spoke of a triumvirate. His downfall in 1708 spelled the end of moderation as a goal in politics.

The Jacobite author of 'The Duumvirate' accused them of usurping the royal prerogative, claiming that:

> Their easy Queen without controle they rule
> And guide, even as a workman guides his Tool.

This allegation speaks volumes for Marlborough's influence in this decade. The duke filled the void created by the death of William III, the soldier king who had rescued English liberty from Popery and arbitrary power and defended Protestant Europe against 'the most Christian king' Louis XIV. Queen Anne as a woman could not live up to this role. The duke's special relationship with her at the outset of the reign enabled him to wield power which to many, including ultimately the Queen herself, seemed to challenge monarchical authority when their paths crossed. The episode of the disposal of Lord Essex's military posts brought this to a head, revealing that in matters of army patronage Marlborough was prepared to insist on the last word. Such arrogance raised the spectre of military rule, and led to the duke being compared with Cromwell.

The threat of a standing army to the liberties safeguarded by the Revolution, which whigs as well as tories had voiced concern about in the 1690s, again seemed very real. That Marlborough entertained any thought of undermining them can probably be dismissed, though he had shown no scruples about being prepared to subvert Scottish independence with armed force if the Union had failed. But at the end of the day, or rather of the decade, his power seemed to contemporaries great enough to make such threats plausible.

In fact such conjectures underestimated the residual powers of the Crown and the personal integrity of the monarch. When Marlborough's request for the Captain Generalship for life seemed to challenge the prerogative, his authority visibly ebbed even among some of his staunchest supporters. When push came to shove in any confrontation with the Crown the monarch could still command more loyalty and support than any mere subject, even a duke of Marlborough. And Anne was not prepared to surrender without a struggle, except in the trying months after her husband's death when her will to fight was sapped. Otherwise the claim that the duumvirs really ruled while she reigned was quite wrong. This might have been the decade of the duumvirate. But at the end of it the Queen emerged as a ruler indeed who could get the better of them both. Moreover Anne was as committed to the Union with Scotland and victory in Europe as much as her Captain General and Lord Treasurer. As Arthur Mainwaring acknowledged in 'An Epistle to the Queen upon the news of the battle of Ramillies':[6]

> While Madam with a mild yet war-like Reign
> You bless your subjects, your allies maintain
> Protect their kingdoms, and your own *unite*
> Give Peace to Britain, and for Europe fight.

It was when Anne determined to give peace to Europe as well as to Britain that the days of the duumvirs were numbered. From this point of view it was as much her decade as theirs.

The Incidence of Contested Elections
1701–1710: A Psephological Note

The incidence of contested elections in the early modern period is a methodological minefield. Even what constituted a contest can be the source of dispute. And the evidence for them is so scattered and disparate that any attempt to extrapolate a coherent pattern from it is bound to arouse criticism. However, an examination of the distribution of constituencies which went to the polls in the decade 1701 to 1710 seems to produce an interesting distribution between different regions of England and Wales.

Carving up the country into districts is of course just as contentious as counting contests. It can be done in any number of ways to suit the researcher who may wish to get the data to fit a convenient breakdown. Nevertheless this current exercise in electoral geography was undertaken before the data were entered into it. The aim was to create three coherent regions with as far as possible a similar number of constituencies in them. The districts selected as 'the South East', 'the South West and Wales', and 'the North and the Midlands' make as much sense as any other three areas to which the counties within them can be ascribed. It is true that the constituencies do not fall equally among them, there being 81 in the first, 100 in the second and 88 in the third. However, to juggle with the boundaries of the regions to produce a more equitable distribution produces more artificial areas than those selected here, while the allocation of constituencies, which gives the South West a disproportionate number, is almost unavoidable since Cornwall alone notoriously had 21 boroughs which returned MPs to parliament.

The South East district contained therefore 30.1 per cent of all English and Welsh constituencies, and the North and Midlands 32.7 per cent and the South West and Wales 37.2 per cent. But the distribution of contests within them was skewed rather differently. The South West and Wales experienced only 26.5 per cent, the North and Midlands 35.5 per cent and the South East 38 per cent. Thus the North and Midlands had very roughly a proportionate share of contests, whereas the South West and Wales witnessed significantly less and the South East more than would have been expected.

There are several possible explanations of this. One is that the evidence records more fully the incidence of contests in the vicinity of London since the most accessible source is the newspaper press, which was based there. Possibly it gave complete coverage to contested elections in the Home counties but failed to report those in remoter parts of the country. However, against this is the fact that the lists of contests are based on a wide range of documentation in the localities as well as in the centre. Furthermore the discrepancy between the South West and Wales and the North and Midlands cannot be accounted for by a bias of the sources towards the South East.

Another possibility is that the size of the electorates in the various constituencies differed significantly. The South West after all contained a high number of small boroughs with fewer than 100 voters. Certainly if we calculate the total electorates in the three regions discrepancies emerge.[1] There were at least 87,332 voters in the South East and only 60,149 in the South West. Thus the average size of constituencies was 1078 in the Soüth East and 601 in the South West. Since the larger constituencies were more prone to contests in the late Stuart period this alone might be assumed to account for the different incidence of contests between regions. However, the total electorate in the North and Midlands was at least 108,542 and the average size of constituencies 1233, so that the numbers of voters and their concentration in large boroughs does not provide the answer to the problem of regional variation.

Above all it does not explain why the lead in the proportion of contests in the South East was not sustained throughout the decade but gradually emerged as the number of general elections grew. At the first general election to take place in 1701 the South East had the smallest proportion of contests, with only 29.3 per cent of them against 34.7 per cent in the South West and Wales and 35.8 in the North and Midlands. At the second 1701 election the North and Midlands had the lion's share of the known contests, while the South West and Wales slipped into third place. It was during Anne's reign that the South East took a clear lead and held it at every general election between 1702 and 1710, while the South West and Wales stayed very firmly in third place.

A political explanation of the phenomenon therefore suggests itself. Partisanship at the polls in William's reign was confused and kaleidoscopic. In the first general election of 1701 it was difficult for contemporaries to analyse the outcome in terms of a majority for the whig or tory party since as the Prussian envoy in London put it 'there are many country members in Parliament who have never joined with these parties to the extent of closely espousing either'.[2] The pressure of events in 1701 concerning the Church, the Succession and above all the question of war with France, however, polarized politicians and made it thereafter easier to gauge election results in terms of gains and losses for the whigs or the tories. Thus in 1708 Sir John Cope could allocate a party label to all the 513 MPs for England and Wales even before parliament met.[3]

The 'rage of party' apparently affected the South East more than the other regions of England and Wales, especially the West country and the principality itself. Perhaps the uneven incidence of the war-time rate of the land tax, which was much heavier in the south eastern counties than in the rest of the country, accounts for this. Again the whig party was probably stronger and more active in the vicinity of London and areas of parliamentary strength in the civil wars than elsewhere, especially the tory shires of the south west. Caution should however be used in making these long-term links, as Suffolk, one of the more 'puritan' counties of the early seventeenth century, became largely tory under Anne.[4] It could even have been the revival of tory activity in whig heartlands under a sympathetic sovereign which ultimately led to the higher incidence of contests at parliamentary elections in the South East during the reign of Queen Anne.

Table A.1

	'01a	'01b	'02	'05	'08	'10	total	%	% cons.*
SE	27	33	35	42	37	50	224	38	30.1
SW	32	20	19	28	24	33	156	26.5	37.2
NM	33	37	31	39	25	44	209	35.5	32.7

NOTES
*cons. = constituencies

SE = South East, comprising the counties of Bedfordshire, Berkshire, Buckinghamshire, Essex, Hertfordshire, Kent, Middlesex, Norfolk, Hants, Suffolk, Surrey, Sussex and including the Cinque ports.

SW = South West and Wales, comprising the counties of Cornwall, Devon, Dorset, Gloucestershire, Somerset, Wiltshire and Wales including Monmouthshire.

NM = North and Midlands, comprising the counties of Cambridgeshire, Cheshire, Cumberland, Derbyshire, Durham, Herefordshire, Huntingdonshire, Lancashire, Leicestershire, Lincolnshire, Northamptonshire, Northumberland, Nottinghamshire, Oxfordshire, Rutland, Salop, Staffordshire, Warwickshire, Westmorland, Worcestershire and Yorkshire.

The number of contests has been derived from the tables in Henry Horwitz, *Parliament, Policy and Politics in the reign of William III* (Manchester, 1977) pp. 329–34 and W. A. Speck, *Tory and Whig: the struggle in the constituencies 1701–1715* (1970, pp. 126–31) updated in the light of subsequent information. The most important change has been in response to Horwitz's criticism that *Tory and Whig* includes 'contests' for which there is no direct evidence of a poll, such as a poll book, or a record of the numbers voting, or of a petition to the Commons from unsuccessful candidates (op. cit., p. 329). The table did indeed record contests 'which are known to have ended in a poll, *or which almost certainly did as far as this could be ascertained from the available evidence* (*Tory and Whig*, p. 124, my italics). The element of uncertainty, however slight, has here been eliminated, and a constituency is only counted as having been contested when there is clear evidence that a poll took place.

Notes

INTRODUCTION: THE 1700s

1. For a discussion of the electoral system in the decade, see W. A. Speck, *Tory and Whig: The struggle in the constituencies 1701–1715* (1970).

2. B. L. Add MSS 30,000D, f. 363: F. Bonet to the Elector of Brandenburg, 17 December 1700; translated in G. S. Holmes and W. A. Speck (eds), *The Divided Society: Party Conflict in England 1694–1716* (1967), p. 19.

3. Cocks, *Diary*, f. 17. Cocks,, a whig sympathetic to dissent, noted that the occasional conformity bill was 'begot by lechery heat of blood without consideration'.

4. T. B. Macaulay, *The History of England from the accession of James II*, ed. T. F. Henderson (1907), p. 343.

5. Huntington library Stowe MSS 58, i, 17: R. Byerley to James Brydges, 12 December 1700.

6. Ibid., 9, 46: Brydges to Godolphin, n.d. (1706). For the impeachments see chapter 2 below; for the tackers see chapter 5.

7. 'The Junto' were Lords Halifax, Orford, Somers, Wharton and, under Anne, Sunderland.

8. *POAS*, vii, 6.

9. Snyder, ii, 999.

10. Shin Matsuzono, 'The House of Lords and the Godolphin Ministry 1702–1710' (Ph.D. thesis, Leeds, 1990), p. 249.

11. Snyder, i, 271.

12. W. A. Speck, 'The choice of a Speaker in 1705', *BIHR* (1964), xxxvii, 30.

13. *Tory and Whig*, p. 72.

14. E. Gregg, *Queen Anne* (1980), p. 166.

15. John Tribbeko, *A funeral sermon on the death of . . . Prince George of Denmark . . . now translated into English* (1708), pp. 23, 27, 34.

16. Gregg, *Anne*, 296.

17. *Wentworth Papers*, p. 142.

18. G. Holmes, *British Politics in the Age of Anne* (1967), p. 210.

19. See below p. 169.

20. T. J. Denman, 'The Political Debate over War Strategy' (Ph.D. thesis, Cambridge, 1985), p. 35.

21. Lord Campbell, *Lives of the Lord Chancellors* (1846), iv, 428.
22. *Addison Corr*, p. 244.
23. Nicolson, *Diary*, p. 129.
24. Defoe, *A History of the Union* (1786), p. 322.
25. G. Lockhart, *The Lockhart Papers* (2 vols, 1817), i, 41, 58.
26. Defoe, *A History of the Union* (1786), p. 323.
27. John Brewer, *The Sinews of Power: War, Money and the English State* (1989); D. W. Jones, *War and Economy in the Age of William III and Marlborough* (Oxford, 1988).
28. Paul H. Scott, *Andrew Fletcher and the Treaty of Union* (Edinburgh, 1992), p. 169.

CHAPTER 1   1701

1. See Appendix, pp. 196–9.
2. 'The Worcester Cabal' *POAS* vi, 310–20.
3. Longleat Thynne papers, vol. xxv, f. 13. R. Price to Lord Weymouth, 21 October 1700.
4. R. Walcott, 'The East India Interest in the General Election of 1700–1701', *English Historical Review* (1956), lxxi, 223–39. For the emergence of two rival East India Companies in the 1690s see above pp. 6–7.
5. H. Horwitz, *Parliament Policy and Politics in the reign of William III* (Manchester, 1977), p. 280.
6. Cocks, *Diary*, f. 79v. The confusion which Harley's association with the tory ministers produced is reflected in Cocks' observation: 'God bless us from the ills they may do: tho for all the opinions of many I cannot believe that Mr Harley in the main to be in any interest but that of the country tho I confess I do not approve of many of his words and actions.' Edmund Gibson wrote to Arthur Charlett on 12 February: 'Mr Harley carry'd it for Speaker against Sir Richard Onslow by some six score voices. His six years opposition to the Court followed by such a sudden turn to that side is made use of by his enemies to his disadvantage.' Bodleian Ballard MSS 6, f. 35. To add to the confusion many years later Anthony Hammond noted that Harley was first elected speaker 'by the best and most honourable (the landed) interest and the Country party'! Bodleian Rawlinson MSS D:37 'The fate of favourites'.
7. Walcott, 'The East India Interest', pp. 238–9.
8. H. D. Schmidt sees this episode as an example of the whig commitment to the new concept of 'Europe' which had replaced older terms such as 'Christendom.' 'The Establishment of "Europe" as a political expression', *Historical Journal* (1966), ix, 177.
9. BL Add 29568, f. 9: Verney to Lord Hatton: 'all this was done with great calmness in less than two hours and I believe above 400 in the House.'
10. Ibid., f. 11. J. Verney to Lord Hatton, 11 March 1701.
11. BL Add 30000E, ff. 67–70. Bonet to the king of Prussia, 7 March 1701.
12. Burnet, iv, 499.

13. R. Coke, *A Detection of the Court and State of England* (1719).
14. BL Add 29568, f. 13. Verney to Hatton, 15 April 1701, iii, 98–9. Lord Cowper told George I that the tories 'set themselves to clog it and indeed render it absurd by some of the restrictions [of the prerogative]'; *Divided Society*, p. 24.
15. BL Add 30000E f. 104. Bonet's despatch, 25 March 1701.
16. Ibid., f. 105.
17. Cocks, *Diary*, f. 77v. According to Cocks, Harley 'was the principall man that had all along contrived their ruin'. Ibid., f. 68v. Harley's partisanship on this occasion poisoned relations between him and the Junto for the rest of the decade.
18. *POAS*, vi, 320. Another version claimed that 'the speaker found the following lines put into his coat pocket' but this is improbable if the date is correct since the House was adjourned due to Speaker Harley's being ill, and only met briefly on 29 April when the adjournment was extended on account of his continued indisposition. The five lines were later swollen to 220. Ibid., 321–33.
19. Sir Edward Seymour accused the five Kentish petitioners of being 'tools of the late ministry' continuing 'that it was high time . . . to put a stop to such proceedings which would destroy our constitution and bring us to 41'. Cocks, *Diary*, f. 73v.
20. Kent Archives Office U1590/019/1, Sir Charles Hedges to Alexander Stanhope, 9 May 1701. The original motion resolved to preserve the balance of Europe, but the word balance was held to be too strong a commitment and was changed to liberties *nem con.*
21. Daniel Defoe put pressure on the whole House in *Legion's Memorial* which claimed to speak on behalf of the electorate. On 14 May tories interrupted a debate on supply to censure this tract. Cocks, *Diary*, f. 72.
22. Luttrell, v, 61.
23. BL Add 22851, f. 183. Lord Delaware to Thomas Pitt, 4 July 1701.
24. Luttrell, v, 94, 100.
25. *Divided Society*, p. 170.
26. See Appendix. The Cinque ports were always treated as a separate entity by contemporaries, but there seems no reason to deal with them so here. Consequently four of them, Dover, Hythe, Romney and Sandwich, are included with the other Kent constituencies. The contest indicated in Dover in *Tory and Whig* was queried by Horwitz and has been dropped from the tally as the evidence for an actual poll is unclear. Had one occurred it would of course have further increased the number held in Kent.
27. HMC *Downshire* i, 810. Henry St John to Sir William Trumbull, 12 November 1701.
28. *CSPD 1700–1702*, pp. 452–3.
29. *Vernon Corr*, iii, 161.
30. *Post Man*, 27–29 November, 2–4 December; *Flying Post*, 27–29 November; reprinted in *The Electors Right Asserted* (1701).
31. Luttrell, v, 121. They also urged 'that the impeach't lords be brought to legal tryalls'.

32. *Divided Society*, p. 125. So far from pursuing the impeachments the Buckinghamshire MPs were required 'that in time of danger, especially, you avoid all such differences disputes and animosities as so lately had like to have undone us.'
33. H. Snyder, 'party configurations in the early eighteenth-century House of Commons', *BIHR* (1972). This was possibly the basis of Bonet's mistaken claim that they had an overall *majority* of 30. *Divided Society*, p. 18.
34. E. Sussex Record Office, Winterton letters, 850. Goulston to Sir Edward Turner, 16 December 1701. See also Henry Whistler's letter to Thomas Pitt, 20 December, predicting that 'the whig party has used all their industry and power to carry it, but will certainly fail', *Divided Society*, p. 25.
35. BL Add 7074, f. 72v.
36. HMC *Cowper*, ii, 443–4.
37. BL Add 7074, f. 77. Ellis to Stepney 30 December 1701.
38. Despite an intriguing story told much later by Harley's brother Edward that William preferred him as Speaker, strictly contemporary evidence leaves no doubt that William signalled his preference for Littleton. BL Lansdowne MSS 885, f. 17. Add 7074, f. 75v; H. Horwitz, *Parliament Policy and Politics in the reign of William III* (1977), p. 299.
39. Hull University Library Hotham MSS DDHo 13/4: Newcastle to Sir Charles Hotham, 7 January 1702.
40. BL Add 17677 XX, f. 165v.
41. Lancs Record Office DDKe correspondence: C. Hutton to George Kenyon, 20 January 1702.
42. Cumbria Record Office D/Lons/W, James Lowther to Sir John Lowther, 27 January 1702. Reference owed to David Hayton.
43. BL Add 22851, f. 121v: James Craggs to Governor Pitt, 25 February 1702.
44. Cocks, *Diary*, II, 5v.
45. BL Add 29588, f. 16.

CHAPTER 2   1702

1. TCD Lyons coll 890: Sir Robert Southwell to William King, 14 March 1702.
2. *A collection of all Queen Anne's speeches* (1714).
3. TCD Lyons coll 901: Bishop of Clogher to King, 2 April 1702.
4. Cocks, *Diary*, i, f. 9. Cocks later noted that rival reflections on the late king kept up the animosities between tories and whigs to the point that, 'I really believe many would rather destroy the opposite party than the French'. Ibid., ii, f. 9v.
5. TCD Lyons Coll 888: Bishop of Clogher to Bishop King, 12 March 1702.
6. PRO/PC2/79–83.
7. TCD Lyons coll 888.
8. *The correspondence 1701–1711 of John Churchill first duke of Marlborough*

and Anthonie Heinsius grand pensionary of Holland, ed. B. Van 'T Hoff (Utrecht, 1951), p. 2.

9. As early as July it was noted that 'the management at Court is now much different from what it was at first. My lords Rochester and Nottingham are not so much heeded as Godolphin and Marlborough and these two latter it is averred by almost every body make interest for my Lords Halifax and Somers'. TCD Lyons coll 927: Thomas Purcell to King, 13 July 1702.

10. BL Add 47025, f. 109. Sir John Percival to Tom Knatchbull, 11 March 1702.

11. Luttrell, v, 160.

12. Cocks, *Diary*, f. 7; BL Add 29588, f. 16.

13. Hereford and Worcester Record Office Lygon transcripts. Ann Bull to William Lygon, 10 March 1702: 'people were in great haste to draw their money out of the Bank upon the death of the king, which now is in such credit that stock rises'. T. Tuckfield to same, 10 March 1702: 'Satterday last when the king was very ill there was a great run upon the Bank and all stocks did fall, but the parliament voting as they did Sunday last stopt the demand on the Bank and advanced the stocks.'

14. *CJ*, xiii, 782.

15. Cocks *Diary*, II, f. 8.

16. T. Forster, *Original letters of Locke, Algernon Sydney and Lord Shaftesbury* (1830), pp. 179–80.

17. BL Add 29588, f. 129.

18. Thus l'Hermitage the Dutch resident noted purges in the vicinity of London but observed that few had occurred elsewhere. ARA Heinsius MSS 792, f. 303, 307. Godolphin and Marlborough were so anxious to retain the services of moderate whigs that on 11 June the lord treasurer wrote to the duke of Newcastle to assure him that the Queen 'never had the least thought of not continuing you in all your authorities'. Among these were the Lord Lieutenancies of Nottingham and the east Riding of Yorkshire. BL Add 70501, f. 113. Even Burnet admitted that 'the queen did not openly interpose in the elections'. Burnet, v, 45.

19. Twenty-five per cent of the freeholders who polled at both contests changed their vote from whig to tory. W. A. Gray, R. Hopkinson and W. A. Speck, 'Computer analysis of poll books: a further report', *Bulletin of the Institute of Historical Research* (1975) xlviii, 64–90.

20. Burnet, v, 45.

21. BL Add 61119, ff 53–4: Hedges to Marlborough, 8 September 1702.

22. Nicolson *Diary*, p. 154.

23. *POAS*, vi, 469.

24. J. R. S. Whiting, *A Handful of History* (1978), pp. 128–30.

25. Bodleian Add MSS A 269, p. 4.

26. ARA Heinsius MSS 792, ff. 427–433. L'Hermitage to Heinsius 23 and 27 November 1702.

27. ARA Heinsius MSS 792, f. 452.

28. Gregg, *Anne*, p. 165.

29. *The Norris Papers*, ed. T. Heywood (1846), pp. 102–7; T. Johnson to R. Norris, 10, 12 and 15 December 1702.

30. Gregg, *Anne*, p. 166. That Anne personally relied on Rochester, who was 'absolute over the party of the Tories in both Houses' to procure support for the perpetual grant, and felt betrayed by his failure to do so, see Lord Coningsby's confused but essentially believable account in *Archaeologia*, xxxviii, 6.

31. *Marlborough–Heinsius Correspondence*, pp. 39–56. At one time Marlborough considered getting Anne to request the increase from parliament in person. Eventually the Commons voted an extra 10,000 troops on condition that the Dutch stopped all commerce and correspondence with the Bourbon powers.

32. ARA Heinsius MSS 792, f. 455.

33. *Journall of the meeting held in the Council Chamber in the Cockpit in Westminster by the Scottish and English commissioners nominat by the Queen to treat of one union betwixt the nations of Scotland and England.*

34. ARA Heinsius 872: L'Hermitage to Heinsius, 2/13, 5/16 February 1703.

35. G. Holmes, *The Trial of Dr Sacheverell* (1973), p. 51. This had earned him the sobriquet of 'the bloody flag officer'.

36. *Divided Society*, p. 122. The witness was preaching to the converted, for according to Burnet 'controverted elections were judged in favour of tories, with such a barefaced partiality that it shewed the party was resolved on every thing that might serve its ends'. Burnet, v, 46.

37. Burnet, v, 51–2.

38. Nicolson, *Diary*, p. 137. The preamble paid lip service to religious toleration.

39. Indeed it only passed a committee in the House of Lords by the narrowest margin of 48 to 48. In a full House that margin would have defeated the measure, since a tied vote was a lost vote by the standing orders. However, when it was reported to the whole House enough absentees on the Prince's side were found to carry it by four votes. ARA Heinsius MSS 792, 22 January/2 February 1702/3. It was a great embarrassment to the Marlboroughs, at a time when relations with Anne were delicate, that their son in law stood out against the Prince's bill. Fortunately the queen appreciated that the duke and Godolphin had spared no effort to get the bill passed. Gregg, *Anne*, pp. 166–7.

40. Nicolson, *Diary*, pp. 137–9; ARA Heinsius MSS 792, ff. 486, 497.

41. ARA Heinsius MSS 792, f. 459. 'But,' he added significantly 'that is not of the same consequence.'

42. ARA Heinsius MSS 729, f. 471. This incident presumably added to the episodes which persuaded bishop Nicolson to move from tory to whig politics. See Nicolson, *Diary*.

43. Burnet, v, 53.

44. Nicolson, *Diary*, pp. 175–6.

45. ARA Heinsius MSS 872: L'Hermitage to Heinsius, 6/27 February 1703.

46. Burnet, v, 58.

CHAPTER 3   1703

1. In a letter to Godolphin of 10/21 August 1702. Snyder, i, 99.
2. Gregg, *Anne*, p. 169.
3. Churchill, ii, 155.
4. *Heinsius Correspondence*, i, 28. L'Hermitage to Heinsius, 13/24 March 1702.
5. Gregg, *Anne*, p. 169.
6. Ibid., pp. 170–6.
7. ARA Heinsius MSS 872: L'Hermitage to Heinsius, 9/20 March 1703. Seymour was reported as saying that it was easier to make half a dozen Lords than to disoblige 300 MPs: 'ainsy on voit que cet avis a este suivy.'
8. Snyder, i, 159, 199.
9. Ibid., i, 165. 9/20 April.
10. Gregg, *Anne*, p. 171. As Gregg points out, the omission of Mr Morley from this letter is significant of a change in the Queen's relationship with the Marlboroughs and Godolphin.
11. *Marlborough–Heinsius Correspondence*, p. 90.
12. Ibid., p. 77.
13. He actually used the word in a letter to Richard Hill, objecting to the view that 'our great effort must still be there [the Low Countries] where we so fruitlessly spent our blood and treasure in the last war and where this method must, in our present circumstances, be still more *useless* and ruinous than it was even in the last war' (my italics). H. Horwitz, *Revolution Politics* (1968), p. 177.
14. *Heinsius Correspondence*, ii, 216, Nott to Heinsius, 30 April 1703.
15. Horwitz, *Revolution Politics*, p. 173.
16. Snyder, i, 221; *POAS*, v, 532, 539. Frank Ellis, who edited this volume, drew attention to an attribution of the poem to 'H: Mor', surmising that this could have been the whig colonel Henry Mordaunt. Ibid., p. 531. If it was by the whig army officer, and Marlborough heard of the attribution, then it would have been even more galling to him.
17. H. Snyder, 'The defeat of the occasional conformity bill and the tack', *BIHR* (1968), xli, 173, note citing T. Sharp, *Life of John Sharp archbishop of York* (1885), i, 368–9.
18. Snyder, i, 259.
19. Kendal Record Office, Levens MSS, Longleat, 27 September 1703. The earl of Clarendon also put pressure on Grahme to be at the opening of the session, adding 'you cannot but know one sort of people will be here to a man'. Ibid., London, 9 October 1703.
20. Snyder, 'Defeat of the occasional conformity bill', p. 175.
21. Gregg, *Anne*, p. 177.
22. Cobbett, vi, 153.
23. Hereford and Worcester Record Office, Lygon transcripts. R. Dowdeswell to W. Lygon, 7 December 1703. 'we do flatter ourselves if a computation is made that it will be flung out by three . . . This

day the Queen and Prince went to Windsor, which we hope will not encourage the passing of it'.

24. Snyder, 'Defeat of the occasional conformity bill', pp. 175-6, 187–92. BL Add MSS 29576, C. Hatton to Lord Hatton 9 December 1703.

25. Snyder, 'Defeat of the occasional conformity bill', p. 175.

26. See G. Best, *Temporal Pillars: Queen Anne's Bounty, the Ecclesiastical Commissioners and the Church of England* (Cambridge, 1964).

27. Paul H. Scott, *Andrew Fletcher and the Treaty of Union* (Edinburgh, 1992), pp. 74–95; 227–31. Fletcher had complained about the subservience of Scottish to English foreign policy in a tract: 'notwithstanding the great and unproportionable numbers of sea and land soldiers that we are obliged to furnish for the support of the war, yet not one tittle of advantage has procured to us by the peace.' Quoted in ibid., p. 90.

28. Arthur Annesley, William Bromley, Robert Byerley, Sir Godfrey Copley, Sir William Drake, Henry Pinnell and Francis Scobel. Interestingly Henry St John and Thomas Coke, who had been appointed commissioners the previous session, declined to stand, a sign that they were moving from following high church leaders like Nottingham into Harley's camp. Luttrell, v, 395.

29. Ibid., p. 403; HMC *Rutland*, ii, 180: Lady Rachel Russell to Lord Granby, 18 March 1704. Byerley was the colonel of a regiment and had not cleared his own accounts. Burnet, v, 112.

30. *Vernon Corr*, iii, 253-4; Luttrell, v, 404, 409–10.

31. For an analysis of the case see Eveline Cruickshanks, 'Ashby versus White', *Party and management in Parliament 1660-1784*, ed. C. Jones (1984), pp. 87–106.

32. Cobbett, vi, 255-7.

33. Ibid., 225–324.

34. Snyder, i, 274-5, 280. In addition to Somerset Nottingham also wanted the archbishop of Canterbury to be banned from Cabinet meetings.

CHAPTER 4   1704

1. *The private diary of William first earl of Cowper* (1833), p. 30.

2. Bodleian Add MSS A 269, f. 6. Gibson to Nicolson, 2 June 1703: Burnet, v, 142: Middlesex Record Office, Jersey MSS Acc. 510/154: Jersey to Richard Hill, 5 May 1704: Hardwicke, *State Papers* (1778), ii, 461. Although Kent was alleged to have got the post by giving the duchess of Marlborough £10,000 he was no whig. *Wentworth Papers*, p. 134. Commenting on Kent's appointment a newsletter noted that 'the whigs have no reason to boast of that change for that noble Lord appeared for the occasional conformity bill and always for the interests of the Church'. BL Trumbull papers, 29 April 1704.

3. BL Trumbull papers newsletter, 29 April 1704.

4. BL Lansdowne MSS 773, p. 29: Charles to Henry Davenant, 21 April 1704.

5. Cobbett, vi, 336.

6. ARA Heinsius MSS 792, fos. 446–7. L'Hermitage to Heinsius, 6/17 1702.

7. Bodleian Ballard MSS 6, f. 93. Gibson to Charlett, 25 April 1704. Sir William Trumbull identified them in December 1703 as 'Musgrave, Harcourt, St John, Mostyn, Copley, Powys, Howe, Coke, Bayerley, Graham, Whitlock, Mackworth.' HMC *Downshire*, i (ii), 817. Three of them had been given office shortly after Anne's accession: Sir Simon Harcourt, the solicitor general; John Howe, the paymaster of guards and garrisons; and Sir Christopher Musgrave, a teller of the Exchequer. Harcourt was already close to Harley at this time, so his continuation in office was not remarkable. Musgrave and Howe, however, were veteran partisans and might well have been expected to resign along with Nottingham and Seymour but in fact retained their places. Two other associates of St John were given minor office when he entered the ministry in 1704 – Sir Godfrey Copley became a comptroller of army accounts (as did Arthur Moore in June, another of the new secretary at war's cronies) and Thomas Coke was made vice chamberlain of the household. Colonel James Grahme had a payment of £234 12s 6d, presumably outstanding from the reign of James II when he was keeper of the privy purse, repaid. Levens MSS. R. Powys to Grahme, 9 May, 6 and 20 July, 8 and 19 August 1704. How Sir Thomas Powys was brought into the Harleian fold, after being one of the managers for the Commons in their meetings with the Lords about the occasional conformity bill, is not known. But only Robert Byerley, Sir Humphrey Mackworth and Sir Roger Mostyn continued in the high church ranks against the Court – in Mostyn's case because of close ties with Nottingham. All three voted for the 'tack' later in the year.

8. BL Trumbull papers. As Francis Annesley saw it, 'the Church party are much divided, the whiggs are entire'. TCD Lyons coll 1080: Annesley to King, 6 May 1704.

9. Snyder, i, 279. Marlborough to Godolphin, 18/29 April 1704.

10. Ibid., p. 283, note 4.

11. Ibid., i, 327.

12. Churchill, ii, 335.

13. Robert D. Horn, *Marlborough: a survey; panegyrics, satires and biographical writings 1688–1788* (1975), p. 41.

14. *POAS*, vi, 28–9, 630–2.

15. Horn, *Marlborough*, p. 51.

16. *POAS*, vi, 15–18.

17. HMC *Portland*, iv, 137.

18. *An Account of the Conduct of the Dowager Duchess of Marlborough* (1742).

19. Carlisle Record Office, d/Lons, James to Sir John Lowther, 14 September 1704; quoted in *POAS*, vi, 15.

20. HMC *Bath*, i, 62; quoted in *POAS*, vi, 15.

21. BL Stowe MSS 222, f. 239v.

22. Paul H. Scott, *Andrew Fletcher ands the Treaty of Union*, p. 108.

23. *An Account of the Conduct of the Dowager Duchess of Marlborough*, pp. 146–7.

24. BL Add 70306: 'October 30 1704 list'.

25. HMC 10th report appendix iv, 338: Ward to Grahme, 3 October 1704; Coxe, *Walpole*, ii, 4–5; Compton to Walpole, 12 October 1704; Cholmondley (Houghton) corr, 359: same to same, 14 October 1704; HMC *Cowper*, iii, 49: St John to Coke, 16 October 1704; BL Add MSS 7078, f. 223: newsletter, 24 October 1704.

26. Snyder, 'defeat of the occasional conformity bill', *BIHR*, (1968), xli, 178–9.

27. BL Add 61123, f. 102, Harley to Marlborough, 14 November 1704.

28. Patricia M. Ansell, 'Harley's parliamentary management', *BIHR* (1961), xxxiv, 92–7.

29. Snyder, p. 181. The meeting had been planned for 22 November but was postponed until Friday the 25th. I here follow Professor Snyder rather than the sequence suggested in my thesis (p. 125). Dating is difficult due to the reliance on undated letters from Godolphin to Harley in the British Library and Longleat House. Snyder could not explain the postponement, perhaps because he dated the first reading incorrectly 24 November. Harley presumably postponed the ministerial meeting to the day following the vote to give it a second reading to have a clearer picture of the alignments on the bill.

30. BL Add 61123, f. 108, Harley to Marlborough, 24 November 1704.

31. Snyder, 'Defeat of the occasional conformity bill', pp. 182–4.

32. Boyer, *Annals*, iii, 157; Churchill, ii, 515, Cutts to ——, 28 November 1704.

33. BL Add 61123, f. 110. Marlborough replied: 'I hope everybody will do you the justice to attribute the greatest share of it to your prudent management and zeal for the public.' HMC, *Bath*, i, 65.

34. 'Faults on both sides', *Somers' Tracts* cd. W. Scott, xii, 691. One of those who apparently voted as he was directed was Lt. Col. Thomas King, deputy governor of the fort of Sheerness, who drew attention to the fact that he had 'vindicated himself as to the tack' when seeking promotion a year later. *Calendar of Treasury Papers 1702–8*, p. 378.

35. NLW Chirk Castle MSS E 4204.

36. Snyder, 'Defeat of the occasional conformity bill', p. 185.

37. BL Add 61123, f. 114, Harley to Marlborough, 5 December 1704.

38. Bodleian Ballard MSS 7, f. 5v: Smalridge to Charlett, 24 December 1704.

39. BL Add MSS 4743, f. 20: Lewis to H. Davenant, 19 January 1705.

40. Bucks Record Office, Verney letters, Fermanagh to Thomas Cave, 4 February 1705 draft.

41. Nicolson, *Diary*, pp. 253–4. *Pace* Trevelyan, ii, 16, Godolphin 'voted for its being read a second time'.

42. Burnet, v, 187.

43. Ibid., pp. 178–9.

44. Ibid., v, 182 note.

45. *Jerviswood Correspondence*, p. 15. cited in Nicolson, *Diary*, p. 240, note 181.

46. I cannot agree with Dr Riley's assertion that 'it was immaterial to them whether there was a settlement of the Scottish question at all'. P. W. J. Riley, *The Union of England and Scotland* (Manchester, 1978), p. 119.

The earl of Dartmouth in his marginal note to a passage in Burnet's *History* dealing with the debate in the English parliament on the Security Act makes whig support of the Lord Treasurer at this juncture not so much altruistic as opportunistic. The whig leaders at first opposed the Treasurer's recommendation that the royal assent be given to the Act. Halifax spoke 'with great outrage about it'. But then Dartmouth saw Wharton doing a deal with Godolphin on the floor of the House of Lords. Wharton then spoke with Somers and Halifax who called off the attack. Godolphin had, according to Dartmouth 'delivered himself entirely into their management, provided they brought him off'. As an example of how the Treasurer had sold out to the Junto, Dartmouth cited the appointment of William Cowper as lord keeper, which he claimed Godolphin himself had led him to understand 'that it had not been done with his approbation: which I did not doubt, knowing it was part of his penance for having passed the Scotch act of security'. Burnet, v, 182–3, 225: Dartmouth's notes. Riley makes much of these notes, claiming they document the Junto's using Scottish issues cynically for their own interests (*The Union of England and Scotland*, pp. 120, 121). Yet Dartmouth, who interpreted what he saw and heard to the mutual disparagement of Godolphin and the Junto, was by no means a dispassionate observer. The notes were made at the earliest in 1734 – the year when the second volume of Burnet's *History of my own Time*, in the margin of which they appear, was published, although they might have been based on memoranda written earlier. That was 29 years after the events they gloss and, more to the point, 24 years after he helped to engineer the downfall of the Treasurer and the whig Lords in the ministerial revolution of 1710. The scene which Dartmouth witnessed in the Lords did not necessarily support his interpretation of it, while strictly contemporary evidence at first hand is clearly at odds with his report of Godolphin's full approval of the appointment of Cowper. In view of this his testimony must be discounted. Cf. Roy A. Sundstrom *Sidney Godolphin: servant of the state* (1992), p. 288, note 114.

CHAPTER 5   1705

1. HMC *Portland*, iv, 146–7.
2. Ibid., ii, 188.
3. BL Add 61123, f. 142, Harley to Marlborough, 27 April 1705.
4. Snyder, i, 423.
5. *Tory and Whig*, p. 107; HMC *Portland*, iv, 189.
6. *CJ*, xv, 38.
7. BL Add 61458, f. 158, Halifax to the duchess, *c.* 10 May 1705. Halifax observed, those who distinguished between the two charters 'would carry that distinction further if they dared'.
8. HMC *Portland*, iv, 180, 188–9. BL Add 61134, f. 53, Somerset to Marlborough, 25 April 1705.
9. Snyder, i, 432–3. Sarah herself had engaged in an altercation with a clergyman at the St Albans election 'pro and con, as to several points of

state'. Frances Harris, *A Passion for Government: The Life of Sarah Duchess of Marlborough* (Oxford, 1991), p. 117.

10.   HMC *Portland*, iv, 189.
11.   *A collection of several paragraphs out of Mr Dyers's Letters* (1705).
12.   *Observator* 28 April – 2 May 1705. The issue for 23–26 May noted that in Berkshire 118 out of 140 clergy voted singly for the tacker Sir John Stonehouse.
13.   *London Post*, 14 May 1705.
14.   *Moderation Display'd* quoted in *POAS*, vi, 63.
15.   Ibid., pp. 59–61, 65.
16.   BL Add MSS 17677AAA, ff. 293–4. He mentioned Aylesbury, London, Middlesex and Wendover (ff. 303, 342). Those for Aylesbury appeared in the *Daily Courant*, 14 May; for London in *The Post Man*, 17–19 May; and for Wendover in *The Flying Post*, 15–17 May.
17.   Snyder, i, 453.
18.   BL Ad 61131, f. 140, St John to Marlborough, 27 July 1705.
19.   Snyder, i, 422 note 5.
20.   BL Add 61123, f. 166, Harley to Marlborough, 29 June 1705.
21.   Churchill College Cambridge Erle papers: James Craggs to Thomas Erle, 26 July 1705.
22.   BL Add 61123, f. 188, Harley to Marlborough, 26 July 1705.
23.   BL Add MSS 70022, f. 256 v., Harley to Price, 14 August 1705; unpublished part of the letter in HMC *Portland*, iv, 223.
24.   For a discussion of the *Memorial* see Alan Downie, *Robert Harley and the Press* (Cambridge, 1979), pp. 80–100.
25.   Snyder, i, 475.
26.   HMC *Bath*, i, 76: Godolphin to Harley 19 September 1705.
27.   HMC *Portland*, ii, 191: Godolphin to Newcastle, 11 October 1705. In this letter Godolphin refers to Harley as 'Mr Guidot'.
28.   This account of the speakership is based mainly on my article 'The choice of a speaker in 1705', *Bulletin of the Institute of Historical Research* (1964), xxxvii, 20–46.
29.   BL Add 61174, f. 84, Harley to Marlborough, 26 October 1705.
30.   BL Add 70285, Godolphin to Harley, 'Tuesday at 2' (6 November 1705).
31.   BL Add 61124, f. 96, Harley to Marlborough, 9 November 1705.
32.   Burnet, v, 211.
33.   J. R. Jones, *Marlborough* (1993), pp. 102–3.
34.   Cobbett, vi, 464–5.
35.   Paul H. Scott, *Andrew Fletcher and the Treaty of Union*, p. 142, argues that the persuasion took the form of financial assistance towards paying Hamilton's debts.
36.   Joseph Taylor, *A Journey to Edinburgh* (Edinburgh, 1903), quoted in Paul Scott, *Andrew Fletcher and the Treaty of Union* p. 139.
37.   Burnet, v, 237.
38.   Cobbett, vi, 452.
39.   Nicolson, *Diary*, p. 320.
40.   Nicolson, *Diary*, pp. 322–5. Years later Dartmouth wrote a note in the margin of Burnet's *History* which recounts an exchange between the

duke of Leeds and the earl of Wharton in the debate on 'the church in danger'. 'Lord Wharton, who never failed to insult, if he thought he had an advantage, desired lords would speak out what their real apprehensions were from? Were they from the queen? The duke of Leeds, who was highly provoked at such a question, answered him, No, but if deerstealers were got into his park he should think his deer in danger, though he had no suspicion of his keeper. Lord Wharton said, he wished his grace would name, who these rogues were that had got into the pale of the church. The duke said, If there were any that had pissed against a communion table or done his other occasions in a pulpit, he should not think the church safe in such hands. Upon which lord Wharton was very silent for the rest of the day, and desired no further explanations.' Ibid., p. 242. This allusion to a notorious incident in Wharton's youth when he had relieved himself in a church is not recorded in any contemporary report of this debate. So far from being silenced by anybody Wharton seems to have made several spirited contributions.

41. Burnet, v, 244. The duke of Marlborough was so pleased with the proceedings in this session that when it ended he wrote to Heinsius that it was 'most certainly . . . the best that ever was in England'. *Churchill–Heinsius Corr*, p. 230.

42. The discussion of the struggle follows that of Geoffrey Holmes in 'the attack on "the influence of the Crown" 1702–1716', *Politics, Religion and Society in England 1679–1742* (1986), pp. 41–7.

43. Longleat house Thynne MSS vol. xlv, ff. 144–5, 152–3: Dyers' news-letters, 22 and 31 January 1706.

44. PRO 30/24/20/114: Sir John Cropley to the earl of Shaftesbury.

45. See J. Cannon and W. A. Speck, 'Re-election on taking office 1706–1790', *Bulletin of the Institute of Historical Research* (1978), li, 206–9.

46. Burnet, v, 246–7.

47. Later in the summer Argyll was urged to return to Scotland to help the Court pass the Union through the Edinburgh parliament. Snyder, ii, 651, 655.

48. Trevelyan, ii, 263.

49. Riley, p. 165. Dr. Riley is particularly critical of Somers' role. Thus he claims that 'Somers seems to have toyed for some time with the idea of a partial union, allowing Scottish representatives at Westminster for the discussion of money bills only – a half-baked proposal which indicates whig desperation.' His source for this comment is a private conversation which Somers had with bishop Nicolson of Carlisle at a dinner held at Lambeth palace on 19 January 1706. In his diary Nicolson recorded how the whig lord 'discoursed me singly with great kindness and Freedome, on the subject of the Union; and we both agreed that, if Scotland were now admitted to a community of trade with England, paying their proportion of the publick Taxes and haveing a like proportionable Number of their Lords and Commons at the passing of Money-Bills, 'twould be sufficient for the present: For that a farther Union (in Religion Laws and Civil Government) must be the Work of Time'. As the editors of the diary observe, 'Somers was the last man to be

prey to the "half baked" ideas Dr Riley attributes to him in this contest (sic.) and his scheme was not the fruit of "desperation".' Instead he was indicating 'that at this stage his own instincts were to move towards a full Union only by careful stages, with parliamentary and commercial union preceding any religious, legal and administrative settlement'. Nicolson, *Diary*, pp. 292, 357–8. Somers' behaviour seems much more in keeping with the view expressed by Trevelyan than it does with the cynicism of Riley. The negotiation of the treaty of Union undoubtedly had its seamy side. But the role of the whig leaders in it was not so much opportunist and self seeking as constructive and far-sighted.

CHAPTER 6   1706

1. Burnet, v, 261.
2. Paul H. Scott, *Andrew Fletcher and the Treaty of Union* p. 155. Other Scottish historians describe the union more as a sell out.
3. Defoe, *History of the Union* (1786), p. 362.
4. Luttrell, vi, 69.
5. Snyder, ii, 629, 636. Cf. Riley, p. 65. 'Apart from the possible threat it represented to his campaigns or the likelihood of its being an objective for a French landing Marlborough seems to have had little interest in Scotland or its affairs.' Nothing could be further from the truth. In August 1706, at Godolphin's request Marlborough undertook to write to James Johnstone 'asking him to urge Roxburghe and the other Squadrone members to support the Union in the Scottish Parliament'. Snyder, ii, 647 and note; when he received a cool reply he informed the treasurer 'I do with all my heart wish good success to the Union, and that you may have as litle to do with those men as is possible'. Ibid., p. 703 and note. In November, when the articles were being debated by the Scottish parliament, Sir David Nairne wrote to the earl of Mar from London: 'all people here show a greater fondness for it [the Union] than ever. My Lord Marlborrow made speeches to me this morning on the subject before all the company.' HMC *Mar and Kellie*, p. 329.
6. J. R. S. Whiting, *A Handful of History* (Sutton, 1978), pp. 146–7.
7. Luttrell, vi, 61.
8. 'An epistle to Sir Richard Blackmore, Knight, on occasion of the late great victory in Brabant', *POAS*, vi, 199.
9. Horn, *Marlborough: A survey*, p. 179.
10. *POAS*, vi, 199. For specimens of them see Horn, pp. 180–230.
11. *POAS*, vi, 174–94.
12. Snyder, ii, 714–15: Godolphin to Marlborough, 18 October 1706.
13. Snyder, ii, 713.
14. *Marlborough–Heinsius Corr*, p. 230.
15. HMC *Portland*, iv, 291: Godolphin to Harley, 22 March 1706.
16. BL Portland MSS, Harley to (Godolphin), 25 September 1706, draft.
17. B. Curtis Brown, *The Letters of Queen Anne* (1935), p. 200: Anne to Godolphin, 21 September 1706. Although Anne described this as

'the expedient I proposed' it bears the marks of a suggestion by Harley.

18. Frances Harris, *A Passion for Government* (Oxford, 1991), p. 127. Godolphin, trying to repair the damage inflicted by this letter, persuaded Anne that Sarah had written 'notion', not 'nation'. Typically the duchess failed to see what difference this made.

19. Snyder, ii, 694–5: Marlborough to Godolphin 26 Sept./7 Oct. 1706. Marlborough clearly intended the copy of his letter to Anne to be communicated to the Junto.

20. Snyder, ii, 724.

21. The proceedings in the Scottish parliament are based on Daniel Defoe's *History of the Union* (1786).

22. HMC *Mar and Kellie*, p. 288.

23. Ibid., p. 292. Mar to Nairne, 16 October. He reckoned only 18 squadrone voted with the Court in this vote.

24. Riley shows that the divisions were very much along predictable party lines, p. 276 and Appendix A; 'one of the main conclusions of this work is that votes for or against the Union were really votes for or against the Court', p. 327.

25. *POAS*, vi, 214, 219.

26. *Letters relating to Scotland in the reign of Queen Anne*, ed. P. Hume Brown (Edinburgh, 1915), p. 105.

27. HMC *Mar and Kellie*, 321, Mar to Nairne 14 November.

28. Ibid., p. 324.

29. HMC *Portland*, iv, 369.

30. *Seafield Correspondence from 1685 to 1708*, ed. J. Grant (Edinburgh, 1912), p. 429.

31. *The Correspondence of George Baillie of Jerviswood 1702–1708* (Edinburgh, 1842), p. 137. Recent historians, for example, P. W. J. Riley and Paul H. Scott, have downplayed the importance of trade to the Scots who supported the Union. It was, however, stressed not only in the negotiations but also in the printed materials which appeared for and against the treaty. See esp. *Scotland's Interest: or the great benefit and necessity of a communication of Trade with England* (1704); *The Advantages of Scotland by an Incorporating Union* (1706); *Triologues* (1706); *A Letter from Mr Reason to the High and Mighty Prince the Mob*. Cf. John Robertson, 'Andrew Fletcher's Vision of Union', in *Scotland and England 1286–1815*, ed. Roger A. Mason (Edinburgh, 1987), pp. 208–9.

32. Snyder, ii, 727. He further informed the duke that some regiments had been ordered to move to the north of England and Ireland in case the mobs got out of hand 'and if there were a reall occasion, I hope some of those at Ghendt would be as near'.

33. *Lockhart Papers*, p. 163.

34. HMC *Portland*, iv, 362.

35. Burnet, v, 290.

36. HMC *Mar and Kellie*, 320. Nairne to Mar, 14 November. Mar's reply was feeble 'we thought it better to let them alone, for it is past time to get verrie many, and few would look worss than none'. Ibid., p. 328. According to Lockhart the Court did attempt to get some pro-Union

addresses 'but could prevail in no place but the town of Ayr, where they got one subscribed but by so pitiful and small a number that they thought shame to present it'. *Lockhart Papers*, p. 168.

37. Defoe, *History of the Union* (1786), p. 245: 'by an arithmetical calculation, or a calculation upon value and payment of taxes, the far greater number opposed the very addressing at all.'

38. Ibid., p. 311.

39. W. Ferguson, 'The making of the treaty of union of 1707', *Scottish Historical Review* (1964), xliii, 89–110; and his book *England's Relations with Scotland; a survey to 1707* (Edinburgh, 1977), pp. 246–52.

40. Trevelyan, ii, 282–3.

41. Riley, *Union of England and Scotland* (Manchester 1978), pp. 256–9, 336–8.

42. *Lockhart papers*, p. 157.

43. Trevelyan, ii, 268.

44. *Lockhart Papers*, i, p. 327.

45. Ibid., p. 166.

46. *Heinsius Corr*, vi, 41. L'Hermitage to Heinsius 14/25 January 1707 (translated). Stair was so important a figure in the Unionist ranks that Lockhart dubbed him the Scottish Judas. *Lockhart Papers*, pp. 88–9.

47. Nicolson, *Diary*, p. 404.

48. NLW Plas yn Cefn MS 2772 cited in Nicolson, *Diary*, p. 393.

49. Kent Archives Office Chevening MSS U1590 C707/5, cited in Nicolson *Diary*, p. 393.

50. Cobbett, vi, 560.

51. Burnet, v, 292. Walpole admitted that 'we pushed through all the articles in the committee'. Kent Archives Office Chevening MSS U1590 C 707/5: cited in Nicolson, *Diary*, p. 393.

52. Cobbett, vi, 561.

53. Luttrell, vi, 144.

54. Burnet, v, 295. The last division, on 24 February, upheld article 22 by 71 to 22.

55. Ibid., p. 295.

56. Nicolson, *Diary*, p. 422.

57. Huntington library Stowe MSS 57, i, 94: Brydges to Cadogan, 10 April 1707. The difference in duty on whalebone between Scotland and England was 90 per cent.

58. Ibid.

59. Snyder, ii, 754.

60. *Heinsius Corr*, vi, 248–9. L'Hermitage to Heinsius, 25 April/6 May 1707. There has been some discussion of Harley's role in this affair. See B. W. Hill, *Robert Harley* (1988), p. 108; Riley, pp. 305–10. Riley's notion that Harley was using the issue to undermine Godolphin and the Union does not quite accord with what little can be gleaned about Harley's behaviour at this juncture. Harley was quite seriously ill, having had what appeared to be a stroke ('estoit tombé dans une espece d'apoplexie') on 26 January. He nevertheless left his sick-bed to appear in a debate two days later, when some tories moved a resolution highly critical of the subsidies granted to the Habsburg claimant to the

Spanish throne, Charles III, and the duke of Savoy, because these had not been appropriated by the Commons. Since these passed through his secretariat he was obliged to defend them, which he did with spirit. He was taken ill as he spoke and said that if he died he wanted it engraved on his tombstone that he was one of those who advised the Queen to give these subsidies. The grants were vindicated by 254 votes to 105. Had they not been, the real target of the tory proposal was not Harley but Godolphin, who would have been censured. Harley therefore was acting in defence of the lord treasurer on this issue. In the brief adjournment on the rebate bill Godolphin took himself off to Newmarket, but returned to support the measure in the House of Lords. *Heinsius Corr*, vi, 69.

61.   BL Lansdowne MSS 1013 f. 78: quoted in Nicolson, *Diary*, p. 396.

CHAPTER 7   1707

1.   Defoe, *History of the Union*, p. 322.
2.   Snyder, ii, 843.
3.   Ibid., 811.
4.   Ibid., 932.
5.   Ibid., 840, note 1.
6.   Gregg, *Anne*, pp. 326.
7.   See especially Iris Butler, *Rule of three* (1967).
8.   Gregg, *Anne*, p. 237.
9.   Frances Harris, *A Passion for Government: the Life of Sarah Duchess of Marlborough* (Oxford, 1991).
10.   *POAS*, vi, 302, 309–10. Cf. Dennis Rubini's review of Harris, in *The American Historical Review* (1993), 98, 158–9.
11.   Burnet, v, 335–6.
12.   Luttrell, vi, 173.
13.   Burnet, v, 332.
14.   Churchill, *Marlborough*, iii, 232.
15.   *POAS*, vi, 286–93.
16.   Cobbett, vi, 595–6.
17.   For a list of peers with political symbols see Cambridge University MSS Mm.VI.42 f. 12. Cf. Shin Matsuzono 'The House of Lords and the Godolphin Ministry' (Ph.D. thesis, Leeds University, 1990), pp. 332–408. The 45 MPs are listed by Walcott, *English Politics in the Early Eighteenth Century* (1956), pp. 233–5 and Riley, pp. 330–4.
18.   Luttrell, vi, 226. Luttrell does not indicate whether it was Francis or Hugh Montgomery.
19.   BL Add 61125, f. 66, Harley to Marlborough, 24 October 1707.
20.   Sheepscar Library, Leeds, Temple Newsam Corr: W. Thompson to Lord Irwin, 16 December 1707.
21.   A. Boyer, *Annals*, vi, 252–7; BL Trumbull MSS, J. Bridges to Sir William Trumbull, 21 November 1707.
22.   Burnet, v, 343.
23.   *Vernon Corr*, iii, 282–5: Vernon to Shrewsbury, 2 December 1707, wrongly dated 4 December by James.

24. *Addison Corr*, p. 83: Addison to Manchester, 16 December 1707.

25. For accounts of the debate on 29 November see Bodleian Carte MSS 244, f. 152: Mountague Wood to Carte, 4 December 1707; *Addison Corr*, p. 82: Addison to Manchester, 6 December 1707; HMC *Lonsdale* pp. 117–18: H. M. to —— (? Henry Mordaunt to Lord Wharton) n.d., and Thomas Hopkins to Wharton, 29 November 1707 (both misdated 1705 by HMC).

26. *Vernon Corr*, iii, 294–6: Vernon to Shrewsbury, 4 December 1707 (misdated 14 by James); HMC *Mar and Kellie*, i, 424: Mar to Erskine, n.d. (4 December).

27. Roxburghe MSS bundle 739: William Burnet to the Countess of Roxburghe. I owe this reference to David Hayton.

28. HMC *11th Report appendix VII* (Lestrange MSS) pp. 114–15: Thomas de Grey to Sir Christopher Calthorp, 13 December 1707 (misdated 1705 by HMC).

29. Ibid., Vernon to Shrewsbury 22 and 24 January 1708 (omitted by James).

30. *Addison Correspondence*, p. 88: Addison to Manchester, 29 January 1708 (misdated 24 January by Graham; cf. *Court and Society from Elizabeth to Anne*, ed. Lord Manchester (1864), ii, 273–4).

31. Burnet, v, 360.

32. HMC *Mar and Kellie*, i, 426–7: Mar to Grange, 5 February 1708; *Addison Corr*, p. 89: Addison to Manchester, 6 February 1708.

33. HMC *10th report, appendix, part iv* (Westmorland MSS) p. 51. Westmorland told George he was for the dissolution of the Council 'because as it was to be an entire Union the nearer we could make it so the better, to be but one people, and that I thought one Council for the whole united Kingdom was sufficient'.

34. 'I had almost forgot to tell your Lordship,' Lord Mar added in a postscript to a letter to the earl of Leven, 'that yesterday the Queen gave the negative for the new militia of Scotland.' HMC *House of Lords*, n.s., viii, 119.

35. *Vernon Corr*, iii, 300–1, 303.

36. Ibid., 288–90; *CJ*, xv, 454.

37. Vernon Corr, Vernon to Shrewsbury, 13 December 1707 (sentence omitted by James).

38. *Vernon Corr*, iii, 298–299: Vernon to Shrewsbury 18 December 1707; *CJ*, xv, 473. Apparently St John had merely listed the regiments present at the battle.

39. *Court and Society from Elizabeth to Anne*, ed. Lord Manchester, ii, 272; Addison to Manchester, 3 February 1708; ARA Heinsius 1330, anon. to L'Hermitage, 30 Jan./10 Feb. 1708. The whigs blamed the Speaker, John Smith, for some of the problems the Court experienced in this debate, saying he had committed two great blunders. First, he should not have allowed the debate to take place in the House but should have moved it into a committee of the whole. Secondly, he should have kept the word 'English' out of the resolution so that foreign troops in Spain could have been included. Ibid., 3/14 February 1708.

40. *Vernon Corr*, iii, 329.

41. Vernon Corr: Vernon to Shrewsbury, 29 January 1708. The version published by James in the *Vernon Corr* reads 'we were this day upon the Spanish affairs, which lasted till three o'clock'. Historians, myself included, have been misled by this into believing that the debate went on until 3 a.m. which has confounded the detailed chronology of the fall of Harley. See Geoffrey Holmes, *Politics, Religion and Society in England, 1679–1742* (1986), p. 59. It might have struck them as intrinsically unlikely that Vernon would write a letter describing the debate before getting some rest. In fact the original has a numeral, 8, which James misread as 3 and compounded his misreading by rendering it as a word.

42. *Vernon Corr*, iii, 335–7: Vernon to Shrewsbury, 3 February 1708.

43. *Faults on Both Sides* a Harleyite tract of 1710 published in *Somers Tracts (1814), xii, 692–3.*

44. P. H. *An impartial view of the two late parliaments* (1711), p. 117, quoted in Geoffrey Holmes and W. A. Speck, 'The Fall of Harley in 1708 reconsidered', *English Historical Review* (1965), ccxvii, 673–698, reprinted in Geoffrey Holmes, *Politics Religion and Society in England 1679–1742* (1986), pp. 57–82 (the quotation appears on p. 57). The account presented here is based on this article with amendments to the chronology necessitated by the correction to the time of Vernon's letter to Shrewsbury of 29 January noted above (note 41).

45. Portland MSS 'order for ecclesiastical preferments', January 6, 1707/8.

46. BL Add MSS 34515 ff. 207–8: Somers to Portland, 14 February 1708; *The Norris Papers*, ed. T. Heywood (1846), p. 167.

47. T. Sharp, *Life of John Sharp* (1885), p. 323.

48. HMC *Bath*, i, 188–9: Harley to Godolphin, 17 December 1707 and reply.

49. *Huntington Library Quarterly* (1951–2), xv, 38–9: Brydges to Cadogan, 24 December 1707.

50. See Holmes, *Politics Religion and Society*, pp. 63–4; *Heinsius Corr*, vii, 96.

51. The duke of Ormonde was designed as Marlborough's replacement, but only if the Captain General refused to go along with the scheme, which would have involved the dismissals of Sunderland, Cowper, Newcastle and Somerset as well as Godolphin. *Heinsius Corr*, vii, 96.

52. HMC *Bath*, i, 190.

53. *Heinsius Corr*, vii, 96. Marlborough's suspicions were aroused not only by the way St John handled the list of troops in the Spanish theatre in 1707, but also by his tactics over a recruiting measure which was another source of difficulties for the Court in the Commons at this time. The duke was convinced that the problems were caused by tory opposition and asked Nottingham in the Lords to call off their attack on the bill. Nottingham only agreed to do so provided Marlborough undertook to transfer troops from the Low Countries to Spain. ARA Heinsius 1330. Anon. to L'Hermitage, 3/14 February 1708.

54. Coxe, *Marlborough*, ii, 191. That Marlborough wrote this on 7 February is documented in *Vernon Corr*, ii, 343: Vernon to Shrewsbury, 10

February 1708. This invalidates the hypothesis in Holmes and Speck, 'Fall of Harley', *Politics, Religion and Society*, pp. 59–60. It is possible that Marlborough was not as completely convinced as Godolphin that Harley was acting treacherously in the debates on Almanza until the 3 February, when the secretary did little to prevent the 'terrible vote of 21,000 absent soldiers.' Burnet, v, 348; PRO 30/24/21/148: Cropley to Shaftesbury, 19 February 1708. This would explain why his attitude towards Harley was more accommodating than Godolphin's at the time.

55. PRO 30/24/21/150: Cropley to Shaftesbury, 19 February 1708.
56. *Swift Corr*, i, 74–6: Swift to archbishop King, 12 February 1708.
57. A. Cunningham, *The History of Great Britain from the Revolution in 1688 to the Accession of George the First* (1787), ii, 142.
58. Devonshire, Newcastle, Somerset and Sunderland. *Heinsius Corr*, vii, 96.
59. *Huntington Library Quarterly* (1951–2), xv, 39–40: James Brydges to Cadogan, 12 February 1708.
60. As Sarah recalled the duke 'was much infatuated' with him at this time. Snyder, ii, 840 note 1.
61. For a discussion of the 'Lord Treasurer's whigs' see W. A. Speck, 'The House of Commons 1702–1714: a study in political management (Oxford D.Phil. thesis, 1966), pp. 186–94.
62. *Addison Corr*, p. 94.
63. Nottingham University Library Portland MSS PWA 1188: Somers to Portland 14 February 1708.
64. PRO 30/24/21/148: Cropley to Shaftesbury, 19 February 1708.
65. Ibid.
66. *Vernon Corr*, iii, 358: Vernon to Shrewsbury, 28 February 1708. The man tipped to replace George was not Orford but Pembroke.
67. *LJ*, xviii, 482–3, 491.
68. As secretary at war Robert Walpole inherited from St John the invidious task of putting a fair face on the figures. A document in his papers hints at the trouble this must have caused him. It consists of the original address and a draft in his hand, much corrected, of an alternative address which considerably reduced the gap between the two sets of figures. Cholmondley (Houghton) MSS B 65. 9a. According to I. F. Burton, 'The supply of infantry for the war in the peninsula 1703–1707', *Bulletin of the Institute of Historical Research* (1955), xxviii, 56–7: 'all the missing men can be accounted for . . . without any suggestion of misappropriation of money.'
69. *CJ*, xv, 551–2.
70. PRO 30/24/21/148: Cropley to Shaftesbury, 19 February 1708.
71. Vernon Corr, Vernon to Shrewsbury, 24 February 1708. Substantial portions of this letter were not published in *Vernon Corr*, iii, 355–6.
72. *Heinsius Corr*, vii, 129.
73. *Heinsius Corr*, vii, 129. Harcourt also voted for the motion, while St John abstained.
74. 'Faults on Both Sides' (1710), *Somers Tracts* (1814), xii, 693.
75. *Vernon Corr*, iii, 355–6.

76.   *Addison Corr*, pp. 94–5: Addison to Manchester, 24 and 27 February 1708.

CHAPTER 8   1708

1.   Luttrell, vi, 269.
2.   Burnet, v, 369. Like Burnet, 'I intend to follow the precedent, as often as I may have occasion hereafter to mention him.'
3.   *Vernon Corr*, iii, 365.
4.   See John S. Gibson, *Playing the Scottish Card: The Franco-Jacobite Invasion of 1708* (Edinburgh, 1988).
5.   *The Jacobites and the Union: Being a narrative of the movements of 1708, 1715, 1719 by several contemporary hands* edited by Charles Sandford Terry (Cambridge, 1922), p. 2.
6.   Ibid., pp. 22–7.
7.   Ibid., p. 30.
8.   Ibid., p. 36.
9.   Ibid., pp. 5, 51.
10.   Historians inclined to the view that Jacobitism was an important force in the eighteenth century see this as yet another lost opportunity for the Pretender. As is usually the case with their writings, however, they commit two methodological errors. Like the Pretender, they mistake anti-government feeling for pro-Stuart sentiment, and give more weight to pro-Jacobite sources than to those of their opponents, and thereby inevitably exaggerate the degree of support for the cause. Both greatly distort the realities of 1708. Much of the anti-union feeling in Scotland came from disgruntled Presbyterians who had nothing to gain from restoring a Catholic Stuart to the throne. There is no need to suspect that their addresses of congratulation to the Queen on the failure of the expedition were insincere. To lend more credence to Lockhart than to Forbin about the military prospects of the expedition is to prioritize the wishful thinking of a country gentleman over the professional opinion of an admiral, thereby reversing the normal priorities of historical method.
11.   Ibid., p. 53.
12.   HMC *Mar and Kellie* p. 436 quoted in Paul H. Scott, *Andrew Fletcher and the Treaty of Union* (Edinburgh, 1992), p. 212.
13.   Burnet, v, 369.
14.   *Divided Society*, p. 109.
15.   *Court and Society from Elizabeth to Anne*, ii, 348–9.
16.   BL Add 61459, f. 39: Arthur Mainwaring to the duchess of Marlborough n.d., 'Saturday seven a clock' [May 1708].
17.   Huntington Library Stowe MSS 57, ii, 27: J. Brydges to Cadogan, 11 April 1708; Levens MSS. There were half-hearted attempts at Bossiney, Lostwithiel, Weobley, Milborne Port, Cricklade, Devizes and Westbury, but they came to nought. HMC *Bath*, i, 190; *Portland*, iv, 489, 491, 495, 500, 515, 517. H. T. Dickinson, 'Henry St John, Wootton Bassett, and the General Election of 1708', *Wiltshire Archaeological and Natural*

History Magazine (1969), *64*, 107–11. When another Harleyite, Sir Simon Harcourt, lost his seat at Abingdon on a petition from a whig candidate in January 1709 it took a year to find him another in Cardigan. By contrast the whigs quickly found seats for prominent members after their electoral defeat in 1710. See Geoffrey Holmes, *British Politics*, p. 320.

18. Kent Archives Office, U1590/C9/30: Chevening MSS Craggs to Stanhope 1 June 1708.
19. BL Add 9102, f. 8. Hamilton to Sunderland, 1 June 1708 (Coxe's transcript); Trevelyan, ii, 413.
20. BL Add 61164, f. 183: Craggs to Marlborough, 21 May 1708.
21. PRO 30/22/24/157: Cropley to Shaftesbury, 'ending of April 1708'.
22. HMC *Mar and Kellie*, pp. 445, 453: Mar to Queen, 14 June 1708 and her reply 24 June; Churchill, iii, 305–6.
23. Queen to Marlborough, n.d. endorsed '27 August 1708'.
24. Kent Archives office, U1590/C9/30: Chevening MSS: Craggs to Stanhope, 1 June 1708.
25. Quoted in J. R. Jones, *Marlborough*, p. 154.
26. *POAS*, vi, 341–4.
27. BL Add 61134, f. 110: Brydges to Marlborough, 7 July 1708.
28. Kent Archives office, U1590/C9/30: Chevening MSS James Craggs to Stanhope, 1 June 1708: 'amidst these dismal things let me give you one glimpse of comfort, which is, that the long Surrey member is adjusted for our next Speaker.'
29. *Private Corr*, i, 142–3: Mainwaring to Sarah, n.d.
30. BL Add 61443, f. 20: Sunderland to Sarah, 9 August 1708.
31. 1 Levens MSS: Hamilton to Grahme, 21 September 1708.
32. HMC *Bath*, i, 192. Harley to Harcourt, 16 October 1708.
33. *Private Corr*, i, 50: Mainwaring to Sarah, [21 October 1708].
34. Trevelyan, ii, 414–15: Sunderland to Newcastle, 19 October 1708.
35. Bl Add 4163, ff. 242–4: transcripts of letters from anon. to Harley, 9 and 23 October 1708.
36. Burnet, vi, 378 and Onslow's note.
37. Huntington Stowe MSS 57, ii, 99: Brydges to Cardonell, 29 October 1708.
38. *Byng Papers* quoted in Henry Snyder, 'Queen Anne versus the Junto: the effort to place Orford at the head of the admiralty in 1709', *Huntington Library Quarterly* (1972), iv, 326.
39. Snyder, 'Queen Anne versus the Junto', pp. 327–9.
40. Huntington Stowe MSS 57, ii, 69: Brydges to Coningsby, 3 September 1708.
41. Levens MSS: Wilfrid Lawson to Grahme, 9 September 1708.
42. Portland MSS Stratford to Harley, 8 October 1708; Finch papers, Bromley to Nottingham, 2 October 1708.
43. HMC *Bath* i, 192: Harley to Harcourt, 16 October 1708. The tory leaders had united.
44. Kendal Record Office; Levens MSS: Ward to Grahme, 2 October 1708; Northants Record Office; Finch papers, Bromley to Nottingham, 2 October 1708; NLW Chirk Castle MSS E994 and 995: Hanmer to

Shakerley, 21 October 1708; Mostyn to Myddleton, 24 October 1708; Northants Record Office; Isham Corr, 1705: Bromley to Isham, 15 October 1708; HMC *Bath*, i, 192: Harley to Harcourt, 16 October 1708.

45. Churchill College Cambridge Drax MSS: Craggs to Erle, 29 October 1708.

46. Kent AO U1590/C9/1311 Chevening MSS; Cropley to Stanhope, 22 November 1708. Walpole told Thomas Erle that he believed Onslow would be chosen Speaker without opposition 'all differences between the whigs are entirely made up'. Cholmondley (Houghton) MSS P6.

47. Boyer, *Annals*, vii, 251. This caused some resentment against the leadership amongst the rank and file of the party who had taken the trouble to get up to parliament to vote for Bromley. 'I believe the Gentlemen will be better informed of an opposition before they will venture such another journey', Thomas Rowney, tory MP for Oxford complained. 'Where the trouble lies I am not a judge, but am satisfied we have been made fools of.' Bodleian MSS Top. Oxon. b. 82, f. 16. Rowney to Clarke, 19 November 1708.

48. Boyer, *Annals*, vii, 251.

49. Kent AO U1590/C9/31 Chevening MSS: Cropley to Stanhope, 27 November 1708.

50. Huntington Stowe MSS 57, ii, 123: Brydges to Cartwright, 3 December 1708.

51. Snyder, ii, 1184.

52. Cocks, *Diary*, ii, f. 5.

53. John Rylands Library Legh of Lyme muniments: Henry Bunbury to [Peter Legh], 1 February 1709. Godolphin had protested to Marlborough in December that 'the method which the House of Commons has taken of trying their elections at the barr of the House, makes it impossible for them hitherto to proceed upon anything but elections one day, and supply the next'. Snyder, ii, 1173.

54. BL Add 61133, f. 160: Walpole to Marlborough, 21 January 1708–9. Luttrell reported that the Commons sat until 3 a.m. and voted Hucks in by '180 and odd voices against 130'. Luttrell, vi, 398. James Brydges observed that they 'turned out Sir Simon Harcourt by a majority of 60 at half and hour after two in the morning'. Huntington Library Stowe MSS 57, i, 153: Brydges to Cadogan, 28 January 1709.The discrepancies presumably arose from the lateness of the hour.

55. BL Egerton 3345 (3): 'Sir Simon Harcourt's speech immediately before he left the House.' Harcourt inveighed in particular against an unnamed politician who had sent Hucks down to Abingdon. This could have been Lord Chancellor Cowper. His diary entry for 3 March 1712 records 'Hucks to be spoken to Abindon'; Herts Record Office, Panshanger MSS.

56. Burnet, v, 396. Bromley informed Nottingham on 7 December 1708 that some resolutions on elections had been taken that even the whigs were ashamed of 'so that some have opposed them & more have withdrawn, yet have taken care to leave enough to carry them'. Northants Record Office, Finch MSS.

57. Burnet, v, 397–399. The precedent was also set that Scottish lords promoted to the peerage of Great Britain, as the duke of Queensberry had been when made duke of Dover, could not vote for the sixteen noble representatives for Scotland.

58. Chevening MSS, U1590/C9/31: Cropley to Stanhope, 15 March 1709.

59. Luttrell, vi, 416.

60. Nicolson, *Diary*, p. 487; Burnet, v, 403.

61. Nicolson, *Diary*, p. 488. He was referring to a popular opinion of cucumbers that they were better thrown away than eaten. Angus Easson, 'Dr Johnson and the Cucumber', *Notes and Queries* (1970), ccxv, 300–302.

62. Burnet, v, 405–6. Nicolson gave the vote as 30–30, whereas HMC *Lords*, viii, 288, gives it as 32–32. Nicolson, *Diary*, p. 489 and note 139.

63. Nicolson, *Diary*, p. 490. Nicolson noted that the next day when he was alone on the bishops' bench the Scottish lords were angry with him for having been in the majority. Ibid., p. 490.

64. Burnet, v, 406–7; Nicolson, *Diary*, p. 488.

65. Nicolson, *Diary*, pp. 492, 494.

66. HMC *Portland*, iv, 523.

67. BL Add 61133, f. 172: Walpole to Marlborough, 8 April 1709. Burnet noted smugly that 'this came up fully to the motion I had made.' Burnet, v, 407.

68. Nicolson, *Diary*, p. 496. Nicolson records a vote of 141 to 73, whereas the *CJ* recorded 141 to 75.

69. Carlisle R O Lonsdale MSS: Lowther to Gilpin, 19 April 1709.

70. Nicolson, *Diary*, pp. 474, 498.

71. Burnet, v, 409.

72. Burnet, v, 409; Nicolson, *Diary*, p. 499 note 206.

73. HMC *Portland*, iv, 521: Abigail Harley to Abigail Harley, 19 April 1709.

74. Nicolson, *Diary*, p. 499.

75. Burnet, v, 410.

76. G. Holmes, *Politics, Religion and Society in England, 1679–1742* (1986), p. 224.

77. Cobbett, vi, 780.

78. Burnet, v, 411.

79. Nicolson, *Diary*, pp. 471, 486. As Burnet observed, 'as I spoke copiously for it when it was brought up to the lords: the bishop of Chester spoke as zealously against it, for he seemed resolved to distinguish himself as a zealot for that which was called high church'. Burnet, v, 411.

80. Burnet, v, 411. Swift wrote in the margin of Burnet's *History* at this point 'dog'!

81. BL Add MSS 31143, f. 313: Peter Wentworth to Lord Raby, 18 March 1709.

82. H. T. Dickinson, 'The Poor Palatines and the Parties', *English Historical Review* (1967), lxxxii, 464–485. According to David Papillon, who took the matter up at the Elector Palatine's court, 'ye reason of their going in so great quantities [was] their extreem poverty, ye plenty of our Isle,

Naturalisation, & ye Queen's allowing ym 5 pence p. diem', ibid., p. 466 note 4.

83. Luttrell, vi, 413–14; Burnet, v, 411–12.

CHAPTER 9   1709

1.   J. Haffendorf, *England in the War of the Spanish Succession: A study of the English view and conduct of Grand Strategy 1702–1712* (1987), p. 201.
2.   Snyder, iii, 1271, 1300.
3.   Ibid., ii, 996.
4.   Huntington Stowe MSS 58, iii, 200.
5.   'Plain English to all who are honest or would be so if they knew how', edited W. A. Speck and J. A. Downie, *Literature and History* (1976), *3*, 101. The draft is dated 24 August 1708. For a discussion see J. A. Downie, *Robert Harley and the Press* (Cambridge, 1979), pp. 105–7.
6.   Downie, *Harley and the Press*, p. 107; Luttrell, vi, 398–9.
7.   Burnet, v, 416: Dartmouth's note.
8.   Lincoln Archives Office Monson MSS 7/12/136: Charles Bertie to Sir John Newton, 28 August 1709. 'and the Dutch to reap the benefit thereof' Bertie added gratuitously.
9.   Colonel Blackadder, quoted in Trevelyan, iii, 18.
10. Snyder, iii, 1359.
11. Burnet, v, 433.
12. For an analysis of the struggle see H. L. Snyder, 'Queen Anne versus the Junto: The Effort to Place Orford at the Head of the Admiralty in 1709', *Huntington Library Quarterly* (1972), xxxv, 323–42.
13. Ibid., p. 330.
14. BL Add 70419; Harley to Stratford, 6 November 1709.
15. Unless other sources are cited the account of the Sacheverell affair which follows is based on the definitive discussion of it in Geoffrey Holmes, *The Trial of Dr. Sacheverell* (1973).
16. Quotations are from H. Sacheverell, *The Perils of False Brethren both in Church and State* (The Rota, Exeter, 1974).
17. King had been a whig candidate for the Speakership in 1708, and had obtained the Recordership as a consolation prize when Onslow was preferred. Heathcote had demonstrated his whig zeal to Godolphin in a conversation with the Treasurer on 8 September. Sir Gilbert said 'pray my lord, don't let us have a rotten peace.' 'Pray tell me' Godolphin replied, 'what you call a rotten peace'? 'I call anything,' he sayd, 'a rotten peace unless we have Spayn, for without it wee can have no safety. And now we have them down, lett us keep them so, till wee gett quite out of the warr.' When the Treasurer pointed out that he and Marlborough were being 'railed at every day, for having a mind as they call it to perpetuate the warr', Heathcote replied, 'They are a company of rotten rogues that tell you so. I warrant you, wee'l stand by you.' Snyder, iii, 1471.
18. Huntington Stowe MSS 57, iii, 127: Brydges to Stanwix, 30 December 1709.

19. BL Add MSS 49360: 'minute book of the Board of Brothers.' That this was little more than a tory drinking club is suggested by one entry: 'Ordered. That all bumpers be excluded the Board except one to Church & Queen to avoid excess and reproach.'

20. Gregg, *Anne*, p. 302.

21. *Wentworth Papers*, p. 103.

22. Ibid., p. 303.

23. Ibid., p. 108.

24. *POAS*, vii, 382–3.

25. *Wentworth Papers*, p. 110.

26. BL Add 70421 Dyer, 4 March 1710.

27. Lincoln Archives Office Massingberd MSS: Burrell Massingberd to Sir William Massingberd, Lincoln's Inn, 28 February 1710.

28. *POAS*, vii, 393.

29. BL Blenheim MSS. Essay on the policy of the Sacheverell trial.

30. See the analysis in Geoffrey Holmes, 'The Sacheverell Riots', *Politics Religion and Society in England 1679–1742*, pp. 217–47.

31. Ibid., p. 246.

32. Snyder, iii, 1440. The Derby sermon was also sentenced to the flames along with the St Paul's sermon.

33. Snyder, iii, 1445. This was presumably a manuscript list. The bishop of Chichester and the earl of Suffolk do not appear on any of the printed lists. See Holmes, *Trial* p.225. Suffolk was absent from the division on 20 March, and voted against Sacheverell on the 21st, when the bishop of Chichester was absent. Ibid., pp. 285, 287.

34. Snyder, iii, 1440.

35. Ibid., p. 1434.

36. Burnet, v, 446.

37. Hamilton, *Diary*, p. 6.

38. *The Wentworth Papers*, p. 146.

CHAPTER 10

1. Burnet, v, 451; *POAS*, vi, 412; 'on the Queen's speech'.

2. Luttrell, vi, 566.

3. See *A Collection of the Addresses which have been presented to the Queen since the impeachment of the Reverend Dr. Henry Sacheverell* (1710).

4. W. A. Speck, 'Staffordshire in the reign of Queen Anne', *Staffordshire Studies* (1991–2), *4*, p. 25. I take this opportunity to correct the statement that the county was never contested in the reign,(p. 31), which flatly contradicts the evidence for a poll in 1708 (p.24 and note 12)! The statement should have read that no poll book has survived for the county during the reign.

5. Luttrell, vi, 563.

6. The present narrative owes much to an analysis of the revolution by Geoffrey Holmes which he communicated to the author thirty years ago and which was unfortunately never published.

7. The possibility of removing Marlborough from the post of commander

in chief seems at least to have been considered. James Cressett was ready to go to Hanover to offer it to the elector when he died in July. Lord Rivers was eventually despatched, though the offer was by then conditional upon Marlborough's resigning. Churchill, iv, 248–9.

8. Hamilton, *Diary*, pp. 25, 85.
9. Ibid., p. 8.
10. Burnet, vi, 9, Dartmouth's note. Dartmouth observed that 'the scheme at that time went no further than for removing the Marlborough family'.
11. Ibid., p. 13. Onslow's note. Speaker Onslow claimed to have heard this from Sir Joseph Jekyll who got it from Somers.
12. Coxe, *Marlborough*, iii, 88.
13. Snyder, iii, 1324.
14. Coxe, *Marlborough*, iii, 86.
15. Burnet, vi, 9 note.
16. Snyder, iii, 1515–16. Godolphin to Marlborough, 2 June 1710. Poulet told Godolphin that he would not accept without his agreement, to which the Treasurer replied that it would be a particular mortification to Marlborough, on which Poulet declined the post. As Godolphin observed 'this gives us a little breathing time, but I doubt it is no more'.
17. Burnet also attributed Sunderland's fall to Anne, saying of it that 'The queen's intentions to make a change in her ministry now began to break out'. Burnet, vi, 8.
18. Snyder, iii, 1532.
19. Hamilton, *Diary*, p. 9. Anne asked Hamilton 'to bring my Lord Godolphin off from the Duchess'.
20. Hamilton, *Diary*, note 49.
21. Snyder, iii, 1575: Godolphin to Marlborough, 21 July 1710.
22. There were meetings held at Halifax's house in mid-July where Harley and Shrewsbury were present. It was reported that a compromise had been agreed whereby the Treasurer was to keep his place but the Chancellor of the Exchequer, John Smith, 'and the other officers' were to be removed 'to make room for some that want to be accommodated with their places'. Nottingham University Library Portland MSS: PW2 (Hollis), 139: W. Jessop to Newcastle, 18 July 1710. Possibly Harley himself was to replace Smith.
23. Gregg, *Anne*, p. 319.
24. Snyder, iii, 1549.
25. Ibid., iii, 1548.
26. Kendal Record Office; Levens MSS Bromley to Grahme, 16 July 1710.
27. Snyder, iii, 1572. James Brydges attributed Anne's hesitancy to dismiss Godolphin to the Bank's unwillingness to lend money 'till her Majesty had made a further declaration that she intended no further changes, nor a Dissolution.' B. W. Hill, 'The change of government and the "loss of the City", 1710–11', *Economic History Review* (1971), xxiv, 401.
28. Burnet, vi, 7: Hardwicke's note.
29. Snyder, iii, 1577.
30. HMC *Portland*, ii, 216: Halifax to Newcastle, 17 August 1710.

31. Hamilton, *Diary*, p. 76, note 57. For some reason the pension promised in the letter was never paid.

32. *Wentworth Papers*, p. 133; *Addison Corr*, p. 233. According to Bromley, Benson owed his place on the commission to the recommendation of the duke of Argyll. Kendal RO; Levens MSS.

33. Snyder, iii, 1597.

34. *Wentworth Papers*, p. 138. The only sop thrown to the high church tories was the offer of a place to Sir Thomas Hanmer, who also refused it. Levens MSS Bromley to Grahme, 1 September 1710.

35. Luttrell, vi, 618.

36. Snyder, iii, 1563, 1603 note. Harley entered the Cabinet as chancellor of the exchequer, which was also unusual since he was in addition only a commissioner of the treasury and not first lord.

37. BL Portland MSS Boyle to Harley 9 July and 11 August 1710; HMC *Portland*, ii, 218: Harley to Newcastle, 12 September.

38. Herts RO, Panshanger MSS: Monckton to Cowper, 28 August; endorsed by Cowper 'Mr Monckton's ltr, a spy of Mr. H.' *Cowper Diary*, pp. 43–5.

39. *Cowper Diary*, pp. 46–7; *Hamilton Diary*, p. 19.

40. *Hamilton Diary*, p. 19.

41. Burnet, vi, 13 and Onslow's note.

42. Kendal RO; Levens MSS Bromley to Grahme, 16 July 1710. It was also reported that Rochester's son, Lord Hyde, was to be made cofferer of the household.

43. BL Trumbull MSS: J. Brydges to Trumbull, 28 July 1710.

44. *Wentworth Papers*, p. 136.

45. Kendal RO; Levens MSS: Bromley to Grahme, 1 September 1710. On 2 September Rochester replaced Godolphin as lord lieutenant of Cornwall. Luttrell, vi, 625.

46. *Heinsius Corr*, xi, 162, 177–8: L'Hermitage to Heinsius, 8/19 and 12/23 September 1710. Amongst Rochester's demands presumably was that Buckingham should succeed Devonshire as lord steward. At all events he and Buckingham were said to be 'in nomination' for the posts of lord president and steward on 16 September, five days before they replaced Somers and Devonshire. HMC *Portland*, ii, 220: Halifax to Newcastle, 16 September 1710.

47. Kendal RO; Levens MSS: Bromley to Grahme, 1 September 1710. On hearing the news Ralph Bridges wrote to Sir William Trumbull on 4 September, 'now we may expect peace & the golden age to come again'. BL Trumbull MSS.

48. Hamilton, *Diary*, p. 21. In 1712 the duchess of Somerset replaced Sarah as groom of the stole.

49. *Life of Sharp*, i, 323.

50. Harley's acceptance of the need to include more tories in his scheme is apparent in a memorandum he drew up on 4 September listing possible candidates for a new admiralty commission to replace the one headed by Orford. Of the 15 names in the list, six were high tories, seven were Court tories, one was a Scottish tory and only three were whigs (BL Add 70333 "Memdm. Navy. Sept:4:1710").

51. BL Add 70333 "Memdms Sept:12:1710". Phrases like 'there remains but

few days to do much business' and 'consider the method of dissolving' indicate Harley's frustration at Anne's attitude.

52. HMC *Portland*, ii, 219.

53. Hamilton, *Diary*, pp. 18 and 80 note 84.

54. *A Collection of all the Addresses* p. 29. Anne ordered the address to be printed in the *London Gazette* 'as a distinguishing favour to them' according to White Kennett, it being 'the only one of all the numerous addresses that have been presented of late that has been printed in the Gazette.' *The Wisdom of Looking Backward* (1715), p. 65. Despite its moderation it had a sting in the tail, expressing opposition to 'all the people that delight in war', a phrase to be echoed in Anne's speech to parliament in December 1711. The address provoked a whig reply 'The Humble Address of the clergy of London and Westminster paraphras'd', *POAS*, vi, 454–61.

55. Hamilton, *Diary*, p. 17. For Sacheverell's 'progress' see Holmes, *The Trial of Dr. Sacheverell*, pp. 243–8.

56. Ibid., p. 250.

57. *The Correspondence of Jonathan Swift*, ed. J. Elrington Ball (1910), i, 208: Swift to King, 10 October 1710.

58. Bodleian Library Carte MSS 244, f. 123: Montagu Wood to Carte, 30 September 1710.

59. Berkeley's appointment was too close to the elections for him to exert much influence over the results. He backed Francis Annesley in Preston, 'being willing to keep an interest that other chancellors have had', but he was beaten by the whig Sir Henry Hoghton. Kendal RO; Levens MSS. Berkeley to Grahme, 26 September. Haigh MSS John Rylands library: Berkeley to Bradshaigh, 30 September 1710.

60. B. W. Hill, *Robert Harley* (1988), p. 133.

61. HMC *Portland*, iv, 551.

62. Abel Boyer, *Quadriennium Annae Postremum* (1718), i, 12.

63. *Journal to Stella* 6 October; *Swift Corr*, i, 208.

64. Huntington Library Stowe MSS 57, iv, 187: Brydges to Geers, 20 October 1710.

65. BL Add 70421.

66. Churchill College Cambridge, Erle MSS. Walpole even predicted that 'from all parts of England our accounts are so very good and our friends so sanguine that I am confident we shall make them hear us next winter'.

67. Carlisle RO, Lonsdale MSS: Lowther to Gilpin, 7 October 1710. Lowther, though employed in the Ordnance office, shared a 'Country' outlook with Stanhope, noting that 'he is a man of learning and eloquence and his honourable promoting of bills to lessen the number of officers in the House when he himself was one, because he believed one time or other they would ruin the Constitution, is a proof of his integrity that will never be forgot'. The Court sun certainly did not shine on Stanhope. 'Some warm inconsiderate persons have set up Mar Stanhope for Westminster,' Harley told Newcastle, 'although they were told that all were engaged for Cross and Medlicott and that Mr Webb had been persuaded to desist in order to quiet the City. But all would not do, and

it has given occasion to much heat.' HMC *Portland*, ii, 222–3. Ironically Newcastle himself was one of the 'warm inconsiderate persons'. Ibid., 222: Heathcote to Newcastle, 30 September 1710.

68. *POAS*, vii, 481.
69. Ibid., pp. 480–6.
70. Nottingham University Library Portland MSS P.W.2.291a: G. Whichcot to Newcastle, 17 October 1710.
71. *Divided Society*, p. 158.
72. Boyer, *Quadriennium Annae Postremum*, i, 20. Although five of the managers were returned, they came in for safe whig seats, like Stanhope, who eventually got into the House on the duke of Somerset's interest at Cockermouth.
73. In two counties he actually supplied numbers: 126 in Kent compared with only five or six who voted whig; 150 in Lincolnshire, compared with only 15 or 16.
74. Christ Church Wake MSSI/256: Thomas Frank to William Wake, 6 October 1710. Frank attributed the false claim to St John, concluding 'some men have a strange knack of fibbing for the truth'.
75. Thus in Essex out of 143 ministers who polled, 125 'plumped' for the single tory candidate. In Rutland, of 43 known clerical votes, 30 polled for the two tory candidates, nine for the two whigs, and four split their votes.
76. Though Dyer claimed that in revenge 'in Essex they tender them the abjuration oath which most of them took and few refused the same'.
77. *Tory and Whig*, p. 25. Trevelyan, iii, 264.
78. HMC *Bath*, iii, 441–2. On 23 September Lord Cheyne, a Buckingham-shire tory, wrote to Harley 'pray if possible make the Quakers for us. They have not declared yet.' Portland MSS.
79. BL Trumbull MSS: Bridges to Trumbull, 13 November 1710.
80. BL Add 61133, f. 210: Walpole to Marlborough, 26 October 1710.
81. Bodleian Carte MSS 244, f. 127: Wood to [Clarke?], 18 November 1710.
82. *Tory and Whig*, p. 123.
83. Christ Church Wake MSS Arch Epis 17: 'Mr Dangworth about the Scots election.'

CONCLUSION

1. *The Duumvirate* Bodleian Carte MSS 208, ff. 397–8, n.d. [?1709].
2. J. A. Downie, *Robert Harley and the Press* (Cambridge, 1979); Michael Foot, *The Pen and the Sword* (1957).
3. J. Brewer, *The Sinews of Power* (1989); D. W. Jones, *War and Economy in the Age of William III and Marlborough* (Oxford, 1988).
4. *POAS*, vii, 19–42.
5. Longleat Thynne MSS xxv, f. 424: W. Ettrick to Weymouth, August 1705.
6. BL Add 61459, f. 3.

APPENDIX: THE INCIDENCE OF CONTESTED ELECTIONS 1701–1710:
A PSEPHOLOGICAL NOTE

1. The figures provided in my *Tory and Whig* were used as the basis of calculating the size of electorates. These were based as far as possible on turnouts at contests. Since these were never 100 per cent then they of course underestimated the electorates. However, it would be a hazardous exercise to revise the figure upwards by some artificial percentage to account for the difference between turnout and the total of those eligible to vote. Keeping to the figures used for *Tory and Whig* at least retains a reasonably consistent basis. And anyway, since we are examining contests which resulted in the polling of voters, then the active rather than the hypothetical electorate seems to provide a more realistic basis.

2. *The Divided Society: Party Conflict in England 1694–1716*, ed. G. Holmes and W. A. Speck (1967) p. 19.

3. Ibid., pp. 29–30.

4 P. E. Murrell, 'The political history of the county of Suffolk and its parliamentary boroughs 1679 to 1715', unpublished Ph.D. thesis, University of Newcastle upon Tyne, 1980.

Index